WALKING THE LAKE DISTRICT FELLS
BUTTERMERE
HIGH STILE, GRASMOOR, GRISEDALE PIKE AND HAYSTACKS

MARK RICHARDS

CICERONE

© Mark Richards 2020
Second edition 2020
ISBN: 978 1 78631 036 1

Originally published as Lakeland Fellranger, 2011
ISBN: 978 1 85284 545 2

 Printed in China on responsibly sourced paper on behalf of Latitude Press Ltd

A catalogue record for this book is available from the British Library.
All photographs are by the author unless otherwise stated.
All artwork is by the author.

 Maps are reproduced with permission from HARVEY Maps, www.harveymaps.co.uk

Updates to this Guide

While every effort is made by our authors to ensure the accuracy of guidebooks as they go to print, changes can occur during the lifetime of an edition. Any updates that we know of for this guide will be on the Cicerone website (www.cicerone.co.uk/1036/updates), so please check before planning your trip. We also advise that you check information about such things as transport, accommodation and shops locally. Even rights of way can be altered over time. We are always grateful for information about any discrepancies between a guidebook and the facts on the ground, sent by email to updates@cicerone.co.uk or by post to Cicerone, Juniper House, Murley Moss, Oxenholme Road, Kendal, LA9 7RL.

Register your book: To sign up to receive free updates, special offers and GPX files where available, register your book at www.cicerone.co.uk.

Front cover: Haystacks from High Wax Knott
Title page: Goat Crag on Robinson seen across Buttermere

CONTENTS

Map key 5
Volumes in the series 6
Author preface 7
Starting points 8

INTRODUCTION 13
Valley bases 13
Fix the Fells 15
Using this guide 16
Safety and access 18
Additional online resources 18

FELLS 19
1 Ard Crags 19
2 Barrow 23
3 Blake Fell 29
4 Causey Pike 39
5 Crag Hill 44
6 Dale Head 53
7 Fellbarrow 62
8 Fleetwith Pike 68
9 Gavel Fell 75
10 Grasmoor 83
11 Great Borne 92
12 Grisedale Pike 100
13 Haystacks 110
14 Hen Comb 120
15 High Crag 127
16 High Stile 134
17 Hindscarth 142
18 Hopegill Head 149
19 Knock Murton 158
20 Knott Rigg 162
21 Low Fell 166

22	Mellbreak	172
23	Outerside	180
24	Rannerdale Knotts	185
25	Red Pike	191
26	Robinson	199
27	Sail	208
28	Scar Crags	214
29	Starling Dodd	220
30	Wandope	229
31	Whiteless Pike	235
32	Whiteside	240

RIDGE ROUTES 246
1 The Newlands Round 246
2 The Buttermere Round 250
3 The Grasmoor Fell-gather 254
4 The Coledale Horseshoe 258

More to explore 263

Useful contacts 264

A fellranger's glossary 265

Alphabetical list of fells in the Fellranger series 269

MAP KEY

Key to route maps and topos

 Route on a defined path

12 **Starting point**

Route on an intermittent or undefined path

4 **Route number** (on topos)

▲ **Fell summit** featured in this guide (on maps)

 Fell summit featured in this guide (on maps)

3 **Route number** (on maps)

N

0   500 m

1:40,000

Harvey map legend

 Lake, small tarn, pond

River, footbridge

Wide stream

Narrow stream

 Peat hags

Marshy ground

Contours change from brown to grey where the ground is predominantly rocky outcrops, small crags and other bare rock.

Improved pasture

Rough pasture

Fell or moorland

Open forest or woodland

Dense forest or woodland

Felled or new plantation

Forest ride or firebreak

Settlement

Boundary, maintained
Boundary, remains

On moorland, walls, ruined walls and fences are shown. For farmland, only the outer boundary wall or fence is shown.

Contour (15m interval)

Index contour (75m interval)

Auxiliary contour

Scree, spoil heap

Boulder field

Scattered rock and boulders

Predominantly rocky ground

Major crag, large boulder

O.S. trig pillar, large cairn

Spot height (from air survey)

Dual carriageway

Main road (fenced)

Minor road (unfenced)

Track or forest road

Footpath or old track

Intermittent path

Long distance path

Powerline, pipeline

Building, ruin or sheepfold, shaft

The representation of a road, track or footpath is no evidence of the existence of a right of way.

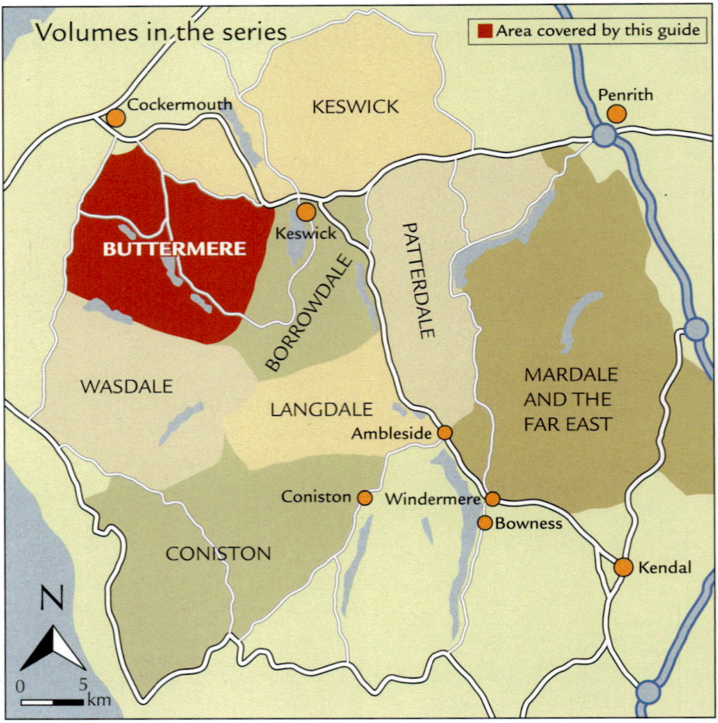

↑ *The Buttermere valley from a wintry Fleetwith Pike (photo: Maggie Allan)*

AUTHOR PREFACE

This land of living dreams we call the Lake District is a cherished blessing to know, love and share. As we go about our daily routines, we may take a fleeting moment to reflect that someone, somewhere, will be tramping up a lonely gill or along an airy ridge, peering from a lofty summit or gazing across a wind-blown tarn and taking lingering solace from its timeless beauty. The trappings of modern life thrust carpet and concrete under our feet, and it is always wonderful to walk the region's sheep trods and rough trails, and to imprint our soles upon the fells. This series sets out to give you the impetus and inspiration to make space in your schedule to explore them time and again, in myriad different ways.

However, the regular paths of long tradition deserve our care. Progressively many of the main paths are being re-set with cobbles and pitching by organisations such as Fix the Fells, to whose work you have contributed by buying this guide. But in many instances, the best consideration we can give these pathways is rest. The modern fellwanderer should show a new 'green' awareness by choosing to tread lightly on the land and to find new ways around the hills. One of the underlying impulses of this guide is to protect these beloved fells by presenting a diversity of route options for each and every fell – and also, in this new edition, recommending 'fell-friendly' routes to each summit which are less susceptible to erosion.

Another feature of this latest incarnation of Fellranger, apart from the smaller size to slip in your pocket or pack, is the addition of a selection of inspiring ridge routes at the end of each volume for those of you who like to spend a little longer with your head and feet in the heavenly realms, relishing the summit views and the connections between the felltops, as well as some accompanying online resources for readers with a digital bent.

Mark Richards
www.markrichardswalking.co.uk

STARTING POINTS

	Location		GR [NY...]	Access	Ascents described from here
1	Grange	Two small verge spaces along Hollows Farm access lane	252 173	FP, B	Dale Head
2	Rosthwaite	Large car park with adjacent Borrowdale Institute parking	257 148	PP, B	Dale Head
3	Seatoller	Large car park by bus turning place	245 137	FP, B	Dale Head
4	Honister Pass	Large visitor centre parking area on the pass (plus NT car park beside YHA hostel)	225 135	PP, NT, B	Dale Head, Fleetwith Pike
5	Gatesgarthdale	Layby below bridge	210 148	FP, B	Hindscarth
6	Gatesgarth	Farmer-owned car park with overflow in yard behind buildings	195 150	PP, B	Fleetwith Pike, Haystacks, High Crag, High Stile
7	Black Sail Hut	Walk/bike-in youth hostel at the head of Ennerdale	195 124	F	Haystacks, High Crag
8	Bowness Knott	Large car park	109 153	FP	Great Borne, High Crag, Red Pike, Starling Dodd
9	Whins	Modest facing laybys	101 165	FP	Gavel Fell, Great Borne, Hen Comb
10	Cross Rigg	Modest verge on N and S side of junction – avoid blocking access	087 182	FP	Blake Fell, Gavel Fell, Knock Murton
11	Felldyke	Compact car park	085 198	FP	Blake Fell, Knock Murton
12	Fangs Brow	Modest verge	105 226	FP	Blake Fell
13	Waterend	Two generous laybys	117 224	FP	Blake Fell, Fellbarrow, Low Fell
14	Mosser	Tiny verge in hamlet	115 250	FP	Fellbarrow
15	Maggie's Bridge	Modest car park	135 210	FP	Blake Fell, Gavel Fell, Hen Comb

	Location		GR [NY...]	Access	Ascents described from here
16	Church Bridge	Small verge over bridge below the pub garden	141 209	FP	Hen Comb, Low Fell, Mellbreak
17	Lanthwaite Wood	Large car park	149 215	NT	Mellbreak, Whiteside
18	Thackthwaite	Limited grass verge	148 237	FP	Fellbarrow, Low Fell
19	Hopebeck	Small roadside recess	169 242	FP	Hopegill Head, Whiteside
20	Swinside	Grass verge parking	176 253	FP	Hopegill Head
21	Hobcarton	Substantial parking area	192 245	FP, B	Grisedale Pike, Hopegill Head
22	Revelin Moss	Large parking area	209 242	FP, B	Grisedale Pike
23	Noble Knott	Generous parking area	223 244	FP, B	Grisedale Pike
24	Braithwaite	Elevated car park with room for a dozen cars	227 236	FP, B	Barrow, Causey Pike, Crag Hill, Grisedale Pike, Hopegill Head, Outerside, Sail
25	Uzzicar	Open space on common	233 217	FP	Barrow, Causey Pike, Outerside
26	Rigg Beck	Small quarry on a hairpin bend just across from new Rigg Beck house	229 202	FP	Ard Crags
27	Chapel Bridge	Small layby	232 194	FP	Dale Head, Hindscarth, Robinson,
28	Keskadale	Small off-road area beside the little bridge and narrow verge parking on S side of road N to the farm	207 188	FP	Knott Rigg, Robinson
29	Newlands Hause	Facing laybys on the pass	193 176	FP	Knott Rigg, Robinson

STARTING POINTS *continued*

	Location		GR [NY...]	Access	Ascents described from here
30	Buttermere	Generous car park in village (plus an NT one just N of village at 173 173 and verge parking above the church)	173 169	PP, NT, FP, B	Crag Hill, Great Borne, Hen Comb, High Crag, High Stile, Knott Rigg, Mellbreak, Rannerdale Knotts, Red Pike, Robinson, Sail, Starling Dodd, Wandope, Whiteless Pike
31	Hause Point	Small parking area	163 183	FP, B	Rannerdale Knotts
32	Cinderdale Common	Generous open verge	162 193	FP, B	Grasmoor, Rannerdale Knotts
33	Lanthwaite Green	Large roadside parking area	159 208	FP, B	Crag Hill, Grasmoor, Hopegill Head, Whiteside
34	High Liza Bridge	Tiny layby (avoid blocking the field-gate)	156 224	FP, B	Whiteside

FP – free parking

PP – pay parking

NT – National Trust (free to members)

B – on a bus route (in season)

F – only accessible by foot or bike

Great Gable over Seat, from Gamlin End on High Crag

Cairn on Dodd with Red Pike rising behind (photo: Maggie Allan)

INTRODUCTION

Valley bases

A perennial favourite with valley-bound tourists and mountaineers alike, the Buttermere valley somehow manages to combine soaring grandeur with serene sylvan beauty at the dale-floor level. The fells included here include all those that make up the skyline of the Crummock Water and Buttermere valley, along with the Loweswater fells and much of the fine fell territory approached from the Newlands and Coledale valleys. Everyone who loves mountains will relish climbing any number of these rugged heights, from Fleetwith Pike, Haystacks, High Stile, Hindscarth and Robinson to that dominant cluster of ridges packed about Grasmoor. This is fellwalking of the highest order. Find here fells that beckon from afar such as Grisedale Pike and Causey Pike, Mellbreak and Whiteless Pike. Your adventures will be memorable.

You can reach the fells of Buttermere, Loweswater and Crummock Water from west Cumbria from the A66 at Cockermouth via Lorton, or from the A5086 via Mockerkin, and a little more remotely from Keswick over Whinlatter Pass or Newlands Hause or over the spectacular Honister Pass at the southern end of Borrowdale.

↑ *Buttermere from Dodd, below Red Pike (photo: Maggie Allan)*

Whiteless Pike and Wandope from Newlands Hause

Facilities

Being right in the thick of the accessible scenic action has its upside. It is no surprise that there is an abundance of luxury hotels, cosy B&Bs and self-catering cottages, as well as hostels and camp sites, all in close proximity to these fells. (The Visit Cumbria website (www.visitcumbria.com, click Accommodation) seems to have the best database or you could just use a search engine.)

There are also excellent village shops in High Lorton and Braithwaite, as well as cafés and/or pubs all around the area, but no supermarkets or petrol stations. Head to Keswick or Cockermouth for these.

Getting around

Buses are limited to the seasonal (April to September) Honister Rambler 77 service. This service circles four times a day from Keswick (beside Booths), via Braithwaite, Whinlatter, Lorton, Lanthwaite Green, Buttermere, Honister Pass, Seatoller, Rosthwaite, Grange-in-Borrowdale and the west side of Derwentwater via Portinscale, while the 77A service runs the same route in reverse. The more regular Borrowdale Rambler 78 service, which plies between Keswick and Seatoller, is far less useful for walks in this guide.

Parking is not to be taken for granted anywhere in this popular park. Always allow time to find an alternative parking place, if not to switch to a different plan for your day or just set out directly from your door – perfectly possible if you find accommodation within any of the main valleys. Always take care to park safely and only in laybys and car parks, not on the side of the narrow country roads. Consult the Starting points table to find out where the best parking places (and bus stops) are to be found. Note that although, in general, one preferred starting point is specified for each route, there may be alternative starting points nearby (for example in Buttermere) should you arrive and find your chosen spot taken.

Fix the Fells

The Fellranger series has always highlighted the hugely important work of the Fix the Fells project in repairing the most seriously damaged fell paths. The mighty challenge has been a great learning curve and the more recent work, including complex guttering, is quite superb. It ensures a flat foot-fall where possible, is easy to use in ascent and descent, and excess water escapes efficiently, minimising future damage.

The original National Trust and National Park Authority partnership came into being in 2001 and expanded with the arrival of Natural England, with additional financial support from the Friends of the Lake District and now the Lake District Foundation (www.lakedistrictfoundation.org). But, and it's a big but, the whole endeavour needs to raise £500,000 a year to function. This enormous figure is needed to keep pace with the challenges caused by the joint tyranny of boots and brutal weather. The dedicated and highly skilled team, including volunteers, deserve our sincerest gratitude for making our hill paths secure and sympathetic to their setting. It is a task without end, including pre-emptive repair to stop paths from washing out in the first place.

Bearing in mind that a metre of path costs upwards of £200 there is every good reason to cultivate the involvement of fellwalkers in a cause that must be dear to our hearts… indeed our soles! Please make a beeline for www.fixthefells.co.uk to make a donation, however modest. Your commitment will, to quote John Muir, 'make the mountains glad'.

Using this guide

Unlike other guidebooks which show a single or limited number of routes up the Lakeland fells, the purpose of the Fellranger series has always been to offer the independent fellwalker the full range of approaches and paths available and invite them to combine them to create their own unique experiences. A valuable by-product of this approach has been to spread effects of walkers' footfall more evenly over the path network.

This guide is divided into two parts. 'Fells' describes ascents of each of the 32 fells covered by this volume, arranged in alphabetical order. 'Ridge routes' describes a small selection of popular routes linking these summits.

Fells

In the first part, each fell chapter begins with an information panel outlining the character of the fell and potential starting points (numbered in blue on the guide overview map and the accompanying 1:40,000 HARVEY fell map, and listed – with grid refs – in Starting points in the introduction). The panel also suggests neighbouring fells to tackle at the same time, including any classic ridge routes. The 'fell-friendly route' – one which has been reinforced by the national park or is less vulnerable to erosion – is also identified for those particularly keen to minimise their environmental impact.

After a fuller introduction to the fell, summarising the main approaches and expanding on its unique character and features, come the route descriptions. Paths on the fell are divided into numbered sections. Ascent routes are grouped according to starting point and described as combinations of (the red-numbered) path sections. The opportunities for exploration are endless. For each ascent route, the ascent and distance involved are given, along with a walking time that should be achievable in most conditions by a reasonably fit group of walkers keen to soak up the views rather than just tick off the summit. (Over time, you will be able to gauge your own likely timings against these figures.)

In many instances a topo diagram is provided alongside the main fell map to help with visualisation and route planning. When features shown on the maps or diagrams appear in the route descriptions for the first time (or the most significant time for navigational purposes), they are highlighted in **bold**, to help you trace the routes as easily as possible.

As a good guide should also be a revelation, panoramas are provided for a small number of key summits, and panoramas for every fell in this guide

Grasmoor from High Nook Farm

can be downloaded free from www.cicerone.co.uk (see 'Additional online resources' below). These name the principal fells and key features in the direction of view.

Advice is also given at the end of each fell chapter on routes to neighbouring fells and safe lines of descent should the weather close in. In fellwalking, as in any mountain activity, retreat is often the greater part of valour.

Ridge routes

The second part of this guide describes some classic ridge routes in the Buttermere area. Beginning with an information panel giving the start and finish points, the summits included and a very brief overview, each ridge route is described step by step, from start to finish, with the summits highlighted in bold in the text to help you orientate yourself with the HARVEY route map provided. Some final suggestions are included for expeditions which you can piece together yourself from the comprehensive route descriptions in 'Fells'.

Appendices

For more information about facilities and services in the Lake District, some useful phone numbers and websites are listed in 'Useful contacts'. 'A fellranger's glossary' offers a glossary to help newcomers decode the language of the fells, as well as explanations of some of the most intriguing place names you might come across in this area. The 'Alphabetical list of fells in the Fellranger series' is a comprehensive list of all the fells included in this 8-volume series, to help you decide which volume you need to buy next!

Safety and access

Always take a map and compass with you – make a habit of regularly looking at your map and take pride in learning how to take bearings from it. In mist this will be a time-saver, and potentially a life-saver. The map can enhance your day by showing additional landscape features and setting your walk in its wider context. That said, beware of the green dashed lines on Ordnance Survey maps. They are public rights of way but no guarantee of an actual route on the ground. For example, a straight-as-a-die bridleway appears to lead straight up from Near Ruddy Beck into Ling Comb, in the shadow of mighty Red Pike, but there is no path here and nothing but erosion to greet the hapless fellwanderer. A mist-blinded bearing based on such a line would indeed be dangerous. Take care to study the maps and diagrams provided carefully and plan your route according to your own capabilities and the prevailing conditions.

Please do not rely solely on your mobile phone or other electronic device for navigation. Local mountain rescue teams report that this is increasingly the main factor in many of the incidents they attend.

The author has taken care to follow time-honoured routes and keep within bounds of access, yet access and rights of way can change and are not guaranteed. Any updates that we know of to the routes in this guide will be made available on the Cicerone website, www.cicerone.co.uk/1036, and we are always grateful for information about discrepancies between a guidebook and the facts on the ground, sent by email to updates@cicerone.co.uk or by post to Cicerone Press, Juniper House, Murley Moss, Oxenholme Road, Kendal, Cumbria, LA9 7RL.

Additional online resources

Summit panoramas for all of the fells in this volume can be downloaded for free from the guide page on the Cicerone website (www.cicerone.co.uk/1036). You will also find a ticklist of the summits in the Walking the Lake District Fells series at www.cicerone.co.uk/fellranger, should you wish to keep a log of your ascents, along with further information about the series.

1 ARD CRAGS 581M/1906FT

Climb it from	Rigg Beck **26**
Character	Narrow lofty ridge above Keskadale
Fell-friendly route	1
Summit grid ref	NY 207 198
Link it with	Knott Rigg
Part of	The Newlands Round

Travellers wending up the Newlands Valley come upon the impressive little ridge crowned by Ard Crags as they take the sharp bend on Rigg Beck. Newcomers might spy the sudden upthrusting ridge of Aikin Knott and wonder what mighty fell soars above them. Although in fact of comparatively modest height, this characterful little fell and its companion Knott Rigg form an elegant, sickle-shaped ridge well befitting the first-time fellwalker.

The routes described here start from the valley floor, maximising the climb and the interest and offering ample opportunity to admire the old oak copse set high on the heather slopes of Causey Pike. Alternatively, a 'there-and-back' outing from Newlands Hause, keeping to the ridge as far as Aikin Knott, will give novices and experienced fellwanderers alike a taste of the magic of fell country, with no doubting their direction.

↑ *Aikin Knott and Ard Crags from Rigg Beck*

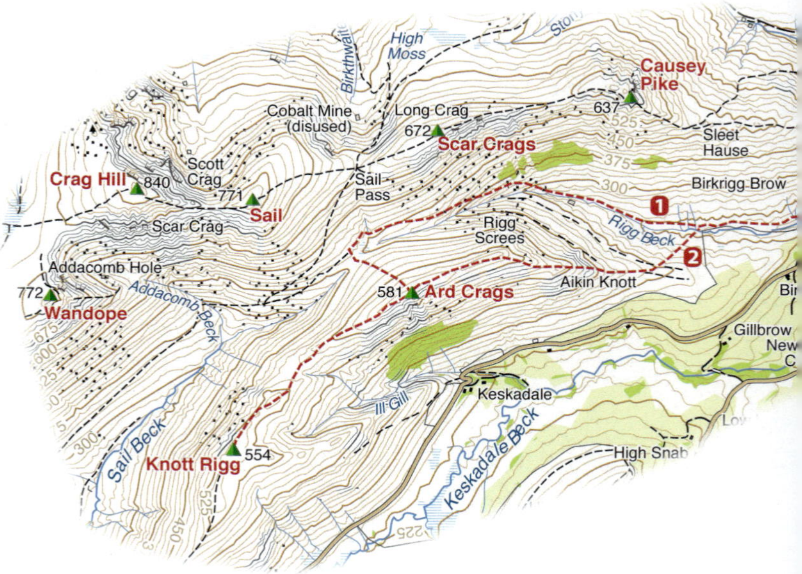

WALKING THE LAKE DISTRICT FELLS – BUTTERMERE

Looking towards Robinson from the spine of the ridge

1 ARD CRAGS

Ascent from Rigg Beck 26

Via Rigg Beck →*2.8km/1¾ miles* ↑*410m/1345ft* ⏲*1hr 20min*

The more circumspect line

1 Set out along the peaceful path leading naturally up the **Rigg Beck** valley which seems to have coped well with the wear and tear of time. Follow it along, roughly west, to the natural level pass. Here curve left to find a tangible if sketchy path slanting half-left up the grassy slope direct to the summit. •

Via Aiken Knott →*2.4km/1½ miles* ↑*410m/1345ft* ⏲*1hr 10min*

The head-on climb

2 Leave the road to follow the path up the valley. Where the wall enclosure ends bear off left, ford the beck and take the long diagonal line to the gently rising ridge. There is a clear path through the bracken. The path comes onto the pasture ridge and moves onto the real meat of the matter – a stiffer, narrower ridge winding through the heather onto **Aikin Knott**. After mounting

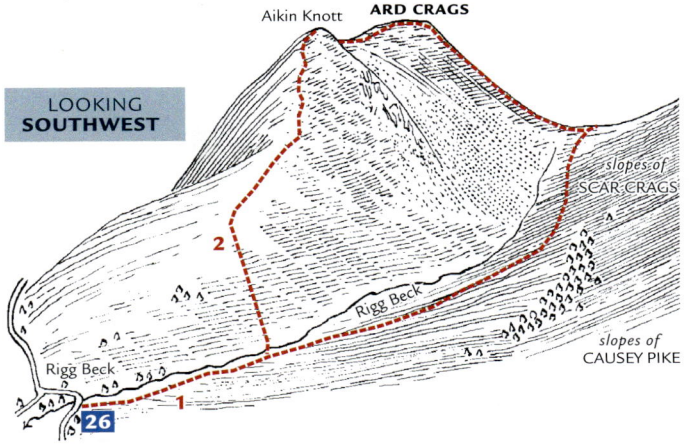

through the heather, reach the best part of the climb as the path runs along the narrow ridge-top to the summit cairn.

The summit

A simple cairn sits on the ridge immediately east of an obvious notch which marks a lovely bird's-eye viewpoint down onto Keskadale Farm. The near bulk of Causey Pike, Scar Crags and Sail contrasts with the balanced perspective on Robinson due south.

Safe descents

Both ascents are reliable in reverse, although the continuing ridge to the NE via Aikin Knott (**2**) is steep and would be uncomfortable in a biting easterly wind.

Ridge route

Knott Rigg → *1.6km/1 mile* ↓*75m/245ft* ↑*50m/165ft* ⏲*30min*
Follow the clear but grassy path SW without complication – a perfect introduction for a novice ridge walker.

Summit ridge

2 BARROW 456M/1496FT

Climb it from	Braithwaite **24** or Uzzicar **25**
Character	A stand-alone ridge rising elegantly from Braithwaite
Fell-friendly route	2 or 3
Summit grid ref	NY 227 218
Link it with	Outerside
Part of	The Coledale Horseshoe

As you travel west along the A66 beyond Keswick, the Northwestern Fells jostle for attention, with the bulk of Barrow coming boldly into view dead ahead. Forming a strong division between the Newlands valley and Coledale, the clean lines of this elegant wedge-shaped ridge rise purposefully and invitingly from Braithwaite at the foot of the Whinlatter Pass. Once a mining community, this charming village is now every inch a tourist haven catering for most pockets, with no fewer than three pubs, hotels, a lively shop, a popular café and the ever-popular Scotgate camp site.

Most approaches (1–6) rise up from the village, with views to the higher fells at the head of Coledale to draw you on, but a couple of back-door southern ascents from Uzzicar are included here, providing the option of a good little round trip (7 for ascent, 8 for descent).

↑ *The heather path to the summit*

WALKING THE LAKE DISTRICT FELLS – BUTTERMERE

Ascent from Braithwaite 24

From the parking area, walk down the final half kilometre of Whinlatter Pass to the first road turning to the right off the sharp bend. Walk along until you pass the green Ivy House Hotel on your right, then turn right to cross the little bridge across the beck to reach the shop.

Via the north ridge →*2.4km/1½ miles* ↑*365m/1200ft* ⏲*1hr 10min*

The first-thought route to the top, with a pleasing variant made up of Routes 2 and 3

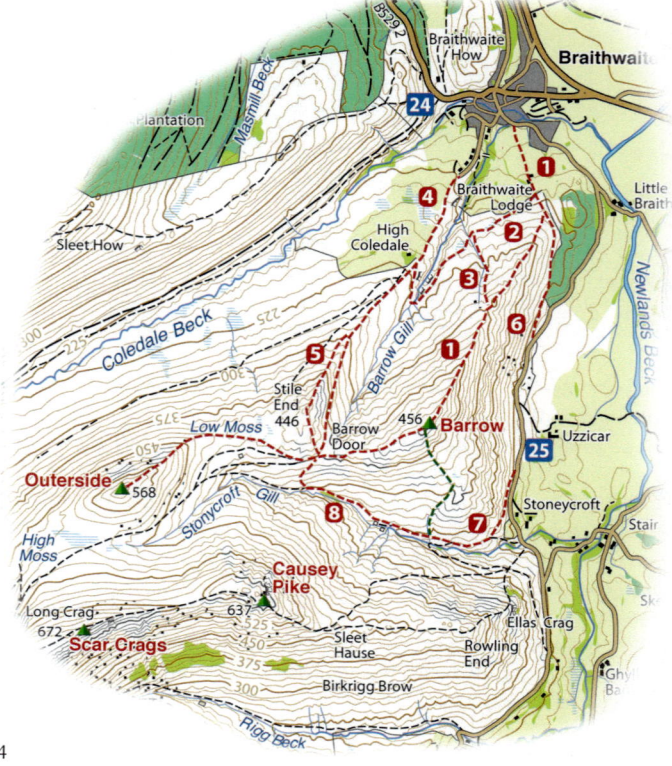

2 Barrow

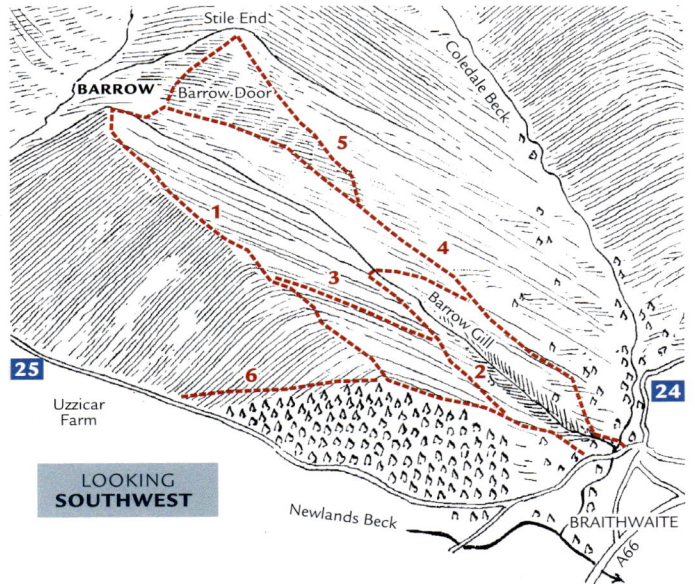

1 From the junction by the village shop follow the Newlands road southeast, passing beyond the final house on the right. Here find a bridleway sign directing from the hand-gate/cattle grid along a metalled lane leading up to **Braithwaite Lodge**. Walk right towards the yew tree by the barns to a fence-stile/gate, where a footpath crosses your way. Head on up the field to a hand-gate, keeping company with the ascending path and coming up above the woodland to branch onto the rising ridge on a heavily used grass trod which soars inexorably up the lovely upper slopes to the summit. **2** Break right from the hand-gate above Braithwaite Lodge and follow a clear path up through the bracken. Ultimately this makes a craggy approach to a ford of **Barrow Gill** to join Route **4** for those who find the lower course of the gill too deep and repelling. **3** Prior to this, an easy route to the left of a tiny grassy gill leads up onto the ridge at the one obvious dip to turn right and join Route **1** to the summit.

Via Barrow Door and Stile End →*2.4km/1½ miles* ↑*400m/1310ft* ⏱*1hr 15min*

A fine way to get a little more out of an ascent of modest Barrow

4 From the village shop follow the lane climbing gently out of the village to the south. Rising and rounding a bend to meet a T-junction, turn left to continue south and follow the tarmac to its end at a gate. Now an open track, the way leads on uphill, passing a reservoir enclosure. As you pass the copse shielding the ruins of **High Coledale**, head straight on, the track now a grassy drove. The path forking left here leads attractively to the ford over the gill. (You could follow this and meet Route **2**, making a short

Stile End from Barrow Gill

round-trip to admire the impressive environs of **Barrow Gill**.) Continue on towards the rising ridge of Stile End but stay with the drove-way along the eastern flank to reach the pass of **Barrow Door** and turn left to climb to the summit. **5** Alternatively, climb the enticing prow ridge of **Stile End**. From here a regular path heads down to Barrow Door to join with Route **4**.

2 BARROW

Ascent from Uzzicar 25

Tackle the fell obliquely from the north with Route 6 or more directly from the south with Routes 7 and 8.

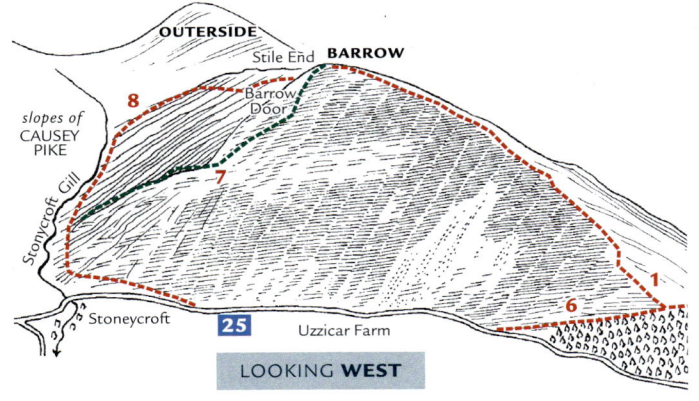

Via the north ridge →*2.5km/1½ miles* ↑*360m/1180ft* ⏱*1hr 10min*
6 From the layby follow the road north to where the bridleway drifts off the roadway by some gorse, gently rising to the left of the woodland wall to turn sharp left and climb the ridge with Route **1**.

Via Stonycroft Gill →*3.6km/2¼ miles* ↑*365m/1200ft* ⏱*1hr 25min*
7 The most direct climbs begin by following the old mine track which leads off the open road immediately south of the layby and enters the valley of **Stonycroft Gill**. The steepest route takes leave of the track where a tiny gill tumbles from the right. Follow this up by a small dammed pool onto a shoulder, then ever more steeply up the heather bank, pathless and breathless, to the summit. **8** Alternatively, stay with the rough mine track to find a trail breaking right, as Causey Pike looms overhead. Take this to reach **Barrow Door** and join Route **4**.

The summit

Summit outcrop

A splendid spot to admire a great view. The Skiddaw massif and Derwentwater take centre stage. Look south over Rowling End to spot Esk Pike and Great End seemingly at the distant head of the Newlands valley.

Safe descents

The north ridge (**1**) makes a simple descent for Braithwaite, as does the path heading W to Barrow Door (**4**), from where you can continue N to Braithwaite or S into the Stonycroft Gill valley (**8**), turning left when you meet the road to reach the Uzzicar verge.

Ridge route

Outerside →*2km/1¼ miles* ↓*130m/430ft* ↑*245m/805ft* ⏲*45min*
Head W to Barrow Door and keep on W, veering over Low Moss to climb the northeast ridge to the summit. The path, rutted in places in the tangle of heather, can be uncomfortable.

3 BLAKE FELL 573M/1880FT

Climb it from	Maggie's Bridge **15**, Waterend **13**, Fangs Brow **12**, Felldyke **11** or Cross Rigg **10**
Character	Centrepoint of a cluster of modest fells above Loweswater
Fell-friendly route	2 or 6
Summit grid ref	NY 111 197
Link it with	Gavel Fell or Knock Murton

Lovers of Lakeland's lesser heights will understandably develop an affection for the seven little fells that gather around Loweswater. The summit cone of Blake Fell does not itself feature in this charming lakeside scene, as it delegates that duty to its northeasterly outlier, Carling Knott. Its strong lines are familiar only to observers from the west, from Lamplugh and Cogra Moss in particular, as it commands the west-Cumbrian coastal plain.

The best of Loweswater nevertheless belongs to the Blake Fell massif. Walkers will find Holme Wood enchanting – you could spend a couple of hours simply strolling round by the shore and past the National Trust's idyllic bothy (holiday let). Up the steeper slopes you can visit Holme Force and loop onto the terrace track (3–4), coming down by High Nook Farm (7) to Maggie's Bridge or, to the north, via Hudson Place (5) or Fangs Brow (6).

↑ *Carling Knott from the shore of Loweswater (photo: Maggie Allan)*

WALKING THE LAKE DISTRICT FELLS – BUTTERMERE

The graded forest tracks of the Cogra Moss basin to the west offer similarly entertaining ascents (8-11), including a gallery path (9) running high and handsome above Cogra Moss and directly below the summit. Note that, although the scattered village of Lamplugh rests closest to its base, there is no permitted access direct from the vicinity of the church, foiling plans to descend from the fell in that direction via Burnbank and Owsen Fells.

3 BLAKE FELL

Ascent from Maggie's Bridge 15

1 Follow the open track leading to and beyond **Watergate Farm**, entering **Holme Wood** at a gate. At once leave the track to join the path rising left on a long diagonal line up the woodland bank, crossing three intervening forest tracks as you mounts to a kissing-gate in the intake wall at the top of the wood. Three options are available from this point – one via Burnbank Fell and two via Carling Knott.

Via Burnbank Fell →*5.2km/3¼ miles* ↑*460m/1510ft*
⏱ *1hr 45min*

Take the fell from the north for handsome views and clear paths en route.

2 Join the green track and turn right, crossing **Holme Beck**. This lovely engineered terrace track leads round the slopes of Burnbank Fell, enjoying handsome views (confirmed by the presence of a strategic seat) over Loweswater towards Low Fell and Grasmoor. Reach a gate and switch up sharp left to the right of the wall (barely a hint of a path) to reach a stile, where a steep fence pitches up, and then clamber by the fence to the cairn on the brow. Alternatively, go through the gate and bear left across the slope to join an

Carling Knott and Burnbank Fell

WALKING THE LAKE DISTRICT FELLS – BUTTERMERE

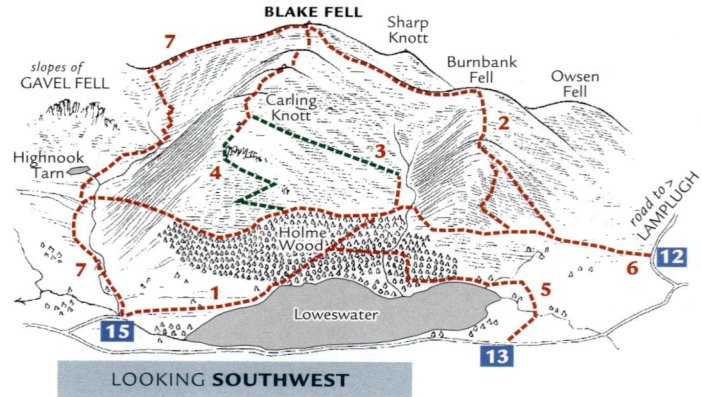

LOOKING **SOUTHWEST**

evident path, coming above an exposure of lateral strata rock to reach the viewpoint cairn marking an extra special fell view – hasten not.

A clear path continues up the broad ridge southwest to the top of **Burnbank Fell**. A modest cairn rests on the far side of the ridge fence. Follow this fence left, crossing a stile and weaving through the heather and across damp ground on a narrow path. The more popular path lies on the west side of the fence. Cross the stile where the ridge path from Carling Knott is met and ascend the short bank, passing a single stunted conifer to reach the summit shelter of Blake Fell.

Via Carling Knott →4.1km/2½ miles ↑465m/1525ft ⊕1hr 30min

Two largely pathless approaches – Route 3 is plain sailing but Route 4, clutching the mossy turf, is rather more vigorous fun!

3 From the kissing-gate in the intake wall bear right on the declining bridle-track, branching left onto a green path just before the slope quickens towards the simple plank-crossing of **Holme Beck**. This shepherds' drove-way leads to a fence-gate. Go through and bear uphill, keeping the fence to your left and the gill over to the right. Ascend steadily, without the benefit of a path but unimpaired, to the ridge. Gain the ridge path and go right to find the summit of **Carling Knott**, a handsome outlying top, the general area quite well clad in heather. There are two ancient cairns, and the main mass has been remodelled into a substantial shelter-cairn. The fell view to the east and south is fabulous and rewards a prolonged stay. The ridge path leads on southwest, dipping via a pool-jewelled hollow to rise via the fence-stile to the summit.

4 As an alternative route, energetic walkers may be tempted to tackle the formidable shadowy ridge-end prow overlooking Holme Wood. In this instance turn left from the kissing-gate, following the bridle-track up to a gate/stile. Bear off the track on a path which dissolves as the mossy bilberry slope steepens. Switch sharp right, and use hands and feet to similar effect in traversing the slope on any trace of a sheep path you may care to find. Either clamber over the right-hand edge above the fence and make your way to the top, or – more interestingly – work back left under the outcropping to thread through a curious quarry-like rift to gain the ridge-top and proceed with Route **3** to the summit.

Ascent from Waterend **13**

Via Holme Wood – link to Routes 2, 3 and 4 →*3.2km/2 miles*
↑*460m/1500ft* ⏲*1hr 30min*

Link route to Route 1

A walker reaches the top of Holme Wood

5 Follow the signposted footpath from the roadside along a confined path leading to a stile. Traverse the field (right) to a stile and a board-walk crossing of the valley marsh, which leads to a gate/stile into the narrow lane leading up to **Hudson Place** (farm). Pass on with the lane, which descends via gates alongside the lakeside meadow and into **Holme Wood**. Wander into the level woodland and take the obvious track angling right, leading up by Holme Force. Continue to where the footpath of Route **1** cuts diagonally across the line of the track. Switch acutely right to join it and then choose from Routes **2**, **3** and **4** at the top.

Ascent from Fangs Brow 12

Via Fangs Brow →*4.5km/2¾ miles* ↑*370m/1215ft* ⊕*1hr 40min*

Link route to Route 2

6 Follow the open track from the roadside gate, staying to the right of the fence as it bends right (due south), after about a kilometre. When the fence soons bends back southeast, part company with it to carry on south and later southeast on a path that soon reaches the cairn on the northeast brow of **Burnbank Fell**. From here join Route **2** as it heads southwest up to the true summit of the fell and on to Blake Fell.

Ascent from Maggie's Bridge 15

Via High Nook Farm →*4.8km/3 miles* ↑*425m/1400ft* ⊕*1hr 45min*

Follow Highnook Beck almost all the way and leave the views to the end.

7 Follow the unenclosed access track to **High Nook Farm** straight out of the car park. (Watch you don't follow the immediate track, to Watergate.) This leads through the gated yard close to the farmhouse and swings up the track above the sheltering copse, which can be alive with croaking rooks. Go through the wall-gate and advance to a track. Stay with the level 'gallery' bridleway – so named because it leads to the famous view over Loweswater from the slopes of Burnbank Fell. As the bridle-track swings right to a small footbridge over **Highnook Beck** ignore this and continue forward on the

3 BLAKE FELL

grassy way to draw close to the outflow of **Highnook Tarn**, where there is evidence of a shallow dam wall.

Pass through the isolated stone gateposts, with their connecting fence long gone. This leads to a higher ford of **Highnook Beck**. Continue on the low ridge, passing a large sheepfold, and begin the climb on a grass trod through the bracken, slanting right then left. Higher on it is less clear for a time, then it returns and turns left in a definite groove. Gaining heather moor, the path leads unfailingly to the tall fence-stile in the damp saddle of **Fothergill Head**. Cross the stile and bear up right, crossing a fence-stile on the brow and continuing north with the ridge path to the summit.

Ascent from Felldyke 11

Via Sharp Knott →*3.7km/2¼ miles* ↑*345m/1125ft* ⏱*1hr 15min*

Quite the most compelling approach, via the fell's sunny western aspect

8 Follow the waymarked path into the lane. Go left and then right through the kissing-gate. Stride along the open track to a kissing-gate, gaining entry into the intriguingly named **Cogra Moss** reservoir and forestry enclosure (Forestry Commission information panel). The track leads on, rock-cut into the flanks of Knock Murton, passing a handsome line of mature beech to arrive at the reservoir dam.

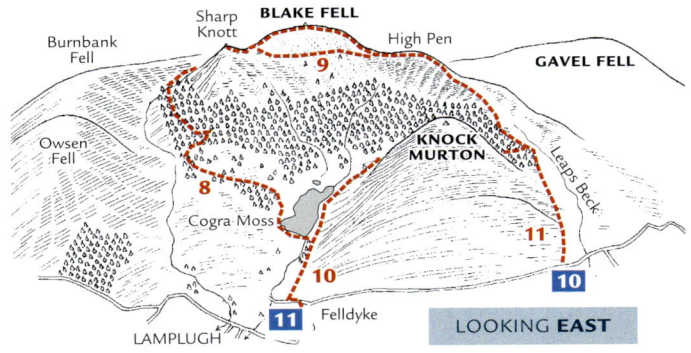

Cross the dam and link to the forest track, keeping left. The track swings round the lower basin, where thoughtful felling is contributing to a greater plan to improve the water quality and benefit the general natural ambiance. The confined track winds up through the middle-aged conifers, and where this ends a path makes its way up the steep bank to the saddle of **Sharp Knott**. Pay this little subsidiary top a visit – beyond the summit cairn is a slate-built shelter in which to sit and muse. Return to the saddle and follow the continuing ridge path to Blake Fell, climbing uninhibited to the summit.

9 Alternatively, having passed **Sharp Knott**, take the path that leads off right from the saddle between Sharp Knott and Blake Fell to follow a sheep path along the high western scarp of Blakefell Screes. Slip under a solitary conifer, the path never more than boot width, and traverse the rough slope to a corresponding saddle on **High Pen**, turning back sharp left to follow the fence a short way before leaving it to trend left (northwest) to the summit.

Via High Pen →4.5km/2¾ miles ↑325m/1065ft ⏲1hr 30min

A straightforward ascent which makes a handsome circuit with Route 8 or 9

10 Set out with Route **8** but carry on with the reservoir-side track past the dam and along under the slopes of **Knock Murton**. (Be alert to fly-fishermen back-casting their lines.) The climb begins where a path branches from the shore track at the water's end. This narrow path, known as the Donkey Trod, ascends the felled bank to meet the forest track from Cross Rigg. Turn left here to climb via Low and **High Pen**, each a lovely viewpoint, and carry on beside the fence. Only after the ridge path from Fothergill Head joins at a stile does the principal path waver from its fence-side duty to bend left, with Route **9**, to the summit.

Ascent from Cross Rigg 10

Via High Pen →4.4km/ 2¾ miles ↑325m/1065ft ⏲ 1hr 25min

Just follow the forest fence for the most direct westerly approach.

11 From the road-verge parking go through the recessed gate and follow the track along the southern base of **Knock Murton**. This leads to a gate and entry into Cogra Moss forestry estate. From here you can either stay on the dark

3 Blake Fell

forest track (along which lurks a fenced iron-mine shaft) or hold right beside the bounding fence. Where the track and fence-side path converge, bear right, falling into step with Route **10** to the summit.

The summit

A large shelter, open to the east, marks the summit. Some 25 metres to the west a shelf makes a fine spot to sit in fair weather to peruse the attractive Cogra Moss basin.

Safe descents

Blake Fell has two dodgy slopes to be aware of: the scree-lined southwestern flank directly below the summit (further compounded by afforestation at its base), and the northern and eastern faces of Carling Knott. The simplest return westbound follows the fence over High Pen (**10**), while for the Loweswater valley it would be best to veer off at the first stile down to Fothergill Head (**7**) and follow the path left, later zig-zagging into the Highnook Tarn basin.

Looking back to Blake Fell from Gavel Fell

Ridge routes

Gavel Fell →*1.6km/1 mile* ↓*130m/425ft* ↑*80m/260ft* ⏲*35min*
This is a fence-driven route. Head naturally SSE off the summit, coming by the fence. A stile at the fence-junction gives access down to Fothergill Head. Either cross this and follow on with the fence to the right, or dip down and remain unfettered, rising S on a prominent path to pass a left-hand fence-corner. By either path, reach the summit cairn.

Knock Murton →*4km/2½ miles* ↓*300m/985ft* ↑*175m/575ft* ⏲*1hr 20min*
Follow the path heading SE well to the right of the fence and keep the ridge fence company as it swings W over High and Low Pen, following the forest-edge path and succeeding track to exit at a gate. Turn acutely right, climbing the bank by the rising forest fence on a strong path, coping with some gorse and mine-disturbed ground. At the highest point veer left, climbing NW to the summit.

Carling Knott across Loweswater

4 CAUSEY PIKE 637M/2090FT

Climb it from	Uzzicar **25** or Braithwaite **24**
Character	Distinctive crinkly ridge-end with a peerless view over Derwentwater
Fell-friendly route	3
Summit grid ref	NY 218 208
Link it with	Scar Crags
Part of	The Coledale Horseshoe

Their distinctive forms and compact arrangement, inviting ridges and deeply incised valleys are what make the Lakeland fells unique. In their midst Causey Pike is a stand-out character in its own right, but also the first peak on a fine 'causeway' of three summits heading to Crag Hill. The situation is eye-catching, the climb rewarding and the view from the top airy and wide.

Climbing over Rowling End (2) or directly to Sleet Hause (1) from Newlands, as most do, your abiding memory will be of the heather. Causey's southern flanks above Rigg Beck also shelter an intriguing copse of ancient oakwood – perhaps a reminder of how the fells may have looked centuries ago before the sheep. Alternative ascents described here also swing round more gradually by Stonycroft Gill (3) or rise up from Coledale over Barrow Door (4).

↑ *Causey Pike from Scar Crags*

WALKING THE LAKE DISTRICT FELLS – BUTTERMERE

Ascent from Uzzicar 25

If the head-on approach of Routes 1 and 2 seems a bit daunting, or you want a good return route after gaining the summit, then Route 3 will appeal.

Via Sleet Hause →2.4km/1½ miles ↑535m/1750ft ⏱1hr 15min

1 Walk about half a kilometre down the road (south) to Stoneycroft Bridge and step off right on the south side of the bridge. The path

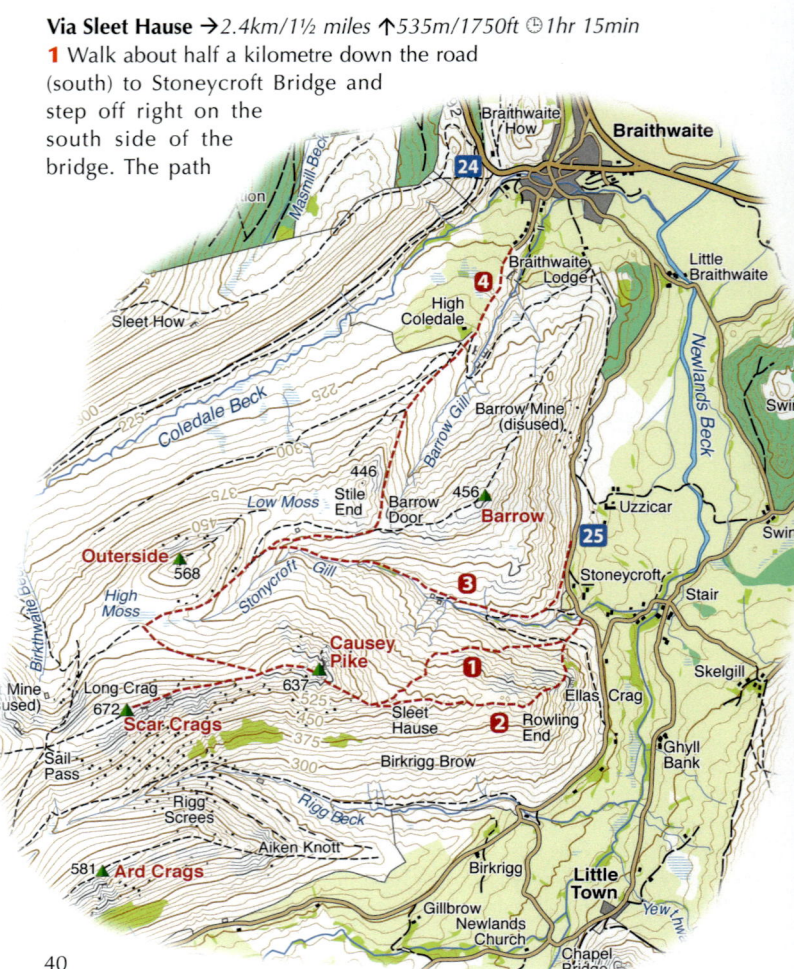

4 Causey Pike

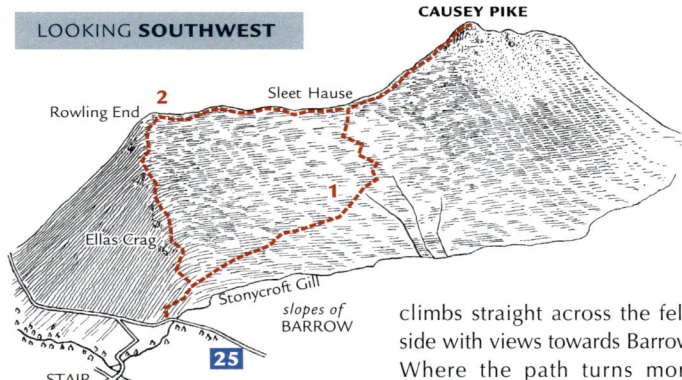

LOOKING **SOUTHWEST**

climbs straight across the fell-side with views towards Barrow. Where the path turns more sternly to the task of climbing to the skyline, a series of zig-zags has been created, securing the trail for many years to come. Climb these to **Sleet Hause** – a fine spot to stop and enjoy the contrasting fellscapes on either side – and turn right to continue steeply up to the summit. The only discomfort is the final scramble. You may be tempted to explore the sheep trod cutting under the outcropping on the left-hand side (not marked) – this avoids the rocks and provides a novel way to circumvent the crag and claim your mountain.

Summit dome as seen from the ascent of Rowling End

Via Rowling End →*2.8km/1¾ miles* ↑*535m/1760ft* ⏱*1hr 30min*
2 Start off with Route **1** but, after crossing a lateral path, keep close to the rising edge above **Ellas Crag**. The hard pull is rewarded by a sumptuous outlook. The ridge path weaves merrily through the heather to **Sleet Hause**, from where the towering dome of Causey Pike beckons. Follow Route **1** to the summit.

Via Stonycroft Gill →4km/2½ miles ↑535m/1750ft ⊕1hr 45min

3 Follow the old miners' track leading off from the parking verge above Uzzicar, which heads up the Stonycroft Gill valley. Keep with the track all the way to High Moss in the southern shadow of Outerside. Here look for a path that goes back east up the grassy fellside, not obvious until you are under way. Follow it to gain the ridge-top, then continue east to the summit.

Ascent from Braithwaite 24

When the buses are running, this leisurely approach would make a good pair with a return down Stonycroft Gill (Route 3).

Via Barrow Door →5.2km/3¼ miles ↑565m/1850ft ⊕2hr

4 From the parking area, walk down the final half kilometre of Whinlatter Pass to the first road turning to the right off the sharp bend. Walk along until you pass the green Ivy House Hotel on your right, then turn right to find the little bridge across the beck to the shop. From the village shop follow the lane climbing gently out of the village to the south. Rising and rounding a bend to meet a T-junction, turn left to continue south (before the sign to the Coledale Inn) and

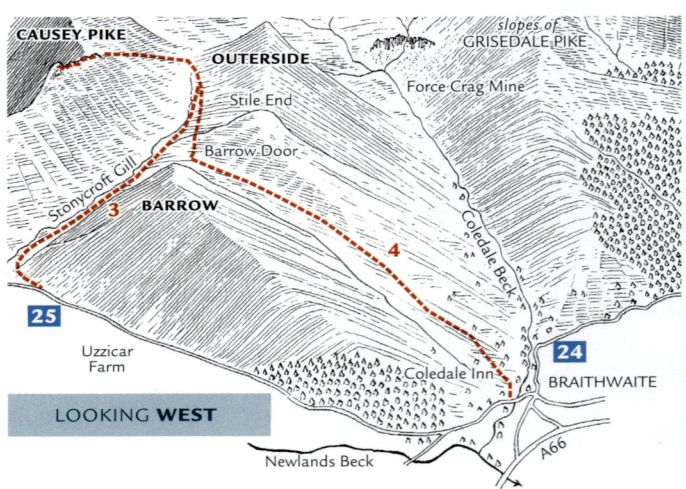

Looking to Helvellyn from the summit

follow the tarmac to its end at a gate. Here it becomes an open track and, after the ruins of **High Coledale**, runs on as a green drove. Continue naturally south, coming up into the gap of **Barrow Door** between Barrow and Stile End. Here veer right on a clear path which joins the old miners' track from Stoneycroft and leads confidently on to **High Moss** with Route **3**.

The summit

The bold knob at the top of the climb from Sleet Hause is probably the summit, but there are up to seven rival tops to the west, each with some trace or more of a cairn, most likely varying in height by only a few centimetres.

Safe descent

The made path from the saddle at the west end of the Causey tops provides a sure line of descent W to High Moss (**3**), where the free-running old miners' track takes you easily right, ENE, and straight down the Stonycroft Gill valley.

Ridge route

Scar Crags → *1.2km/¾ mile* ↓*55m/180ft* ↑*90m/290ft* ⏲*30min*
You would be hard pressed to get lost on this ridge route – although in misty conditions you could slip past the modest summit cairn and arrive at Sail Pass, bemused! The ridge runs slightly S of E, passing some peat hags and cotton-grass tufts, onto the edge that climbs to the summit.

5 CRAG HILL 839M/2753FT

Climb it from	Braithwaite **24**, Lanthwaite Green **33** or Buttermere **30**
Character	Commanding convergence of ridges from Buttermere and Braithwaite
Fell-friendly route	1 or 2
Summit grid ref	NY 193 203
Link it with	Grasmoor, Sail or Wandope
Part of	The Coledale Horseshoe

Crag Hill is a classic mountain – a culmination of handsome ridges tempting travellers over Newlands Hause off the tarmac to reach its dizzy heights. Seen from the north it is the craggy dalehead attraction above Coledale, while from the south its gullied face towers above Sail Beck, spilling into the corrie of Addacomb Hole.

The focus of many popular northwestern circuits, worthy approaches lie at all points of the compass. Reach it from the north along Coledale (1), from the east over the summit of Sail (6), directly from Buttermere to the south over Whiteless Pike (5) and from the shores of Crummock Water to the west along Gasgale Gill (4). Each route can be paired with another to make up a truly great mountain day, with the option of a magnificent traverse between Braithwaite and Buttermere, taking the Honister Rambler bus back to base (in season!).

↑ *Crag Hill from Sand Hill, overlooking Coledale Hause*

5 CRAG HILL

Ascent from Braithwaite 24 *off map NE*

A direct line along the old mine track up Coledale, with two variants in the final stages, offers a tough clamber up a loose scree trail (Route 2) or an extension avoiding Eel Crag altogether (Route 3).

Via Coledale Hause →6.8km/4¼ miles ↑760m/2500ft ⏱2hr 30min

1 Take the footpath leading directly south from the car park and resist the urge to step up right towards the ridge. Instead follow the wide track that contours under Grisedale Pike above the beck. Where the track forks, short of the derelict buildings associated with the old **Force Crag Mine**, veer down left to ford **Coledale Beck**. Stick firmly to the main rough trail leading west which climbs above the side-ravine with a fine view of Low Force. Cross the beck again (at GR 195 212) and follow the path up to where the Fix the Fells team have made a tidy serpentine section up the steeper slope, which comes under Eel Crag to reach **Coledale Hause**. Turn left to tackle the steep path up **Eel Crag** and carry on easily to the summit.

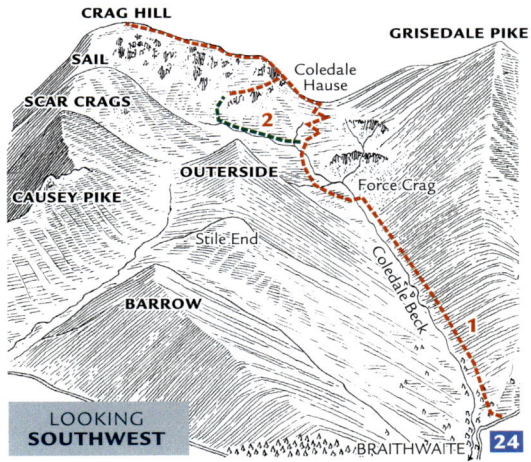

WALKING THE LAKE DISTRICT FELLS – BUTTERMERE

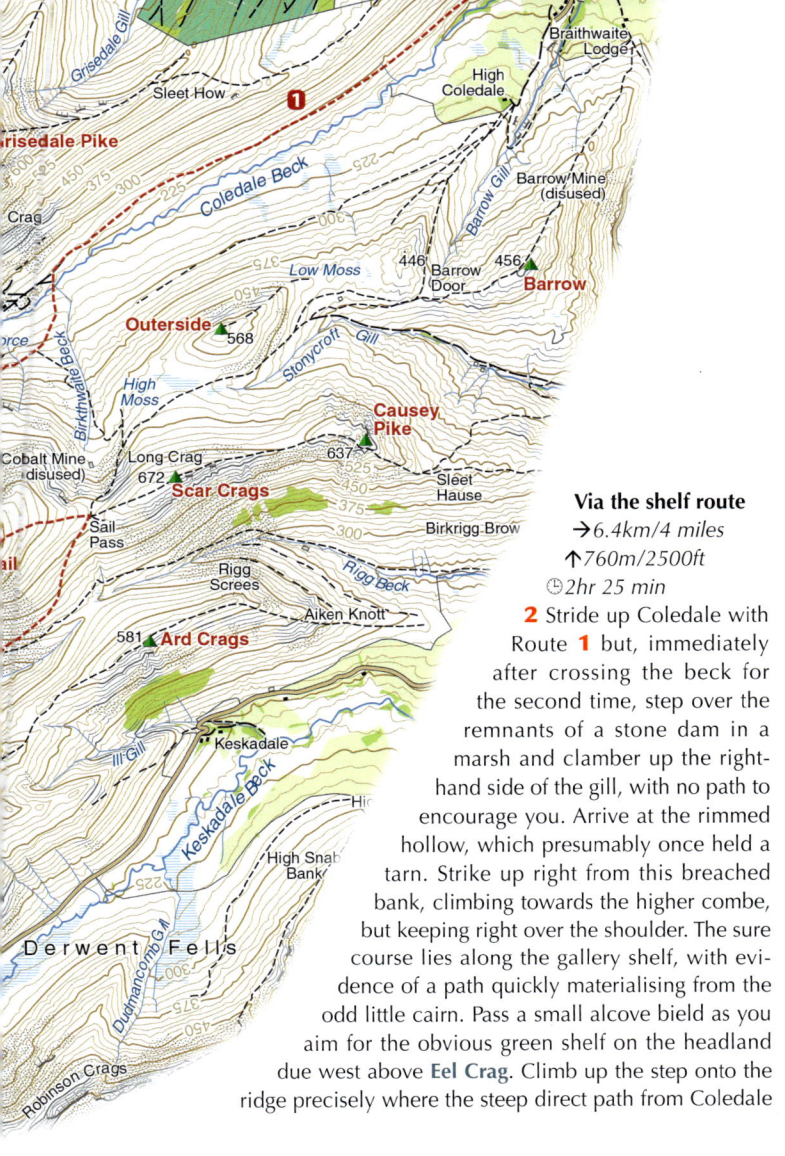

Via the shelf route
→ 6.4km/4 miles
↑ 760m/2500ft
⏲ 2hr 25 min

2 Stride up Coledale with Route **1** but, immediately after crossing the beck for the second time, step over the remnants of a stone dam in a marsh and clamber up the right-hand side of the gill, with no path to encourage you. Arrive at the rimmed hollow, which presumably once held a tarn. Strike up right from this breached bank, climbing towards the higher combe, but keeping right over the shoulder. The sure course lies along the gallery shelf, with evidence of a path quickly materialising from the odd little cairn. Pass a small alcove bield as you aim for the obvious green shelf on the headland due west above **Eel Crag**. Climb up the step onto the ridge precisely where the steep direct path from Coledale

Sail and Crag Hill from Coledale

Hause joins the ridge-top. Bear naturally left, joining Route **1** and climbing easily to the summit.

Via upper Gasgale Gill →*6.8km/4¼ miles* ↑*760m/2500ft* ⏲*2hr 40min*
3 Take Route **1** as far as Coledale Hause. Here the made path continues southwest beside the headstream of Gasgale Gill to the nameless saddle between Crag Hill and Grasmoor, with its peaty pool. Turn left up the strong path, climbing easily over grass northeast to the summit.

Ascent from Lanthwaite Green **33**

Via Gasgale Gill →*5.2km/3¼ miles* ↑*790m/2590ft* ⏲*2hr 35min*

A scenic approach up a deep ravine, best attempted in dry weather

4 Cross the open common to the footbridge and either follow the beck upstream, coping with an entertaining rock-step beside a handsome waterfall, or clamber up the fell, taking the right-hand branch off the ascending path to

5 Crag Hill

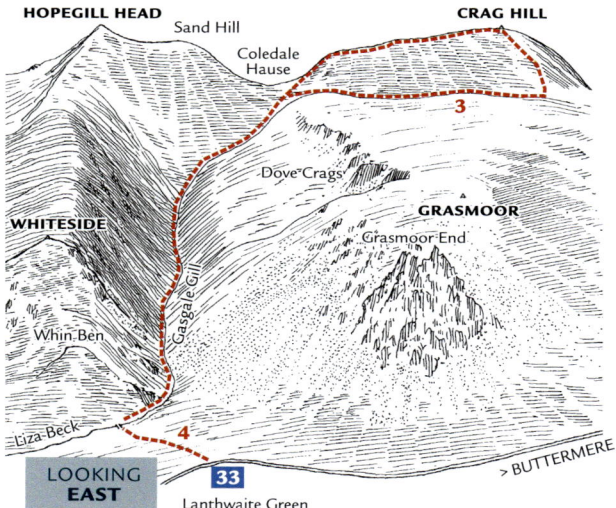

Whin Ben. This goes over a stepped rock-step to meet up with the beckside path, running on up the wild valley. There is no doubting the path, although heavy rain has caused notable landslippage. The beck has some lovely cascades near the top. Come onto the level grassy saddle of Coledale Hause. Head up the facing scree slope to join Route **1**. The stones are loose so **take care** and minimise the wear, tear and disturbance for those who follow you.

Ascent from Buttermere 30

Via Whiteless Pike →5.2km/3¼ miles ↑745m/2450ft ⏲2hr 25min

The fell highway

5 From the National Trust car park, pass to the right of the facing quarry, walk up the bank and, from the fence-stile, cross the High House Crag brow. Head up the fellside on one of two turf paths clear of bracken that lead naturally up Low Bank to the saddle at the head of **Squat Beck**. Look out for the winding path climbing north, coming onto the western shoulder to the back of **Whiteless Breast**. Here set to work on the more earnest part of the climb. Apart from one minor rock-step high up, the climb is obvious, and with modern pitching supporting the heavy use, the way is never in doubt. From the summit of **Whiteless Pike** continue on with the ridge via **Saddle Gate**, then take the lovely ridge by **Thirdgill Head Man** onto the broad expanse of grass leading to the saddle cross-paths. Here turn right (east) to the top.

Via Sail Beck →7.6m/4¾ miles ↑835m/2740ft ⏲3hr

A good route for a return from Route 5, and a grand way in its own right

6 From the National Trust car park at the northern approach to the village, either walk straight over the road and, from the stile, cross the High House Crag brow, or go right with the road and bear off left, guided by the footpath sign, past the cottages to a gate, and follow the field boundary to meet up with the path from the wooded dell. Again, at this point there are two routes up the **Sail Beck** valley. The more common path, a shepherds' drove, makes a deliberate break up left, just where the fence ends and before the final length of wall. Take this and move comfortably through the bracken on **Whiteless Breast**. It

Crag Hill from Sail

5 CRAG HILL

OS column looking to Grasmoor

swings into the re-entrant valley, then up and across **Bleak Rigg** bank to enter and ascend from the **Third Gill** valley before it embarks on a long traverse across the slopes of Wandope. This leads over **Addacomb Beck** and across a gullied section of path, and climbs through heather to an obvious cairn and path-fork. Bear up left with this path, climbing handsomely to **Sail Pass**, the saddle with Scar Crags. Cut back onto the ridge on the unsightly path and continue over the intervening summit of **Sail** and along the narrow connecting ridge which climbs the exhilarating east ridge onto the summit plateau.

WALKING THE LAKE DISTRICT FELLS – BUTTERMERE

The summit

A stone-built OS column stands back from the edge on a domed summit bereft of rock features. From this pedestrian meeting place and well-loved viewpoint right in the heart of the Northwesterns, the panorama is generous, rivalling Grasmoor in all but airiness, until you stand on the edge and look north.

Safe descents

For all the remote situation, there are reliable routes to get you to safety in hostile weather. For Braithwaite descend SW to the saddle (**3**) and follow the engineered path N to Coledale Hause, bearing NE (right) into Coledale itself entirely on good footing.

Ridge routes

Grasmoor →2km/1¼ miles ↓120m/395ft ↑135m/445ft ⏲40min
Descend SW to the saddle and continue up the corresponding steep trail to pass a prominent cairn. The path trends to the southern edge to revel in the spacious views and reach the large compartmentalised summit shelter-cairn.

Sail →0.8km/½ mile ↓100m/330ft ↑30m/100ft ⏲25min
Descend ESE, curving to the E as the ridge narrows through the dip and rises over slabs to the plateau. The summit cairn lies a little to the left, off the strict line of the regular ridge path, beside peaty pools.

Wandope →1.2km/¾ mile ↓105m/345ft ↑35m/115ft ⏲20min
Descend SW, but well short of the saddle veer S, coming along the edge above the hanging valley of Addacomb Hole to reach the little cairn on the grass at the tip.

Whiteless Pike →2.1km/1¼ miles ↓220m/720ft ↑60m/195ft ⏲35min
Leave the trig point SW. The prominent path leads down to a cross-ways in the depression: here turn left (S) to Thirdgill Head Man and continue down narrow Whiteless Edge to finally rise swiftly from the narrow nape onto the summit.

6 DALE HEAD 753M/2470FT

Climb it from	Honister Pass **4**, Seatoller **3**, Rosthwaite **2**, Grange-in-Borrowdale **1** or Chapel Bridge **27**
Character	Conclusive headwall of the Newlands valley
Fell-friendly route	6
Summit grid ref	NY 223 153
Link it with	Hindscarth

Looking down haughtily on the Newlands valley, Dale Head lends both dignity and grandeur to its wild upper reaches, but as a lynch-pin feature hereabouts it fulfils many other roles. Apex of the great ridges of High Spy and Hindscarth and a bridge-head to the western fells on Honister Pass, its lower slopes also have an elegant presence in Borrowdale, below the sub-plateau of High Scawdel, in the form of High Doat, a lowly ridge attractively fringed with native oakwood.

Striking when viewed from the head of Gatesgarthdale are its series of riven ridges and the remnants of slate-quarrying caverns, far too dangerous to explore casually, and in its northern shadowed lap lies evidence of copper mining, with the Rigghead slate quarries in Tongue Gill providing added interest. Dalehead Tarn is the largest sheet of water in the Northwestern Fells, with several lesser sparkling jewels close by on High Scawdel to detain you on your fell journey.

↑ *Dale Head from Fleetwith Pike (photo: Maggie Allan)*

WALKING THE LAKE DISTRICT FELLS – BUTTERMERE

Naturally for such a landmark, routes lead up from all directions. Described here are approaches from Honister Pass (1), Borrowdale (2–5) and Chapel Bridge to the north (6–7). Not many walkers linger long to enjoy the wide views from the summit – but don't let that stop you from savouring this memorable spot.

Ascent from Honister Pass 4

Simple and short but a stiff challenge all the same

Direct →*2km/1¼ miles* ↑*395m/1300ft* ⏲*1hr*

1 Cross the road from the parking area to the right-hand side of the fence and follow it north. (Alternatively, reach this point by the old road from Seatoller, criss-crossing today's tarmac highway.) The path is not exactly faithful, drifting away from the fence at an early stage as it passes an old fold, before coming back into line. Suddenly the fence ends, having served its purpose in defending the dangerous quarried hollows – although a metal fence did once continue to the top. There are intermittent cairns to guide you on – the natural line is a little west of north – direct to the summit cairn.

Path from Honister as it reaches the summit

6 Dale Head

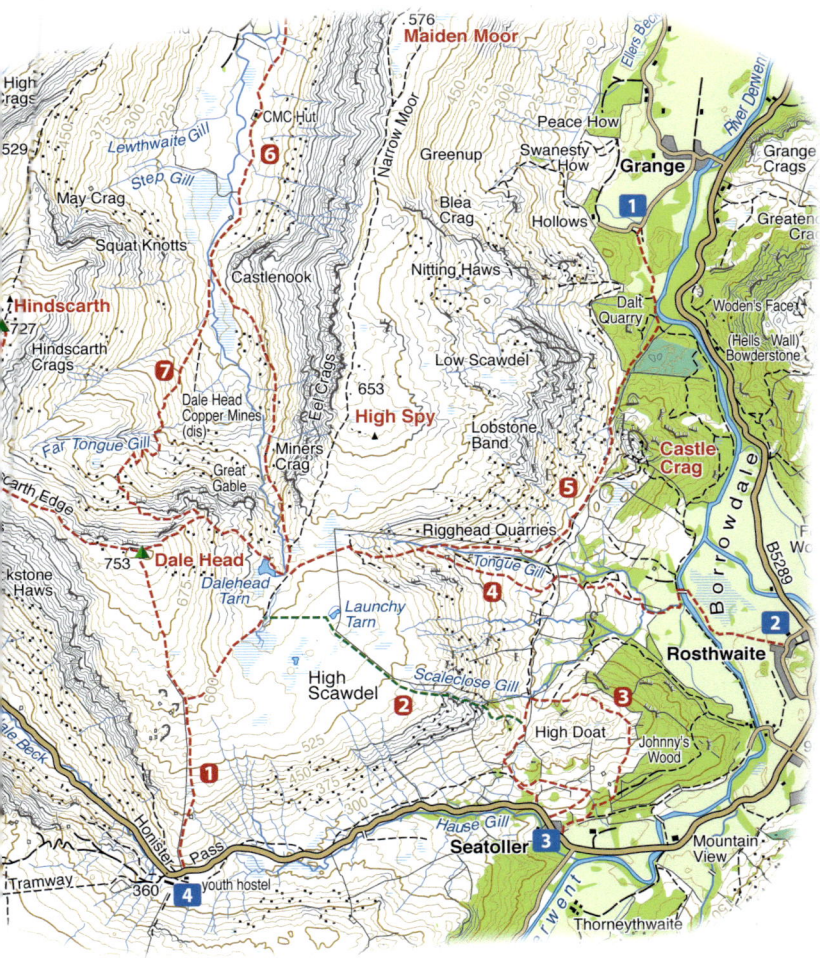

WALKING THE LAKE DISTRICT FELLS – BUTTERMERE

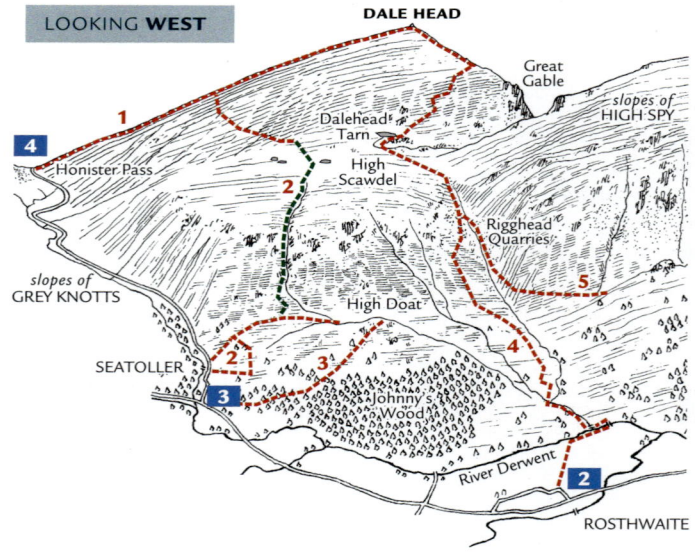

Ascent from Seatoller 3

The fellwanderers' route, largely pathless, starts up from Seatoller via two options – the choice is yours.

Via High Scawdel →4.8km/3 miles ↑655m/2150ft ⏲2hr 15min

2 You can bear right at the first gate at the top of the car park, facing the track-bridge on the left, which leads to a row of cottages, and follow the old road by two further gates as it switches back across the fellside. Alternatively, ascend the tarmac road to the first bend to step up through the hand-gate and climb more directly. As the two routes come together, bend up the grass-bank path to a hand-gate to follow on north beside the wall. After three walls come together, set back to the right, march on a further 60 metres in the same direction (north) to find a small boulder beside the path on the left.

Leave the regular path and climb the steep pathless bank, avoiding bracken and outcropping, and as the slope eases find traces of a path

6 Dale Head

leading to a hand-gate in a stout wall. From here there is little evidence of a path, but the route simply follows the upper course of **Scaleclose Gill** and the subsequent fence to the sharp fence-corner, then bears right to reach **Launchy Tarn**. From here head due west to join the path running south, south of **Dalehead Tarn**. Follow this as it gently rises and curves right to meet the fence above the highest re-entrant quarry. Turn right and follow the fence and subsequent cairns north to the summit with Route **1**.

3 The boulder where you leave the path can also be reached via High Doat. Leave the car park at its eastern end, cross the stile and follow the green-way straight ahead, climbing via a gate into light woodland. Continue with a fence right to go through a gateway and climb onto the bracken slopes of **High Doat** on a clear path, then continue on through a further gateway. The path runs handsomely over the felltop, curving west down by a wall-stile and, after crossing the bracken-free hollow, clambers over a wall-stile onto the bridleway. Turn left beside the wall and quickly come to the boulder beside the path, from where Route **2** leads onwards.

Ascent from Rosthwaite **2**

Via Rigghead →*5.6km/3½ miles* ↑*685m/2250ft* ⏱*2hr 20min*

A natural line on clear paths with lots of points of interest

4 Follow the walled lane from the Flock-in café. This leads to and over New Bridge. Here bear immediately left to the double footbridge. Cross the stile after the first footbridge, now following the flood-bank west beside **Tongue Gill**. Cross a plank-bridge to a stile. There take the winding track up the bank (ignore the inviting ladder-stile), rising to pass through a gate. Bear up half-left onto the lateral track and, in effect, step straight over it to find a green corridor path that leads up the ridge, avoiding bracken, to reach a wall-stile. The continuing path mounts the slate spoil, passing to the right of the old quarry dwelling (now a locked mountain hut) and running on level over slate shards to join the ascending path from Tongue Gill. Keep with this fascinating trail via steps, passing mine cavities and ruined sheds to reach the fence-stile at the top of the valley. Follow the clear path onwards to ford the outflow of **Dalehead Tarn**, skirting to the left of the large outcrop to wander by the north side of the large rushy pool. Embark on the now well-pitched trail, climbing

Ascent from Grange 1

Via Rigghead →6.8km/4¼ miles ↑715m/2350ft ⏲3hr 20min

A side-door approach, full of scenic surprises

5 Follow the Hollow Farm access lane leading south from the middle of the hamlet. Keep left off the metalled roadway at the fork, and pass between camping fields to come by the river. After the second footbridge bear right up the track via a gate onto the part-pitched track leading through the impressive defile of Broadslack Gill on the west side of **Castle Crag**. After coming over the brow, follow on, choosing the right-hand track where it forks. This old mine approach leads up into the **Tongue Gill** valley and climbs via a stile to join forces with Route **4** at the flight of slate steps.

Mallard on Dalehead Tarn

6 DALE HEAD

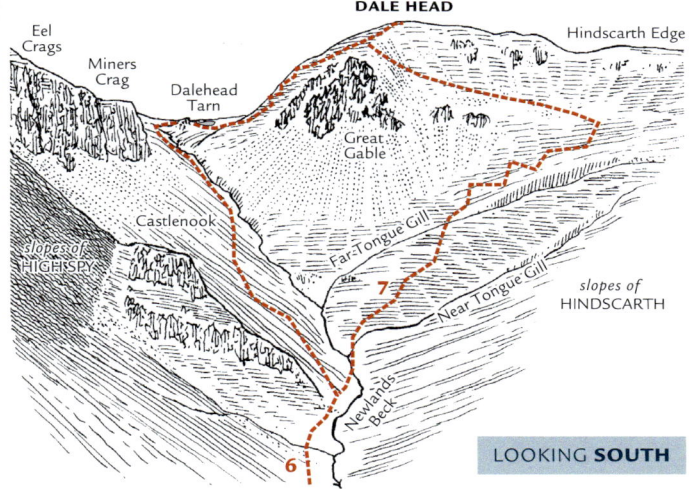

Ascent from Chapel Bridge 27 *off map N*

Chapel Bridge is a springboard for two fabulous climbs of great scenic merit.

Via Dalehead Tarn →*6.4km/4 miles* ↑*610m/2000ft* ⏲*3hr 30min*
6 Walk up from the bridge-side parking area to Little Town to take the valley track south. Continue past the **Carlisle Mountaineering Club Hut** about a mile up the valley and pass under the **Castlenook** spur, by mine spoil banks. The track fades as it approaches a fork. Here bear uphill, climbing steadily over rough ground – you may keep beside the beck and inspect the impressive sequence of cascades, but the higher path is the preferred way. This leads up beneath the line of cliffs marshalling High Spy to come above the upper ravine and ford the beck, the outflow of **Dalehead Tarn**, in harmony with Routes **4** and **5**. Continue with Route **4** to the summit.

Via Dale Head Copper Mines →*5.6km/3½ miles* ↑*610m/2000ft* ⏲*2hr 20min*
7 Start out with Route **6** and then, after passing beneath **Castlenook** spur, ford **Newlands Beck** as **Near Tongue Gill** feeds into the valley beck. Follow

the green-way, an old miners' track, climbing steadily south to ford the more impressive **Far Tongue Gill** with its slabby walls. The green-way now follows a sequence of hairpins as it climbs to the site of the upper copper mine.

Copper-mine ruin backed by Great Gable Crag

Pass the ruined shed on a clear path which works southeast, up to the highest adit on the steep slope directly below the fell's headwall. A narrow trod ventures onto the shoulder to join Routes **4**, **5** and **6** as they converge. You may be tempted to descend to view the dramatic dale scenes from the top of Great Gable Crag, with gullies falling on either side, but you must backtrack to continue, as there are no safe ways down. Follow Route **4** to the summit.

The summit

Summit cairn (photo: Martin Graham)

Here stands a cairn that does real justice to the situation, a worthy rival to High Spy's handsome standard, albeit set a few strides east of the true summit for good reason. Given a half-decent day, the temptation to sit on the brink and soak up the long view down the Newlands 'glen' to Skiddaw is hard to resist.

Safe descents

The one sure recourse in foul weather is the path S to Honister Pass (**1**). A chain of cairns and then a fence make this a reliable way in mist. But if your

6 Dale Head

The Newlands valley from Dale Head (photo: Andrew Locking)

destination is lower Newlands then you need to follow the ridge path NE, watching for the right-hand turn leading onto the pitched path tilting down to Dalehead Tarn. Ford the outflow and follow the path, above the beck's right bank, into the valley (**6**).

Ridge route

Hindscarth →*2km/1¼ miles* ↓*95m/310ft* ↑*70m/230ft* ⏲*30min*
The ridge path has little to hamper its progress W, and the modest outcropping prior to the descent to the wide saddle is passed on the south side – although watch out for the low metal stumps of the old fence that once ran along the ridge. Along Hindscarth Edge a natural lateral path has evolved which shortcuts the way N to the summit.

7 FELLBARROW 416M/1365FT

Climb it from	Waterend **13**, Mosser **14** or Thackthwaite **18**
Character	Retiring pastoral fell, guardian of Lorton Vale
Fell-friendly route	1
Summit grid ref	NY 132 242
Link it with	Low Fell

Lying at the northern extremity of a gently swelling ridge of grassy little heights, Fellbarrow belongs to the pastoral landscapes of the lower Cocker rather than the mighty fells of Crummock and Buttermere. The underlying Skiddaw slate ensures rolling slopes and acres of grass for the contentment of sheep, cattle and the melodious lark. The summit reveals long vistas towards Cockermouth and the coast.

The whole massif has a chequered history on the access front. At the Fellbarrow end, walkers have long approached the summit from the Hatteringill fell-lane off the old green road linking Low Lorton with Mosser. This southward-branching lane, used by Wainwright disciples and equipped with stiles both to and within the access land, is indeed scenic but the farmer at Mossergate retains the right to challenge and turn you back, and so it is not recommended here.

↑ *Fellbarrow from Low Lorton, the summit just out of view between Smithy Fell and Hatteringill Head (photo: Tim Thornton)*

7 FELLBARROW

The walker who loves a round-ramble will enjoy a circuit taking in the string of little connected ridge summits on this massif – Darling, Low, Sourfoot and Smithy Fells and perhaps Hatteringill Head – or spending a low-level day exploring the lanes to the north (3) and visiting the smallest nature reserve in England, the unimproved hay meadow beside Sandy Beck. If the summit of Fellbarrow is your sole aim, the most natural, legal ascents are from the northern tip of Loweswater (1), Mosser to the west (2) and Thackthwaite in Lorton Vale (4–5).

Ascent from Waterend 13

Via Mosser Fell Road →*3.7km/2¼ miles* ↑*290m/950ft* ⏱*2hr 10min*

1 Opposite the parking area find a metalled lane signed 'Askill B&B/bridleway to Mosser Fell Road'. As the tarmac switches to concrete bear left then smartly right into the green lane, rising via gates to meet the Mosser Fell Road. Turn left and follow the lane for about 0.8km (½ mile) until you reach a recessed track access on the right, leading through a galvanised gate into the fell enclosure. Follow this over **Mosser Beck** to enter open pasture, the green track advancing to the foot of a gorse-cloaked slope. Follow the obvious path which slants diagonally left up through the gorse. Once free of the low leg-tickling shrubs head east, drifting northeast as the semblance of a path materialises, to reach the summit pillar.

Ascent from Mosser 14

Via Mosser Gate →*2.8km/1¾ miles* ↑*265m/870ft* ⏱*2hr 15min*

Consider a brief visit to the hidden up-field setting of the Chapel of St Michael (southwest of the hamlet) before setting off.

2 Follow the road signed 'Loweswater – unfit for motor vehicles'. This leads through the blue-painted Mossergate Farm and tidy **High Mosser**, retaining a moderately metalled surface. After a

Remote St Michael's, Mosser

WALKING THE LAKE DISTRICT FELLS – BUTTERMERE

walled stretch the lane briefly opens up and here a track breaks left to a galvanised gate onto the fell. Take this to continue with Route **1**.

Low-level circuit →8.7km/5½ miles ↑170m/560ft ⏲3hr

A useful low-level round-ramble entirely on firm track or metalled road

3 Walk up through the hamlet and beyond to take a green lane setting off east towards Low Lorton. This charming lane straddles the northern slopes of the fell – but sadly there is no right of way onto the fell. It leads by Catgill Bridge and Crinkley Hill down to Low Lorton Bridge, rebuilt after the floods of November 2015. After about 3km (2 miles), as the road starts to hairpin to the left, turn left (north) on an appealing track leading from High Bank to High Rogerscale. At the end, turn left (west) along the tarmac road to walk about a kilometre to Sandybeck Bridge, with access to the **Sandybeck Meadow National Nature Reserve**. Continue to a left turn along the metalled **Mirk Lane**, keeping left and passing through **Toddell Bridge** and **Aikbank Mill** to return to Mosser.

Ascent from Thackthwaite 18

Via Thackthwaite House →2.8km/1¾ miles ↑485m/1590ft ⏲1hr 15min

The most entertaining route to the top, particularly if you include Watching Crag

4 Climb out of the centre of the village on the narrow lane to Thackthwaite Farm, signed 'Low Fell'. This leads up by the garden of Thackthwaite House to a kissing-gate into an open field. Ascend, with the line of trees and ditch to the right, to a second kissing-gate, and complete the rise to the open fell at a third kissing-gate. The green-way veers right, taking a pleasing bracken-free line through two further fence-gates and swinging up into the combe to embark on a neatly cut sequence of zig-zags.

Keep on the main path to the kissing-gate in the saddle. Go through this and bear left by the old sheepfold (sliced through by the ridge fence) to stand on top of the tiny crest of **Watching Crag**, the perfect place to linger and enjoy a charming view over the eastern scarp of Sourfoot Fell into the lovely Vale of Lorton. Backtrack through the kissing-gate in the saddle and keep left,

Looking south to the High Stile range from above Thackthwaite

crossing the top of **Sourfoot Fell**. Follow the fence onwards over **Smithy Fell**, another minor swelling barely deserving of a distinguishing name. At a fence-junction cross the stile to the left and another stile after that on the climb to the summit.

5 Alternatively, if you're happy to skip **Watching Crag**, at the second left-hand hairpin above the combe, branch off on a contouring shortcut path direct to the fence-junction, rejoining Route **4** for the final stretch to the summit.

The summit

The stone-built OS column stands seven metres west of the fence, with a clump of rushes and a small cairn some ten metres further to the west and, another 70 metres west again, a horseshoe of stones – a back-rest more than a shelter. A good half of the view is dominated by the flatter landscape from the low country of the rivers Marron and Cocker, dotted with old working villages and woods, to the coastal fringe of Workington, with the Scottish hills far beyond.

7 Fellbarrow

To visit Hatteringill Head from here, follow the fence north, crossing a fence-stile during the easy descent and later crossing a ladder-stile over the wall at the foot of the slope. Bear half-left to pass the small outcrop and then rise over the saddle to find a cairn.

Safe descents

All approaches are safe in reverse. If heading W over Mosser Fell (**1**) be sure to bear left into the gorse on a sheep trod, uniting with an open tractor track lower down.

Ridge route

Low Fell →*2km/1¼ miles* ↓*85m/280ft* ↑*90m/295ft* ⏲*40min*
Follow the watershed ridge with its attendant fence. Descend S, and at the foot of the slope cross a fence-stile, putting you on the east side of the fence. Keep company with the ridge fence over Smithy Fell, and in the next decidedly damp hollow bear left, contouring to the saddle with its kissing-gate. Go through and keep to the ridge path, which leads up to a fence-stile and smartly onto the top of Low Fell.

Looking southeast from the ridge fence towards Grasmoor

8 FLEETWITH PIKE 648M/2126FT

Climb it from	Gatesgarth **6** or Honister Pass **4**
Character	Striking chiselled ridge rising from the head of Buttermere lake
Fell-friendly route	3
Summit grid ref	NY 206 142
Part of	The Buttermere Round

Viewed from Buttermere village or across the lake from Burtness Wood, Fleetwith Pike commands the fellwalker's attention. A fell to climb by one sure ridge from dale-bottom to top, it perfectly complements the rugged complexity of Haystacks across the wild hollow of Warnscale Bottom. Near the top of this combe lies Dubs Bottom, a hanging valley where the final traces of Ice Age ice lingered longest. Watch out for the beck draining sluggish and deep through the blanket peat.

Motorists and cyclists alike enjoy the challenge of the crawl to the top of Honister Pass. The journey up Gatesgarthdale is memorable, with ice-scoured rock, overbearing cliffs and ribbons of scree. That from Seatoller is steep but more pastoral. Closed in 1989 after four centuries of mining blue-green slate at the site, Honister Slate Mine was reopened in 1997 by Mark Weir, who developed it into a tourist attraction with mine tours and via ferratas.

↑ *Fleetwith Pike from Haystacks*

8 Fleetwith Pike

As well as the direct route up Fleetwith Edge (1), approaches are described here from Gatesgarth along old slate miners' tracks via Dubs Bottom (2) and along the Old Tramway from the pass (3). On Route 1 notice the white cross erected for Fanny Mercer who tumbled to her death here in 1887, a reminder of the perils of a momentary stumble (and just round the corner from a regular rescue practice ground for Cockermouth Mountain Rescue Team on upper Warnscale Beck).

Ascent from Gatesgarth 6

Via Fleetwith Edge →2km/1¼ miles ↑535m/1755ft ⏲1hr 20min

Direct and delightful

1 Follow the road through the trees. Beyond the cottage leave the open road at the track and 'Open Country' sign and immediately stride up the pasture to the foot of **Low Raven Crag**. The pitched path sets to work climbing over this initial rocky obstacle, passing the white cross. At first glance the fell's west ridge, known as Fleetwith Edge, appears to climb in one mighty leap, but it

Fleetwith Pike from Horse Close on the southern shore of Buttermere (photo: Andrew Locking)

WALKING THE LAKE DISTRICT FELLS – BUTTERMERE

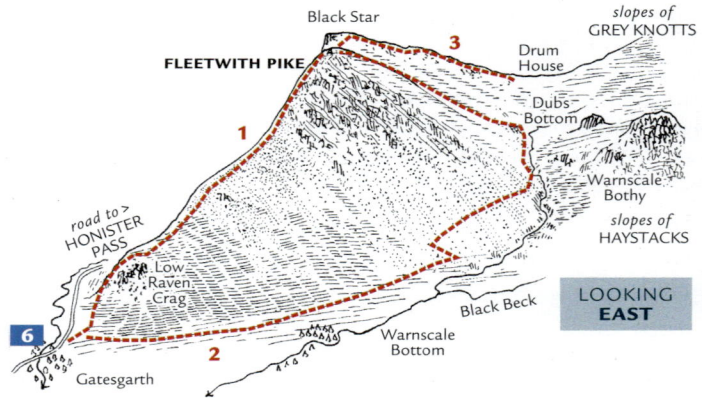

has several clear-cut stages on which to pause and indulge in backward glances. Higher up, the smooth conformation of Skiddaw slate makes a sudden transition to volcanic intrusions, and coarser rock and heather

Fanny Mercer memorial cross on Low Raven Crag

8 FLEETWITH PIKE

replace the grass underfoot. A gully to the right gives a handsome view down into Warnscale Bottom. The ascent culminates precisely and elegantly upon the summit cairn.

Via Warnscale Beck and Dubs Quarry →*4.1km/2½ miles* ↑*535m/1755ft* ⏲ *1hr 50min*

Follow in the footsteps of the miners through wild Warnscale.

2 Head south, following the open track that leads below Low Raven Crag to enter the Warnscale valley, coming above a pine copse. Ignore the fork to the broad footbridge and keep on to a ruin, where the path switches up and begins a steady ascent across the steep fellside of Fleetwith Pike. It curves south to a tight bend above the deep upper ravine of **Warnscale Beck**. The

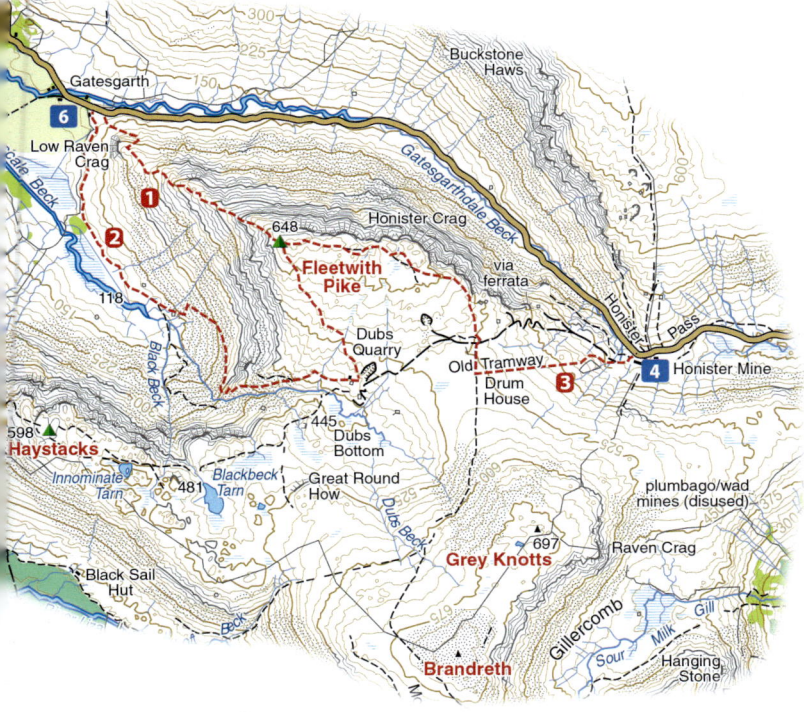

engineered track, now rather loose, winds attractively up to the ruins connected with **Dubs Quarry**. One has a roof and is used as a mountain hut. Directly after this and before the quarry entrance, break left on a narrow path which climbs northwest to the summit.

Ascent from Honister Pass 4

Via the Drum House incline →*2.8km/1¾ miles* ↑*300m/985ft* ⏲*1hr 10min*

The least strenuous route to the same stunning views

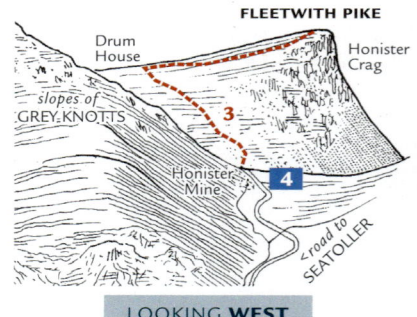

3 From the private Honister Mine parking area, take the footpath that climbs with the modified slate-quarry incline (the **Old Tramway**) towards Drum House, peeling left (west) almost immediately off the open track. (The track itself can be busy with lorries and

Drum House incline (photo: Maggie Allan)

8 Fleetwith Pike

The summit ridge from the top of Honister Crag

minibuses heading to the via ferrata or the mine tour.) On reaching the remnant retaining walls of **Drum House** at the top, bear right off the level track at a right angle, crossing the grassy moor to reach the open quarry track lined with tall slate stones. Bear left and then smartly right onto a clear path, which rises to the right of the still-active slate quarry. The path leads easily upwards, giving walkers scope to venture to the edge and view the upper section of the via ferrata, on the line of the old mining incline, with a workshop shelter set into a re-entrant quarry. The ascending path draws close to the top of **Honister Crag**. Make the move onto this knoll. From this point the ridge is a delightful mix of outcrops and marshy pools and the path winds naturally on to the summit.

The summit

Summit cairn, looking to Great Gable, Scafell and Kirk Fell

A classic situation with a triumphant cairn and a grassy perch where you may wish to linger long. To the northwest Buttermere and Crummock Water lead the eye out to the Solway Firth and the Scottish hills. Closer at hand, to the south are Great Gable, Scafell and Pillar above the sombre crags of

WALKING THE LAKE DISTRICT FELLS – BUTTERMERE

Haystacks. Swinging round to the north past the High Stile range, the bulky mass of Robinson, Hindscarth and Dale Head is clearly seen.

Safe descents

Retracing Route **2** to Dubs Quarry (S then SE) puts you on the most secure track down into Warnscale for Buttermere. Due E along the summit ridge by the top of Honister Crag (**3**) a clear path leads faithfully to the quarry road and so down to Honister Pass on paths that are very reliable in mist.

The ridge from Black Star (photo: Maggie Allan)

9 GAVEL FELL 526M/1726FT

Climb it from	Maggie's Bridge **15**, Cross Rigg **10** or Whins **9**
Character	Gable-like little height in the company of Hen Comb and Blake Fell
Fell-friendly route	9
Summit grid ref	NY 117 185
Link it with	Blake Fell or Hen Comb

Strictly speaking, Gavel Fell is the southernmost section of the Blake Fell massif, and the peak is seldom climbed in isolation, with many walkers energetically embracing it during a clean sweep of the Loweswater Fells. Its profile is clearest viewed from the charming little hamlet of Croasdale to the west, but sadly access is no longer permitted from this direction, or even from nearby Banna Fall which might otherwise have made up a charming round, perhaps taking in the tiny cairnless summit of Floutern Cop.

All the same, there are many plausible approaches to the summit, from the west and from the north. It makes a good short-day walk from High Nook (1–5) – if climbed by Black Crag (2) the route is immersed in the heather on the ridge to the summit – or a fine short climb from Cross Rigg (6–8) or Whins (9).

↑ *Black Crag (photo: Andrew Locking)*

WALKING THE LAKE DISTRICT FELLS – BUTTERMERE

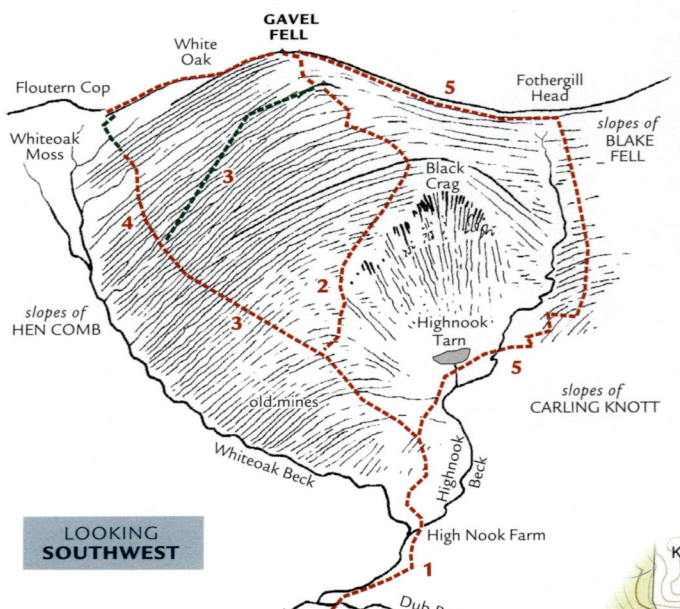

Ascent from Maggie's Bridge 15

Via Black Crag →*4.8km/3 miles* ↑*425m/1395ft* ⏲*1hr 50min*

The direct line up through the heather

1 Follow the **High Nook Farm** access track from Maggie's Bridge (spurning the immediate track to Watergate). This leads through the gated yard close to the farmhouse and swings up above the sheltering copse. Go through the wall-gate and advance to a track fork after about 80 metres. There are four ways to the summit from this point.

9 Gavel Fell

2 Bear left and follow the rising grass bridle-track. As it eases, and with the approach of bracken on the right, bear off right on a tangible trod which works up the steep slope via a shallow hollow, gaining height above **Black Crag** and offering views over the Highnook Tarn basin. Coming onto the heather-clad ridge, keep an eye and ear out for grouse with their 'get back, get back' calls. Bend gently southwest, over a cairned subsidiary top, to reach and cross the stile at the fence-junction just short of the summit.

North from the ridge above Black Crag

Via the Whiteoak Beck drove-way →*3.7km/2¼ miles* ↑*415m/1360ft* ⏱*1hr 15min*

A grassier variant

3 Alternatively, from the fork, instead of branching off with Route **2** continue south on the original track contouring above **Whiteoak Beck**. Some 60 metres after passing through a forlorn stone gateway arrive at a gate. Here climb up right, keeping the fence close to your left. Directly after a fence-junction on the opposite side, take a convenient opportunity to clamber over the fence and continue, now with the diagonally rising fence to your right. The grassy pasture is more comfortable underfoot here. Reach a small fenced enclosure and here recross the fence. Head up away from the fence and rise past a double-enclosure sheepfold onto the subsidiary top to join the ridge path of Route **2** at the cairn.

Via White Oak Moss →*5km/3 miles* ↑*425m/1395ft* ⏱*2hr*

A little longer and a little damper

4 Follow Route **3** as far as the gate after the stone gateway. Go through this gate, maintaining company with the level green track and stepping over an

9 Gavel Fell

area of wash-out. Go through another gate, contouring into the marshiness close to White Oak Moss, where the path dissolves. Curve right (pathless) to meet and cross the fence, climbing over White Oak to reach the summit cairn.

Via Fothergill Head →5.2km/3¼ miles ↑430m/1410ft ⏲2hr 10min

Follow the boundary markers to the top.

5 Set out on Route **1** and stick with the level bridleway leading into the combe. The track swings right to a small footbridge over Highnook Beck. Spurn this to continue forward on the grassy way and draw close to the outflow of Highnook Tarn, where there is evidence of a shallow dam wall. Pass through the isolated stone gateposts, with their connecting fence long gone, and continue up to a higher ford of Highnook Beck. Continue on the low ridge by a large sheepfold and begin the zig-zag climb. Follow a grass trod through the bracken, slanting right then left – higher up it is less clear for a time, then reinvents itself and turns left in a groove. On gaining heather moor the path leads unfailingly to the tall fence-stile in the damp saddle (with a boundary marker at its base with the initials 'I' and 'G' divided by a line). This is Fothergill Head. Do not cross this stile, but instead turn left and follow the fence to the summit. En route notice an old stoop stone lying at the left-hand bend in the fence – another old boundary marker.

Ascent from Cross Rigg **10**

Make your own way over the Comb Gill ravine or follow the old path to Fothergill Head.

Via Godworth →3.7km/2¼ miles ↑310m/1015ft ⏲1hr 20min

6 From the roadside parking an open track leads from the facing gate, with gangly thorn bushes close left part-screening the heathery bulk of Knock Murton. Beyond the next gate the track advances to a fence-corner and continues through a shallow hollow, rising by the gorse to a gate in the intake wall. There are two ways forward.

7 Go straight ahead and gently rise to the cairn surmounting grassy Godworth. Cross over and traverse the shallow hollow to join a quad track leading on by a dyke on the heather moor. Keep with the sheep trods as this

Drove-track from Cross Rigg to Godworth

dissolves, skirting the rushes at the head of a side-gill to arrive at the attractive **Comb Gill** ravine. Slip through by a small waterfall, noting the sheepfold below. Swing right round the rush-filled hollow to ascend beside the largely dry course of **Ill Gill**, and continue uneventfully direct to the summit.

8 The second option from the intake wall-gate is to follow the more obvious path swinging left. This skirts the summit of Godworth on the north side and rises gradually across the slopes of Saddler's Knott, becoming more pronounced as it rises northeast on the slope of **High Pen**. Approaching the fence in the saddle of **Fothergill Head** and short of the stile, bear right on an evident path through the heather, slipping by the left-hand fence-corner to reach the summit.

Ascent from Whins **9**

Via Floutern Pass →*4.5km/2¾ miles* ↑*390m/1280ft* ⏲*1hr 45min*

9 From the laybys a bridleway signpost 'Buttermere 4.5 miles' directs along a confined hedged lane. After the path fords a small gill a second lane joins

9 Gavel Fell

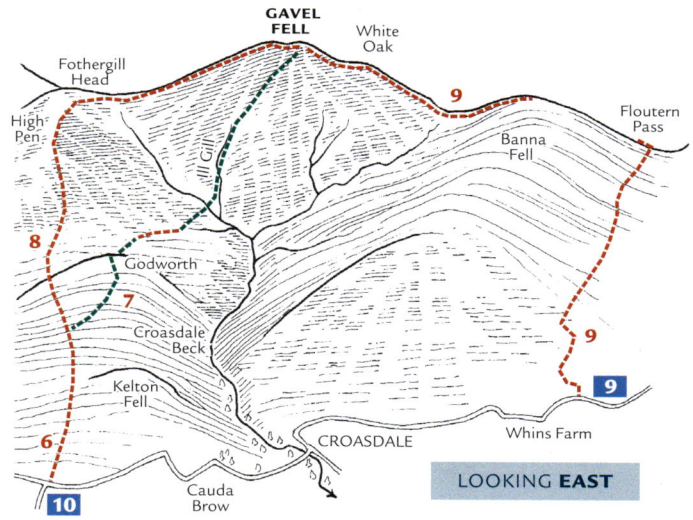

from the left. From here follow the obvious part-walled, part-fenced track via gates. After the third gate the track runs open up a pasture, coming to a fence. Switch left up to a further gate after which the track enters rough pasture on the south slope of **Banna Fell**. Keep faithfully to the track to reach a gate/stile in the fence marking the top of **Floutern Pass**. Go through and either bear immediately left following the fence or nip up the cairnless tor of **Floutern Cop** first then switch back pathless to the fence-corner. Follow a faint path west beside the fence to its junction with the Banna Fell fence. Clamber easily over by the loose rope, turn right, and after a damp depression climb over the subsidiary top of **White Oak**. Complete the ascent with the fence close right to the summit.

Looking along the southerly fence toward Floutern Cop

The summit

All maps pinpoint the north top of Gavel Fell as the summit but cairn builders have preferred the more obvious little swelling south of the fence-junction. To the west you should spot the historic port and mining town of Whitehaven and to the southwest, on a clear day, Snaefell on the Isle of Man. To the northwest you may feast your eyes on Loweswater and lowly Low Fell.

Safe descents

Not a fell to fear. In dire conditions take one of the following routes: for Loweswater follow the fence ENE from the fence-junction stile, thereby joining a green track leading N to High Nook (**3**); for Kelton/Cross Rigg keep beside the fence, zig-zag NW then N to the Fothergill Head stile, and there switch left (W) on the clear path running down the easy slopes of High Pen and Saddler's Knott (**8**).

Ridge routes

Blake Fell → *1.6km/1 mile ↓80m/260ft ↑130m/425ft ⏱40min*
Fences define the route. Follow the fence running NW then N to the Fothergill Head saddle. Continue NW up to the skyline fence-stile and, keeping the fence to the right, advance naturally to the summit.

Hen Comb → *3.2km/2 miles ↓190m/625ft ↑175m/575ft ⏱1hr 15min*
Accompany the fence descending SE and S over White Oak. After slipping through a damp hollow, ignore the first fence-junction, continue to the second fence-junction and cross the fence, now following the fence trending ESE. Where this switches down right to Floutern Pass, keep forward over a marshy patch, climbing over the dry crown of Floutern Cop (no cairn). The descent leads to a fork in the path; let yourself be guided half-left with a quad track (passing the site of an old cairn marked on maps – though there is nothing visible on the ground). The tangible path rises to cross a simple fence-stile and continues purposefully, climbing NNE to the summit of Hen Comb.

10 GRASMOOR 852M/2795FT

Climb it from	Lanthwaite Green **33** or Cinderdale Common **32**
Character	Mighty presence above Crummock Water
Fell-friendly route	5
Summit grid ref	NY 175 204
Link it with	Crag Hill or Wandope
Part of	The Grasmoor Fell-gather

The paternal elephant of the range stands with his back proud of all else, and with his mighty wrinkled head frowning benignly down upon Crummock Water. On either side are deeply incised wild valleys, notably Rannerdale Beck and Gasgale Gill. Despite the name, which suggests that shepherds knew it as the high pasture or 'grass moor', much of the fell's western flanks are draped in heather and not a little scree, and only the eastern aspects have scope for any grass.

A high proportion of walkers choose to reach the summit from the east by Coledale Hause (3) or Wandope Moss (4) a little further south, rejecting the more obvious, energy-sapping direct assaults. But this is a fell to bring out the best in you, and demanding climbs – including routes described here via Grasmoor End (1), Dove Crags (2) and, for the more cautious, Lad Hows (5) – are well rewarded.

↑ *The fell's distinctive western face – Grasmoor End*

WALKING THE LAKE DISTRICT FELLS – BUTTERMERE

Ascent from Lanthwaite Green 33

Via Grasmoor End →2.4km/1½ miles ↑700m/2300ft ⏱2hr 30min

Choose a fair-weather day to get the best out of the craggy environs and impressive outlook of the west ridge.

1 Cross the open common and take the inviting bracken-free path up the gentle slope southeast, short of the footbridge. Ahead looms **Grasmoor End**. It looks like a daunting climb, on the angle between the north and west faces, but it's straightforward once you get going. A stream of light scree gives a clue as to the line to be taken. The path makes its way up into the heather, gaining an open grass gully which climbs to a heather and bilberry-draped shelf. Move round to the right and up a rock-step. Although you are now on rockier ground, the whereabouts of the path is never in question. A further rock-step and the rocky terrain invites you on. Continue into a longer, tighter gully, this time a bit more demanding on your energies. This brings

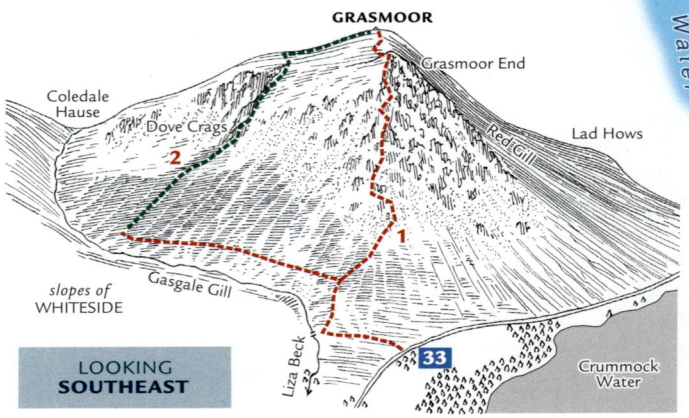

LOOKING **SOUTHEAST**

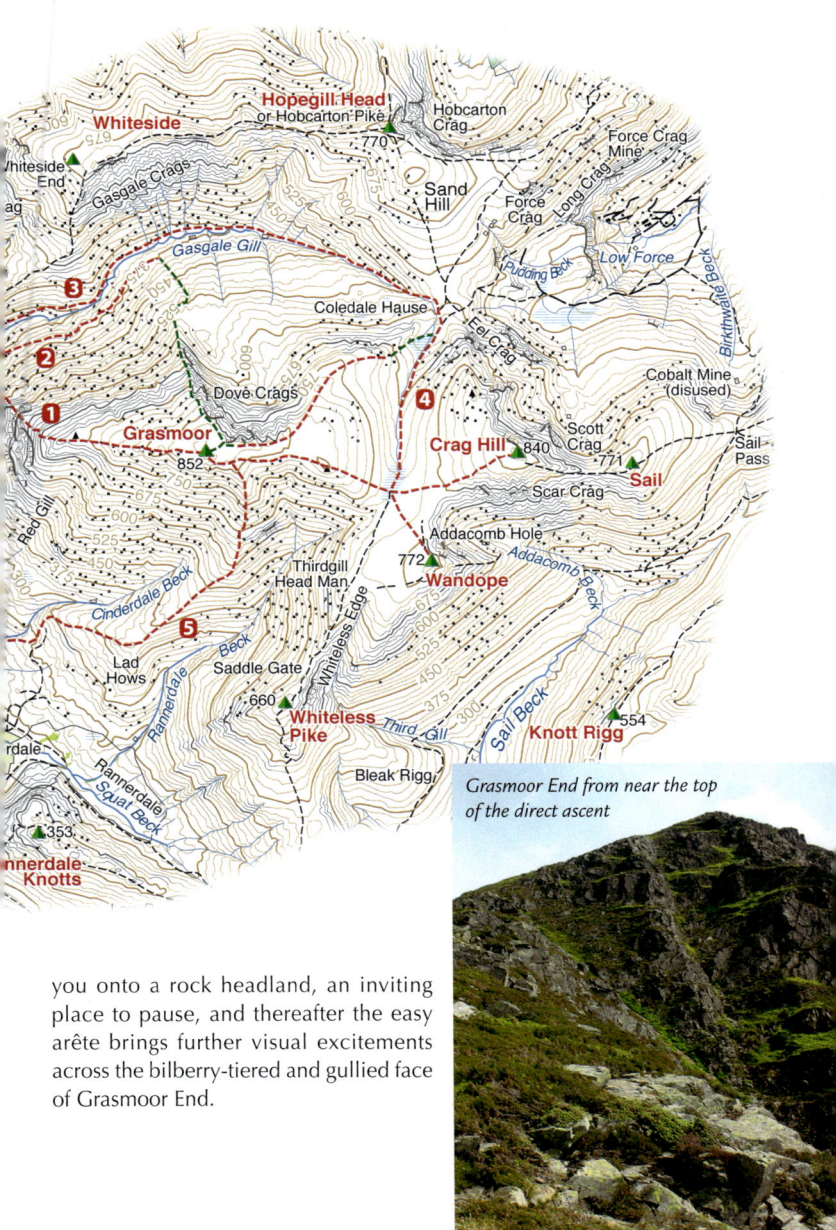

Grasmoor End from near the top of the direct ascent

you onto a rock headland, an inviting place to pause, and thereafter the easy arête brings further visual excitements across the bilberry-tiered and gullied face of Grasmoor End.

The ridge continues like a step ladder, with sprigs of prostrate juniper clinging to the rocks. Driving ever upwards the ridge eases, delivering you onto a tame grassy top adorned with a small cairn – divert right momentarily to enjoy the crest-top view down Grasmoor End. The ridge from here is broad, open and interspersed with gravelly scree at an easy angle, and leads up by a second little marker to the summit shelter.

Rock-step beside Dove Crags

Via Dove Crags →*3.2km/2 miles* ↑*700m/2300ft* ⏱*2hr 10min*

A route for walkers whose nerve fails as they confront Grasmoor End

2 Start out with Route **1** and, short of the pale scree, veer left along the narrow trod in the bilberry bushes, passing above a solitary larch tree and contouring into the Gasgale Gill valley on the northern slopes of Grasmoor. The narrow path undulates as

Dove Crags in sunshine

10 GRASMOOR

it comes across scree and, passing a little alcove structure, moves along the heather slopes below the high scree-streaked slopes. After the scree, watch for the first grass slack up the heather bank. This leads steeply but surely to the corrie lip, where you bear right up onto the rising edge of **Dove Crags**. There is one slab section, but nothing to hinder steady progress. The climb eases, with some marvellous arêtes and gullies to gaze down upon, and duly gains the plateau at the corrie edge. At this point bear southwest to reach the summit.

Via Coledale Hause →5.6km/3½ miles ↑700m/2300ft ⊕2hr 35min

Savour the drama of the gill all the way to the hause and choose from a couple of options at the top.

3 Cross the open common to the footbridge spanning **Liza Beck** and then you have a choice. Follow the beck upstream, coping with an entertaining rock-step beside a handsome waterfall. (Or, to avoid this – not marked on the map – clamber up the fell, taking the right-hand branch off the ascending path to **Whin Ben** to miss the outcrop above the gorge.) There is no doubting the path

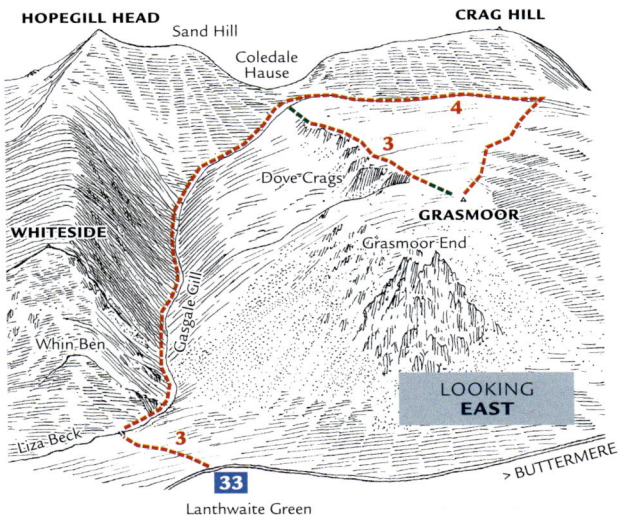

up the valley, although heavy rain has caused some notable landslips. The beck has some lovely cascades near the top. Come onto the level grassy saddle of **Coledale Hause**. Turn up with the beck and step off the engineered path, crossing the beck. After some 200 metres angling southwest onto the rising slope, pick up a path which brings you onto the northeast ridge to meet the re-entrant edge of the Dove Crags corrie. Head directly to the summit with Route **2**.

Via upper Gasgale Gill →*6km/3¾ miles* ↑*700m/2300ft* ⏲*2hr 50min*
4 Follow Route **3** as far as **Coledale Hause** and follow the engineered path as far as a junction of five paths with attendant pool. Bear up right after the initial bank, pass a prominent cairn and follow on along the edge, revelling in the southerly prospects, to reach the summit.

Ascent from Cinderdale Common 32

Via Lad Hows →*2.8km/1¾ miles* ↑*760m/2495ft* ⏲*1hr 50min*

A really grand climb, with a good path all the way

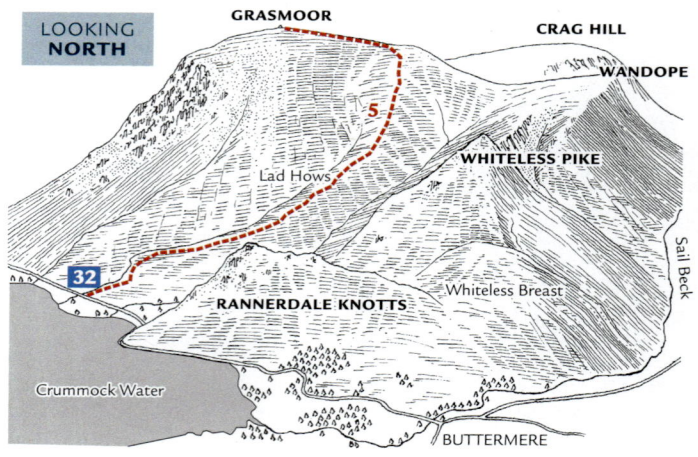

10 Grasmoor

5 Begin by following **Cinderdale Beck**, but break up the bracken bank among rocks as you near the cascades. The path bears southeast onto the ridge, climbing onto **Lad Hows** to weave through the heather. It keeps to the high ground as it turns northeast then climbs inexorably northwards, sustaining the steep ascent until the scarp top is reached, where the route follows the edge path left to the summit.

The summit

To fellwalkers the summit is a place to idle after the rigours of the climb and survey a magical mountain scene. Most eye-catching of all is the crowd of fells to the southeast, backed by the Scafells.

Safe descents

The Lad Hows ridge leading S then SW from the plateau edge (**5**), some 200 metres east of the summit, may seem steep, but it presents few difficulties in reaching the road by Crummock Water. In a similar league is the path that heads E to the cross-path saddle (**4**), from where you head N for Coledale Hause and then either W down the Gasgale Gill valley (**3**) or E down Coledale for Braithwaite.

Ridge routes

Crag Hill →*2km/1¼ miles* ↓*135m/445ft* ↑*120m/395ft* ⏱*40min*
Head E, descending from the prominent cairn down a bank to the cross-paths. Maintain your easterly course on a clear path which rises and curves NE to the summit OS column.

Wandope →*1.6km/1 mile* ↓*110m/360ft* ↑*30m/100ft* ⏱*30min*
Head E, descending from the prominent cairn down a bank to the cross-paths. From here veer SE through the grass to the summit cairn poised on the tip above Addacomb Hole.

WALKING THE LAKE DISTRICT FELLS – BUTTERMERE

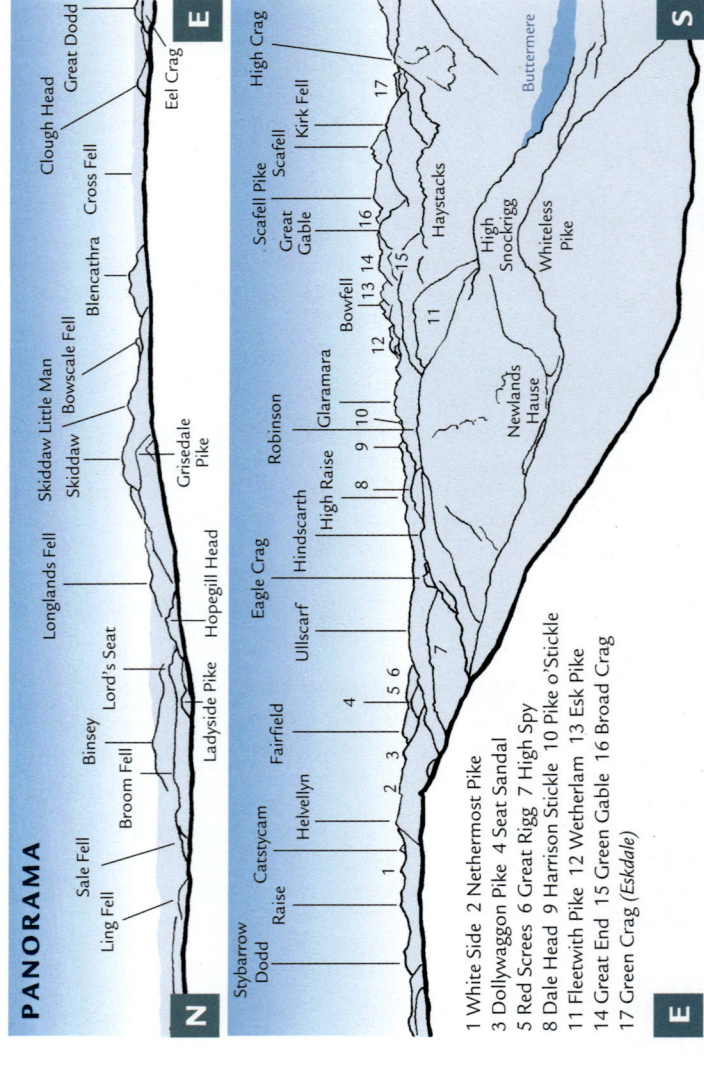

10 Grasmoor

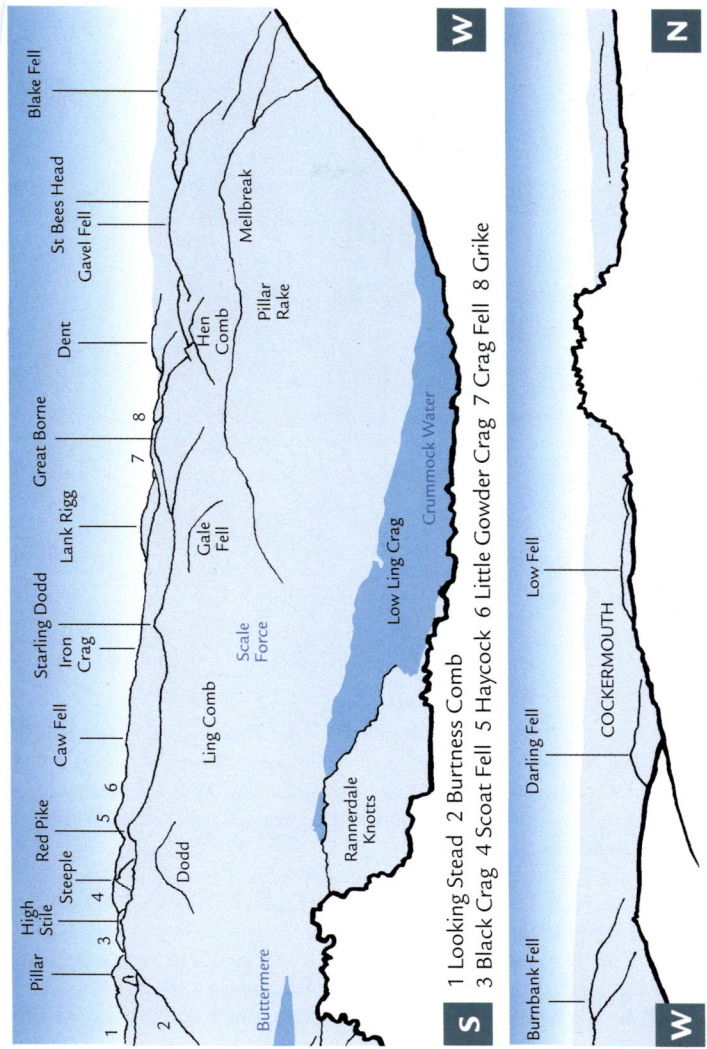

1 Looking Stead 2 Burtness Comb
3 Black Crag 4 Scoat Fell 5 Haycock 6 Little Gowder Crag 7 Crag Fell 8 Grike

11 GREAT BORNE 616M/2021FT

Climb it from	Bowness Knott **8**, Whins **9** or Buttermere **30**
Character	Western end of the long spine of rough high fell to the south of Buttermere, facing over lower Ennerdale
Fell-friendly route	5
Summit grid ref	NY 124 164
Link it with	Starling Dodd

Stand at the outflow of Ennerdale Water and Great Borne is the clear guardian of the dale. Stand on the summit of Crag Fell above Anglers' Crag and it seems the natural springboard to the mighty High Stile range. At its feet lies the rugged headland of Bowness Knott, on which the heather is slowly re-establishing itself after much tree-clearing.

A feature of the fell's scree-covered southern slopes are fox traps known as goose bields. Halfway up Rake Beck on a rocky knoll lies a perfect specimen built semi-igloo fashion, with an apron of boulders on the fellside affording easy access to the lip of the bield. A dead goose would have been hung from a plank across the interior, tempting foxes to jump into a pit from which they could not escape. Look out also for the foundations of a Viking farmstead beside Smithy Beck, with curious double walls.

↑ *Great Borne from Ennerdale Water*

11 GREAT BORNE

Despite the scree, there are at least four approaches possible from the south (1–4), and another gentle scree-free option from the west at Whins (5). One more line from Buttermere is also included (6) for those looking for a longer day out, and perhaps a return along the ridge.

Ascent from Bowness Knott 8

Via Rake Beck →2.4km/1½ miles ↑490m/1610ft ⏲1hr 20min

The direct ascent, with scope to add in Bowness Knott for a different perspective on Ennerdale

1 Walk back north along the approach road, beneath the conifer-screened craggy slopes of Bowness Knott. Where the road bends left find a stile on the right. Rise directly from **Rake Beck**, climbing the bracken bank ahead. Clip the corner of the forest fence and keep left where the path forks, then climb to reconnect with Rake Beck. The right-hand path is the direct access to the summit of **Bowness Knott**.

Should you wish to include Bowness Knott in your tramp then follow this path to a currently broken fence-stile. The path follows on up the bilberry

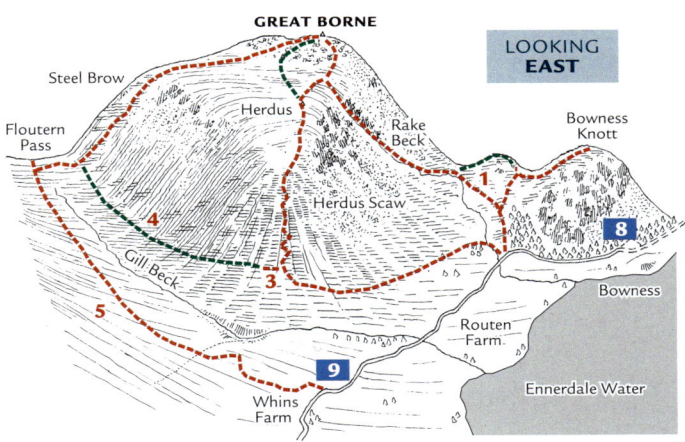

bank then keeps well to the right to mount the final crest. The view is superb over the lake, across to Crag Fell and east up the long, wild mountain corridor of Ennerdale. Return to the stile and follow the fence right to cross over Brown How and meet up with the main path beside Rake Beck, before a large erratic and a sheepfold.

Walk up beside Rake Beck on a well-used path. Coming above a rocky knoll find a perfect-specimen goose bield. The path continues up the east side of the ravine, amid bilberry and heather. (The state of the path makes progress quite slow and it is ill-suited for descent.) The beck makes a grand leap, with crags forming the west side of the ravine. As the ravine eases the path angles right (east), thereby missing the cairn on the top of **Herdus**. Weave up through boulders to mount north to the summit cairn.

Via Clews Gill →*5.2km/3¼ miles* ↑*540m/1770ft* ⏲*2hr 10min*

An off-the-beaten-track ascent laden with interest

2 Follow the opening strides of the Ennerdale access track down by the lakeside and let yourself be lured left with the sign for the Smithy Beck Trail. This well-maintained woodland path leads to and over a footbridge in front of a picturesque little waterfall. On joining a forest track go left and, at the crossing of **Smithy Beck**, take the second, slightly less confident path right.

Foundations of a curious double-walled Viking building

This leads past a cluster of Viking farmstead foundations. Sheltering beneath the pines, the path fords Smithy Beck awkwardly and rises past sheepfolds to bend left and exit the forestry at a padlocked gate. Cross the adjacent fence.

A green path sets your course heading

11 GREAT BORNE

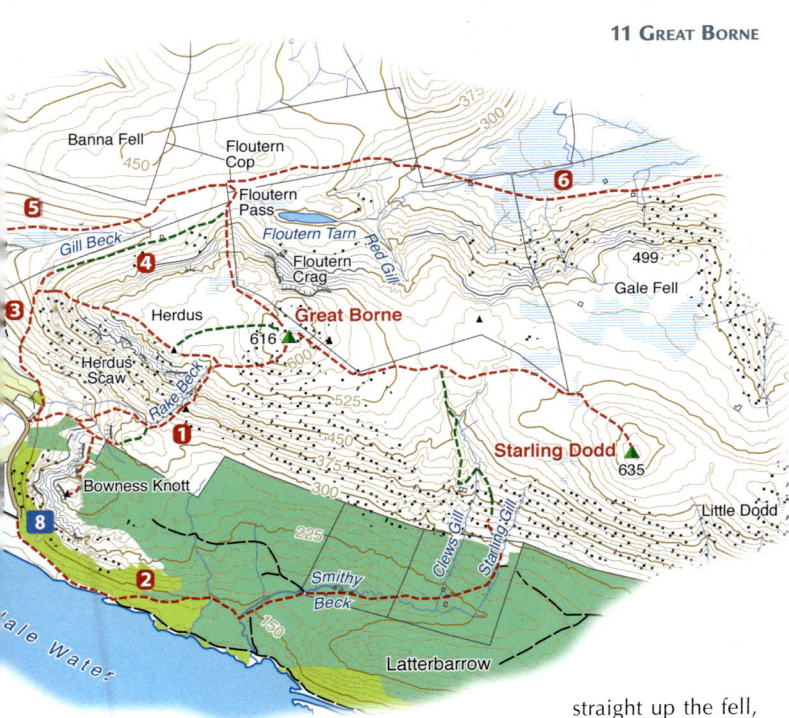

straight up the fell, avoiding the worst of the bracken. Where the bracken ends, contour left and slip through **Clews Gill**. It is possible to continue within the gill, but far more entertaining to bear left, trending back down the slope towards the sheepfold. At the sheepfold climb upon the boulder-and-heather mid-ridge, rising between boulder hollows, devoid of any hint of a path. A grand little passage culminates at rocks and a ruined goose bield. Descend into Clews Gill and keep to the main left-hand gill at the confluence, with pink exposure apparent. The ravine is well endowed with grass, which makes progress easy in comparison to the flanking heather moor. Passing a spring, the gully opens and leads easily up to the ridge path. Here bear left, soon to accompany the ridge fence to the summit.

Bowness Knott from the path below Herdus Scaw

Via Herdus →3.2km/2 miles ↑490m/1610ft ⏲2hr

A steep climb to take in a subsidiary summit

3 Set off with Route **1**, cross the stile off the road and follow the beckside path. From a ford keep the wall close left, and as this curves left join the green-way rising easily up the slope. Where a secondary drove-way crosses diagonally, bear right with this. Climb up to and through the gorse, drifting left under the scree of **Herdus Scaw** and over the brow to come above the fence.

From here, tackle the blunt west ridge of **Herdus**, climbing quite steeply with an evident path through the heather to reach the crest. Watch that you do not get confused by sheep trods that lead diagonally left – keep to the rounded ridge. A handful of stones marks the first skyline top, from where the ridge levels and broadens. Keep to the right-hand scarp edge to reach the tiny cairn marking the top. A brief wander down the south slope will reveal the craggy character that gave the hilltop its name. From here there are two routes on to the summit of Great Borne. The least used traverses the heather and marsh on a contouring line slightly north of east to mount the broken slope.

11 GREAT BORNE

More commonly walkers descend into the shallow combe and pick up the top of the Rake Beck path (Route **1**).

Via Floutern Pass →3.5km/1¼ miles ↑490m/1610ft ⏲1hr 45min
4 Follow Route **3** as far as the point where it turns right to climb from the Gill Beck valley up the ridge. Here continue to contour above the fence and a later sheepfold to reach the next fence-junction at **Floutern Pass**. Now ascend the blunt ridge of **Steel Brow**, with the fence to the left. As you gain the ultimate high ground swing right, away from the fence, to claim the summit.

Ascent from Whins 9

Via Floutern Pass →3.7km/2¼ miles ↑520m/1705ft ⏲1hr 50min

The pastoral route to the pass

Herdus from the Floutern bridleway above Whins

5 Set off on the bridleway leading off the road and signposted 'Buttermere 4.5 miles' along a confined hedged lane. Ford a small gill. A second lane joins from the left. From here follow the obvious part-walled, part-fenced track via gates. After the third gate the track runs up a pasture, coming to a fence and gate where a notice warns walkers not to attempt to reach Herdus Scaw's west ridge over non-access land through the adjacent fence-gate. Switch up left with the green-way to a further gate, from where the track enters rough pasture on the south slope of

Banna Fell. Keep faithfully to the track to reach a gate/stile in the fence marking the summit of **Floutern Pass**. Bear off right, crossing the marsh to the fence-stile and continuing to a second fence-stile in the pass-traversing fence. Follow Route **4** to the summit.

Ascent from Buttermere 30 *off map E*

Via Floutern Pass →*8.4km/5¼ miles* ↑*450m/1475ft* ⏲*2hr 30min*
6 Leave Buttermere by the Fish Hotel. The lane veers left, then after a gate take the lane right (southwest) at a kissing-gate. This leads to the gated Scale Bridge spanning Buttermere Dubs, the river that links Buttermere with Crummock Water. Cross and bear right. After the Far Ruddy Beck footbridge, keep left on a path that traverses rough ground. There are in fact two paths running across this fellside, and the higher drier path has become the more popular. This veers up after some 250 metres but is quite eroded during its upward step. Both routes arrive at a kissing-gate in a rising wall then descend a flight of pink-stoned steps to the foot of the Scale Force ravine. Cross the footbridge and follow the continuing path across the steep fellside.

Outflow of Floutern Tarn, looking to Gale Fell

11 Great Borne

The path duly contours under **Gale Fell**, keeping to the drier side of the marshy basin at the head of Mosedale. The bridleway passes through two stile/gates in wet conditions and rises to the top of **Floutern Pass**, passing the minor grassy knoll of **Floutern Cop**. Short of the gate bear left, crossing the fence-stile, and skirt round a fenced bog to a second fence-stile. Now head down, and begin the steep climb up Steel Brow to the summit with Route **5**.

The summit

A large shelter and a stone-built OS pillar mark the summit. Pink-hued, fractured and rounded bedrock predominates. The fence that sidles across the felltop cuts you off from much of the upper dome but no matter. Standing on the western end of the High Stile ridge, your attention will inevitably be drawn southeast to Starling Dodd and the main summit mass of Red Pike.

Safe descents

Consider only two lines. The safest in mist is Steel Brow (**4**). Follow the fence NW, steep but bereft of hazard, to Floutern Pass, then turn right for Buttermere (**6**) or left for Whin in Ennerdale (**5**). The western extension of the fell, Herdus, drops away equally steeply, but as long as you stick to the path (**3**) there is no problem. Once off the ridge trend S to reach the road, turning left for Bowness Knott. Keep out of Rake Beck.

Ridge route

Starling Dodd →2.4km/1½ miles ↓120m/395ft ↑135m/445ft ⏁50min
The fence provides the lead SE from the summit – curiously a double fence for a while. The clear path naturally crosses the head of Clews Gill well to the right of the fence before coming by the fence again, which comes to a sharp point. Climb on freely SE onto the summit dome.

12 GRISEDALE PIKE 791M/2595FT

Climb it from	Braithwaite **24**, Noble Knott **23**, Revelin Moss **22** or Hobcarton **21**
Character	A genuine peak, admired from Keswick perspectives, the summit a rapturous viewpoint
Fell-friendly route	5
Summit grid ref	NY 198 225
Link it with	Hopegill Head
Part of	The Coledale Horseshoe

The soaring ridge of Grisedale Pike grabs your attention from afar, especially from the eastern approaches to Keswick. Between its northeast and east ridges lies the secluded valley of Grisedale itself, its lower depths consumed by conifers. Seen from this direction the peak has a commanding presence over Whinlatter Forest Park. It is also the first prominent summit on the perennially popular Coledale Horseshoe which, once gained, makes the remainder of the horseshoe nigh-on irresistible.

↑ *Southwestern aspect of Grisedale Pike*

12 GRISEDALE PIKE

Due south of the summit, beside Coledale Beck, lies the Force Crag Mine, dramatically backed by Low Force. Above this, the hanging valley of Pudding Beck further encourages cautious exploration in this mined landscape, where deposits of copper, zinc, lead and barytes were extracted from the 16th century until final closure in 1991. (Guided mine tours are available through the National Trust.)

In the main, the steepness of the fellsides keeps walkers resolutely to the ridges (2–6) but the miner's track up Coledale (1) and the gentle approach up the Hobcarton valley (7) provide interesting alternatives. On Route 7, the close-up view of Hobcarton Crag, beneath Hopegill Head, ensures consistent entertainment.

Ascent from Braithwaite 24

Route 1 makes a good, sheltered, low-level return route from the more popular ridge path (Route 2).

Via Coledale Hause →*7.6km/4¾ miles* ↑*700m/2295ft* ⏲*3hr 30min*

1 Leave the car park past the barrier and follow the old mine track along the lower slopes of **Kinn**. As you near the mine buildings of the former **Force Crag Mine**, Grisedale Pike's southern slopes soar above your head. Veer left at the

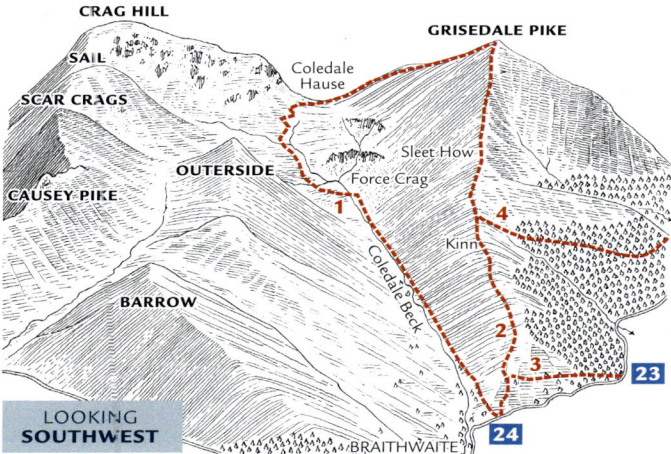

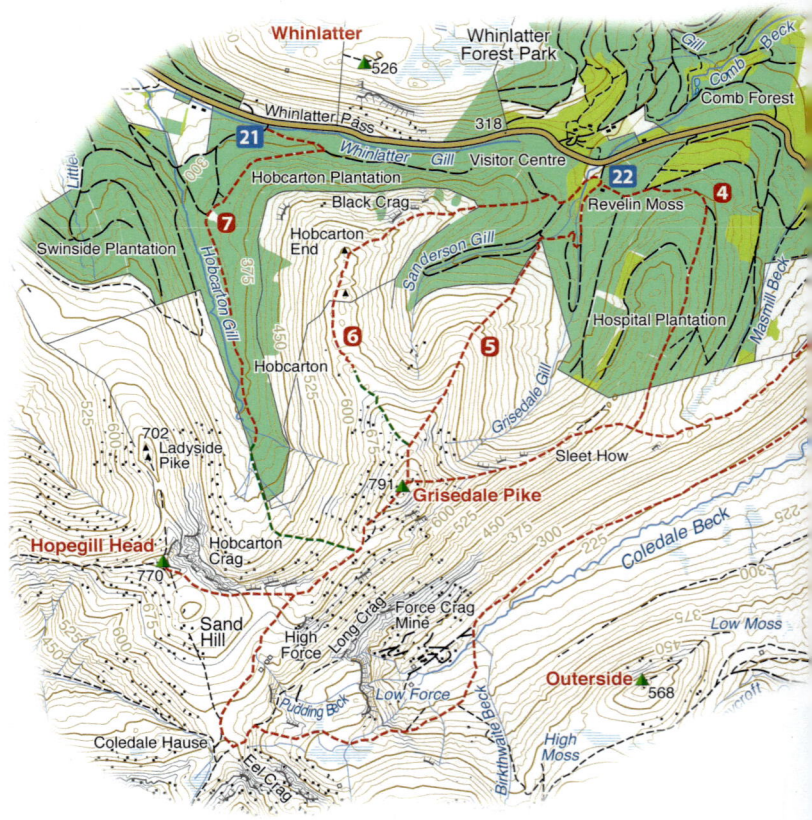

track fork just before the mine and, after fording **Coledale Beck**, set to work on the rough trail leading initially south, which curves west as the higher combe is entered. Excellent repair work has been done on the trail, especially higher up on the serpentine way to the saddle of **Coledale Hause**. Turn right when you reach the hause, then take the right-hand path at the fork to head northeast well above the **High Force** cliff. At a junction turn right again to join the ridge path from Hopegill Head and continue up the well-defined ridge to the summit.

12 GRISEDALE PIKE

Via Kinn →*4.8km/3 miles* ↑*730m/2395ft* ⏱*2hr 30min*

2 The path from the car park quickly steps up the bank on the right, climbing to a fence-stile. From here the grass path eases through the bracken onto the ridge-top of **Kinn**. Stride along on a marvellous promenade above the deep trench of Coledale Beck. As the **Masmill Beck** valley terminates on the right, the path swings right, naturally pitching up onto the heathery skyline of **Sleet How**. Follow the narrowing ridge, which becomes steeper and rougher on the abrupt climb up the east ridge, to reach the summit.

Ascent from Noble Knott 23

Via Kinn →*5.2km/3¼ miles* ↑*630m/2070ft* ⏱*2hr 20min*

An alternative starting place for the classic ascent when the lower car park is full

3 Step up from the car park, passing the forestry post with the vertical legend 'Heavy Sides Trail'. The path levels and then descends to meet a path

The head of Coledale on the promenade from Kinn

WALKING THE LAKE DISTRICT FELLS – BUTTERMERE

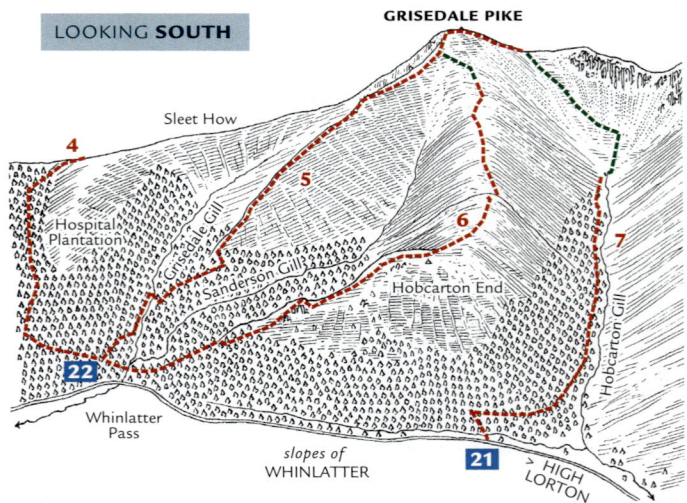

coming up from the left. Now on a gentle rise, meet up with a level forest track. Go left and follow this to the turning bay. A footpath sign 'Grisedale Pike' directs you on through to a stile in the forest-bounding fence. Walk forward only a matter of 40 metres to link with the path rising through the bracken from the Braithwaite car park. From here follow Route **2** to the summit.

Ascent from Revelin Moss 22

Via Hospital Plantation →*3.2km/2 miles* ↑*700m/2295ft* ⏱*2hr 15min*

A back-door route to beautiful Sleet How

4 Strike out from the car park along the forest track leading southeast. As this ascends, keep left at the first junction and then right at the fork (forest post 45), rising into cleared space with open views to Skiddaw and the Bassenthwaite valley. At the next junction keep right as the route continues its gentle rise before levelling out and exiting the forest at a fence-stile after the seat and turning bay. Traverse the fell-slope ahead on a thin sheep trod, avoiding the

12 GRISEDALE PIKE

Ascending the east ridge

bracken as best you can, and link up with Route **2** part-way up its climb onto the skyline ridge of **Sleet How**.

Via the northeast ridge
→ *2.8km/1¾ miles*
↑ *700m/2295ft* ⏱ *2hr*

The first of two fine but little-walked northerly ridges

5 Leave the car park past the barrier and follow the track to find and cross the footbridge spanning **Grisedale Gill** – the watercourse from which the fell is named. The path curves round to join a forest track at a wide bend. Here go right, and at the next junction keep left to find a prominent sign directing left off the track to 'Grisedale Pike'. Cross a fence-stile and ascend beside the old wall (evidence of a subsequent metal fence is almost lost). A steady plod ensues up the northeast ridge, which gives a good excuse to pause periodically and glance back at the view which gradually extends over a series of intervening ridges towards the distant Helvellyn range. A 'bench' outcrop might tempt a pause before the final steady rise to the bare rock summit.

Via Hobcarton End → *3.2km/2 miles* ↑ *700m/2295ft* ⏱ *2hr 20min*
6 Step back down from the car park and follow the open forest track left to cross Comb Beck (the combined waters of **Sanderson** and **Grisedale Gills**). The track passes down by their confluence and rises, all beneath a mantle of mature conifers. Where the track makes an exaggerated bend at a junction go round right with it and at the next fork bear left into a dark tunnel. A second fork left, with orienteering post, brings you into an unmarked and ever more forbidding tunnel path, which curiously includes four strides of path

pitching. Thankfully, you ultimately emerge from the dense labyrinth onto heather moor. What joy!

The path winds handsomely onto the ridge, from where you can revel in the view. It tends to the left, avoiding the ridge-end cairn, but the cairn is worth a detour for the view of the Lord's Seat group across the pass. Follow the heather ridge, crossing a fence-stile by cairned knolls. The ridge path leads to the next, more considerable step and then dissolves on the final rise to the summit. Veer half-left to join the old wall (and Route **5**) on the final section of the northeast ridge.

Ascent from Hobcarton 21

Via the Hobcarton valley →*3.6km/2¼ miles* ↑*490m/1610ft* ⏱*1hr 45min*

A fabulous dalehead route, perfect for admiring Hobcarton Crag in its wild and lonely setting

7 From the car park head east past the barrier on the forest track, turning sharp right at the first track junction – this is the main forest track leading into the Hobcarton valley. Where the track ends, at a lightly fenced turning circle,

Forest track in the Hobcarton Valley

12 GRISEDALE PIKE

slip down the continuing gravel bank into rushy ground leading to a fence-stile. Cross the stile and follow the fence, keeping it close left, to its termination – in its latter stages it takes the form of a gathering fence for a triangular fold. From the top post angle half-left, climbing across the grassy slope. The scree is easily avoided as a broad mossy grass strip leads on up to the skyline. On meeting the old wall and ridge path go left to the summit.

The summit

The bare slate summit, with its hazardous remnants of an old metal fence, has a modest cairn. A block of tilted slate provides an eastern shelf on which to rest, shielded from prevailing westerlies. (Older OS maps show a mythical man-made 'shelter'.) The view holds the gaze on the eastern fells across upper Coledale and, beyond, the Helvellyn range. From here, to the south, Scafell Pike directly overtops Great Gable.

Safe descents

If Braithwaite is your destination, and comfort underfoot more important than issues of time, then follow the ridge SW (**1**). Cross the nameless intermediate height, and on the subsequent descent fork left down to Coledale Hause, from where a clear winding trail leads E to ultimately ford Coledale Beck and join the mine track. The east ridge is steep and stony at the top, and a far better choice is the northeast ridge (**5**), which brings you easily down to the forest tracks of Whinlatter Forest Park and Comb Bridge.

Ridge route

Hopegill Head →*2km/1¼ miles* ↓*115m/375ft* ↑*95m/310ft* ⏱*40min*
A broken ridge wall descends then climbs over the nameless intermediate hill above the deep wild dalehead of the Hobcarton Gill valley. The path splits at a cairn at the beginning of the descent, so be on the lookout for it and keep right. Hold to the clear ridge path, watching in foul weather to avoid the perilous edge on the right, and climb naturally to the summit, which has all the same bare rock characteristics of Grisedale Pike.

WALKING THE LAKE DISTRICT FELLS – BUTTERMERE

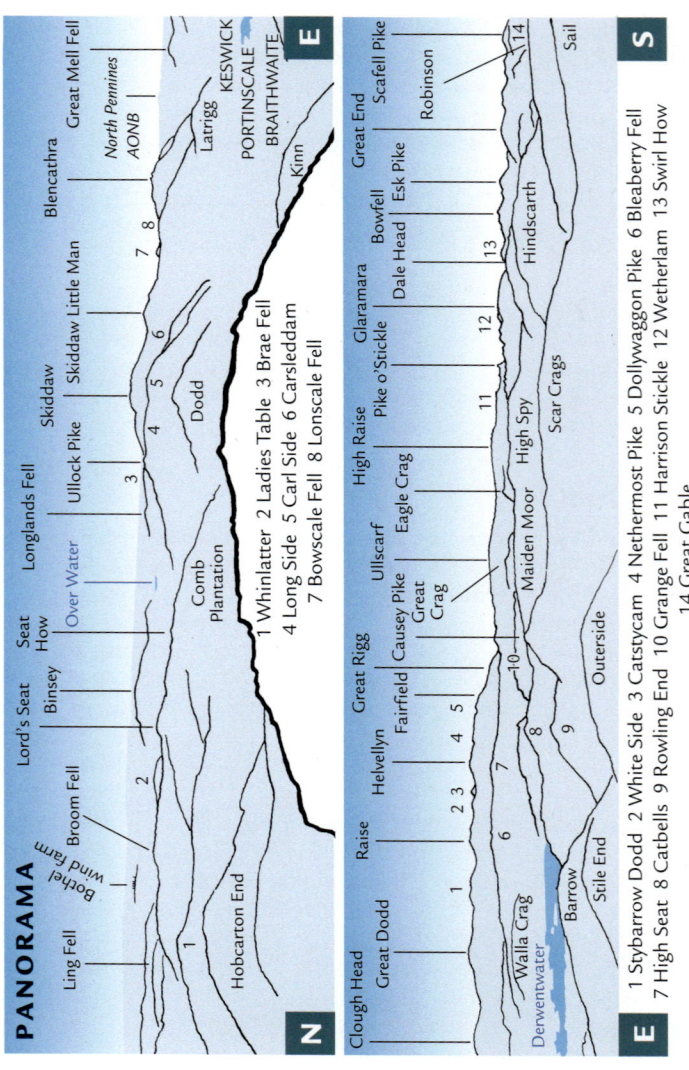

PANORAMA

1 Whinlatter 2 Ladies Table 3 Brae Fell 4 Long Side 5 Carl Side 6 Carsleddam 7 Bowscale Fell 8 Lonscale Fell

1 Stybarrow Dodd 2 White Side 3 Catstycam 4 Nethermost Pike 5 Dollywaggon Pike 6 Bleaberry Fell 7 High Seat 8 Catbells 9 Rowling End 10 Grange Fell 11 Harrison Stickle 12 Wetherlam 13 Swirl How 14 Great Gable

12 GRISEDALE PIKE

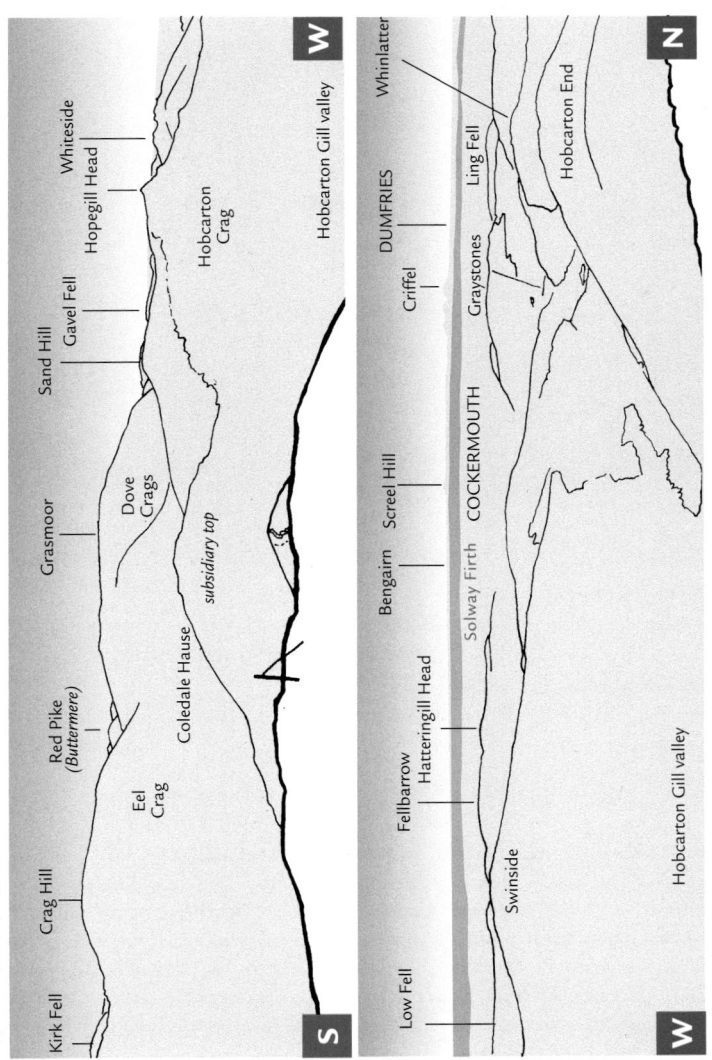

13 HAYSTACKS 598M/1962FT

Climb it from	Gatesgarth **6** or Black Sail Hut **7**
Character	An enigmatic, rugged tangly ridge of pools and dense heather, casting dark shadows over Warnscale
Fell-friendly route	1 or 4
Summit grid ref	NY 193 132
Link it with	High Crag
Part of	The Buttermere Round

Haystacks is the near-perfect distillation of a Lakeland fell – rocky knolls and crags, paths deftly spun through tangled heather and sparkling pools, and outlooks into Buttermere and upper Ennerdale, all within a small area. The romance of a great mountain day is assured, without many miles or mighty heights to conquer. Despite its popularity, much of the plateau is little visited and ripe for exploration, from the lava-topped rocks of the northern scarp to Blackbeck Tarn, and not forgetting Innominate Tarn, teeming with wildlife and the photographer's favourite.

↑ *Haystacks from Gatesgarth Farm*

13 HAYSTACKS

The plainer sunny side of the fell belongs to walkers venturing into Ennerdale, many of whom opt for a night at Black Sail Hut Youth Hostel. This former shepherd's shieling rests at the foot of the fell's southern flank, adding hugely to its mountain magic, and is only accessible on foot or by mountain-bike – the warden's Land Rover excepted.

Routes described here come up from Gatesgarth Farm (1–3), via Scarth Gap or Warnscale Bottom (look out for the high-set circular sheepfold, similar to those found in southern Scotland), or from Black Sail Hut (4–5). Those drawn to tackle this characterful fell from Buttermere could include both sides of the well-maintained shoreline path in their quest.

Ascent from Gatesgarth 6

Via Scarth Gap → *2km/1¼ miles* ↑*470m/1540ft* ⏱ *1hr 10min*

Best in late spring when the slope is a rapture of bluebells

1 Traverse the meadows at the head of Buttermere by the gate-marshalled lane. Cross **Warnscale Beck** via **Peggy's Bridge**, and through the gate rise directly beside the small copse on a pitched path. At the acute corner, where paths radiate, bear up left, maintaining company with the fence and the

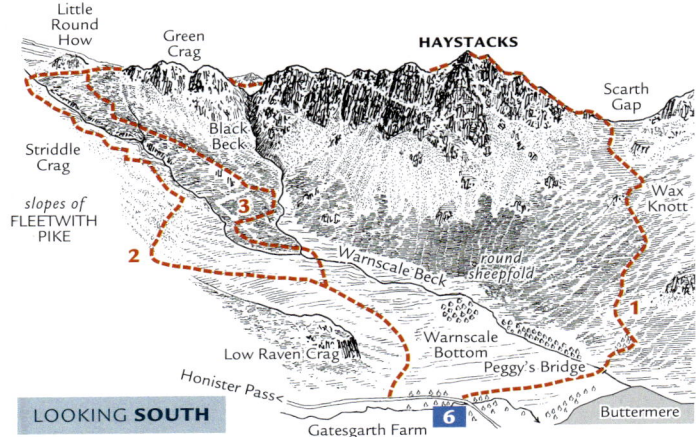

pitched path. The path mounts onto **Wax Knott**, a pronounced shelf where many walkers pause to admire the great basin of Warnscale, encircled by the craggy heights of Fleetwith Pike and Haystacks. The path leads through a wall and continues up to the pass to a large cairn. Turn up left – the path, while pummelled by a million boots, might still be unclear for those new to this rocky fell environment. Strike boldly on and the rock-steps will become evident close up. Pass the pool and reach the summit outcrop, with cairns at either end of a north–south bare rib of rock.

Blackbeck Tarn

Via Warnscale →4.5km/2¾ miles ↑490m/1610ft ⏲2hr 15min

Two routes weave up this wild valley steeped in history.

2 Leave the open road above the sheltered Gatesgarth hamlet on the bridle-track leading south. Follow this round to get your first really special view of Haystacks over the copse of Scots pine as you enter Warnscale. Spot the circular sheepfold on the facing lower slope of the fell, a curious place for a holding pen. The green track advances sweetly into the amazing crag-circled amphitheatre. A fork in the way brings a moment of choice – two means to a common end.

Ignore the inviting footbridge. Keep to the main track, which switches left then right after a ruin to steadily gain height across the growing slope of Fleetwith Pike. This comes to a tightly engineered bend above the ravine of **Warnscale Beck** and winds up towards Dubs Quarry. Just short of the quarry ford the beck at the obvious point. Follow the regular path southwest, advancing close under **Little Round How**, a classic example of the raw, irresistible

113

effects of a glacier on stubborn rock. Repaired in places, the path runs on behind the mighty bulk of **Green Crag** to descend close to the outflow of **Blackbeck Tarn**. The view through the upper ravine into the Buttermere vale is superb. The path weaves on over rocky ground to come along the shores of **Innominate Tarn**. Thereafter, either of the two strongly marked paths will ensure your westward progress to the ultimate rocky top.

3 A pleasing variant path breaks right from the Warnscale Bottom track, crossing the broad wooden footbridge over **Black Beck**. Quickly fording the beck, this heads south until forced sharp right by a change in the terrain. The path briefly comes close to Black Beck, then winds left on an easterly bias over the rough ground on a miners' trail. It is easy to miss Warnscale Bothy, built for slate workers at Dubs Quarry. If you find it, please respect this vital resource for climbers. The path weaves up to meet the Route **2** path at a bare, ice-incised rock shelf; here turn right to the summit.

Ascent from Black Sail Hut 7

Via Scarth Gap →*2km/1¼ miles* ↑*295m/970ft* ⏱*55min*

4 Scarth Gap is perhaps the most commonly used pedestrian link with the outside world from this unique location. The open access track leads west to

Contorted lava high above Scarth Gap

13 HAYSTACKS

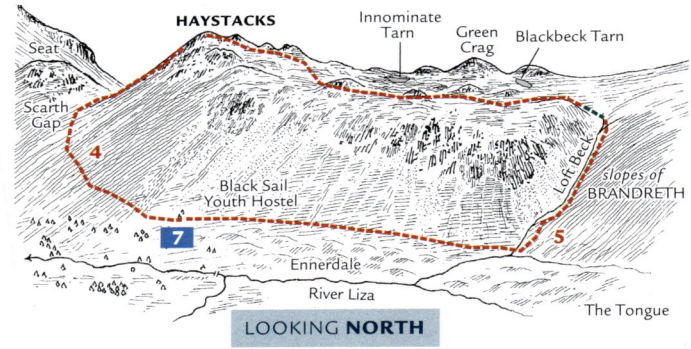

a gate at the entrance to the forest land. Ignore this and instead bend up right with the pitched path beside the fence, climbing unwaveringly into the hause, where you turn right to join Route **1**.

Via Loft Beck →3.7km/2¼ miles ↑310m/1020ft ⊕1hr 30min

A delightfully quiet and leisurely way to reach the summit just behind the hut

5 Two paths lead from the hostel door, so make sure you follow that leading east-southeast, not the trail leading southeast down to the Liza footbridge. Adopted by the Coast to Coast Walk, the higher path runs along the upper edge of a extensive field of glacial moraine. Ford **Loft Beck** and bear up the narrow valley on a continuously pitched path. As the beck opens bear left to cross a marshy hollow and cross the fence-stile. Keep left beside the fence (west then northwest) along the southern skyline of the fell, with many a rocky twist and pool to negotiate en route to the summit.

Looking towards the head of Ennerdale from the summit

The summit

At the top sits a bare rock rib aligned north–south with cairns at either extremity, that to the north probably the higher. A rock-girt pool occupies the little hollow to the west. In good weather, the view will occupy you for some time – especially the upper realms of Ennerdale, with Great Gable and Pillar close by. Since the summit is low set, the view is limited, but the summits of Scafell Pike above Beck Head, Helvellyn above Drum House and Skiddaw above Hindscarth Edge can all be glimpsed.

Safe descents

The fell's defences are dark and gloomy. There are unforgiving cliffs on many fronts, and red-alert danger to the north. Should you head ESE to retrace Routes **2** or **3** past Innominate Tarn, from the Blackbeck Tarn outflow ford keep resolutely to the main path. On no account consider descending Black

Beck as there is no way down. If you hold to the near path on the rise from the ford be very careful not to be lured by the innocent green shelf that seems to be the beginning of a downward path. **It is not – it is a death trap!**

Ridge route

High Crag →*2km/1¼ miles* ↓*175m/575ft* ↑*325m/1065ft* ⏲*1hr 20min*
Leave the summit W, following the steep-stepped popular way down to Scarth Gap. Cross the saddle W, join the pitched path climbing onto the heather-clad headland and curve NW to pass the handsome little cairned summit of Seat. There is a consistent path, which declines into a damp depression before mounting a modified assault on Gamlin End and continuing to the summit. The Fix the Fells Project had no option but to put effort into this scree-ridden path, and they have done a fine job.

From Dubs Quarry (photo: Maggie Allan)

WALKING THE LAKE DISTRICT FELLS – BUTTERMERE

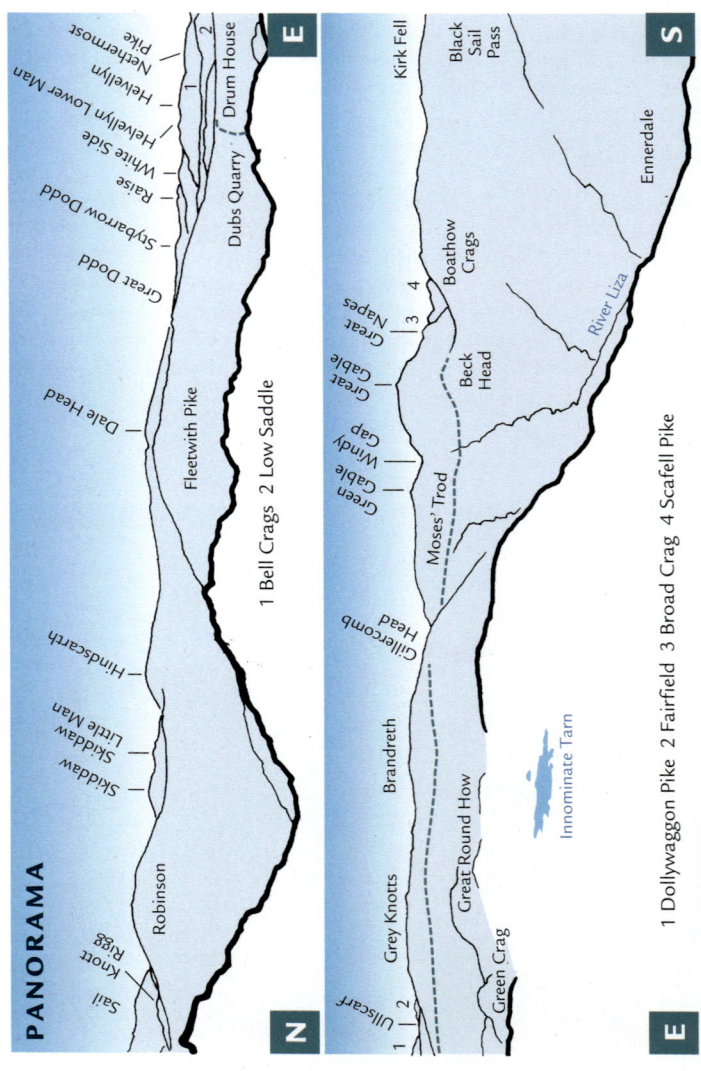

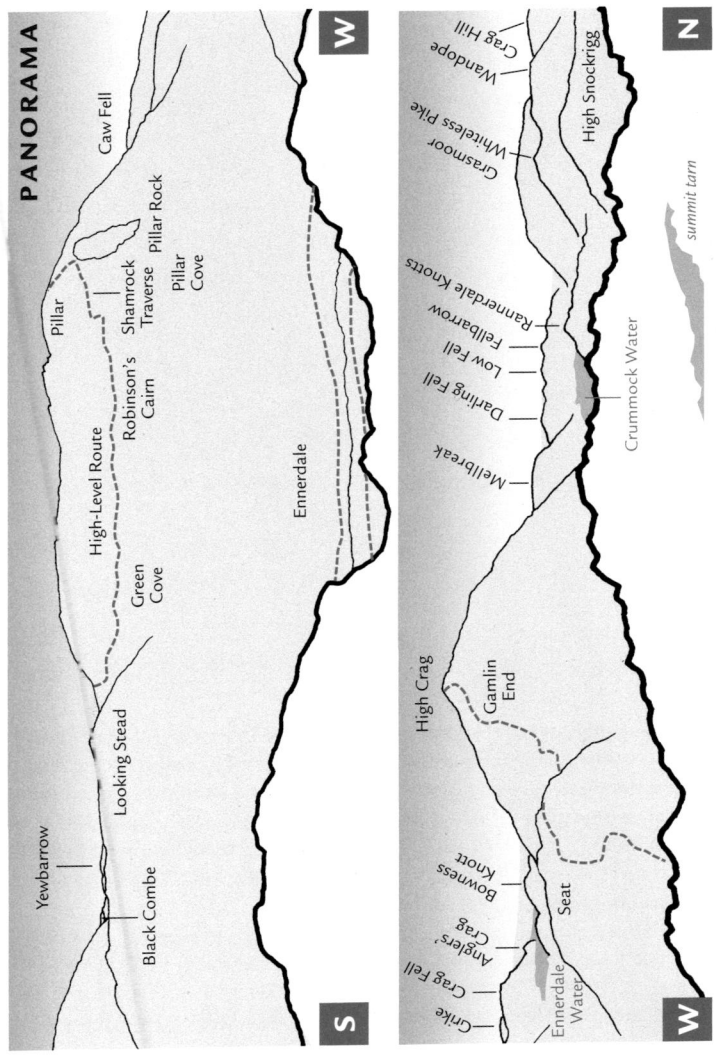

14 HEN COMB 509M/1670FT

Climb it from	Church Bridge 16, Maggie's Bridge 15, Whins 9 or Buttermere 30
Character	Modest north–south ridge bounding Mosedale
Fell-friendly route	1
Summit grid ref	NY 132 181
Link it with	Gavel Fell

Hen Comb (traditionally pronounced 'hencum'), rising ever so gently up due south from the southern tip of Loweswater, has no commanding profile, craggy outcrops or discernible points of historic or geological interest to recommend it. Further discouraging casual exploration with a horseshoe of marsh, it is ticked by summit-baggers and few others. But it stands in a fine situation and the true fellwanderer will find its summit a lovely place to idle with the larks on a sunny day and muse over its handsome surround of fells.

There are many ways to reach this peaceful spot if you don't mind getting your boots wet. The most natural run down from the north (1–4), following the valleys on either side or ambling up the northern slopes, but you could also gain the summit from Whins over Floutern Pass (5) or from Buttermere across the foot of Scale Force (6).

↑ *Hen Comb from Gavel Fell*

14 HEN COMB

Ascent from Church Bridge 16

Three watery approaches, the first two involving the fording of Mosedale Beck and therefore not recommended in or after heavy rain

Via Little Dodd →4.1km/2½ miles ↑400m/1300ft ⏱1hr 40min

The natural, direct approach

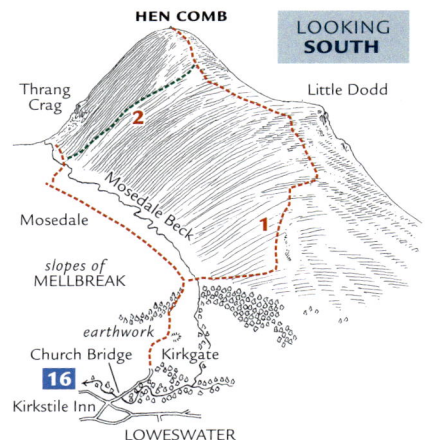

1 Follow the lane up the rise by **Kirkhead House** and the white-washed **Kirkgate Farm**, with a contemporary view-orientated barn-house adjacent. The unmetalled walled lane leads on towards Mellbreak. Where it makes a sharp left bend notice the shallow banks of an **earthwork** in the field over to the right. Pass through a gate and keep right along the track below the conifer plantation.

As this track ends bear down right off the track with the wall, going through the hurdle-gate to ford **Mosedale Beck**. Immediately to the left is the beck's narrowest point, but this is also beside a decidedly deep plunge pool (useful for a dip at the end of a walk on a blazing hot day). The shallower ford is to the right – heavy rain can make this a difficult crossing. Walk up the pasture with the wall on your right. As the wall shapes to swing away right, and before a fence comes in left, bear left on the quad track in a groove. Follow this through grass to a faint cross-path and turn right to climb over the fence as it abuts a length of wall. The path mounts the ridge and drifts over the left-hand shoulder of **Little Dodd**. A brief detour brings this minor top underfoot, its craggy southern slope an attractive feature overlooking Whiteoak Beck. The ridge path levels and advances to a step over a fence, from where the path faces the final modest pull to the summit.

Via Mosedale →3.9km/2½ miles ↑405m/1330ft ⏱2hr

2 Start out with Route **1**, but where the plantation ends keep with the open grass track, striding with ease into coy Mosedale. As the track forks keep right, moving west across the valley towards the beck. Take your chances in fording it and clamber up to swing over the fence in the corner. Climb entirely pathless up the steep bracken bank, with the fence reasonably close on the right. Where this fence switches right, keep straight up the grassy fell to join Route **1** and the ridge path.

Round Thrang Crag →5.5km/3½ miles ↑420m/1380ft ⏱2hr 30min

3 Start out with Route **2**, but rather than heading down to ford the beck, wander on south with the bridleway to cross a footbridge over **Mosedale Beck**. Up to this point the firm track has been fine and dandy. The next stage, running round the southern base of the fell, is, shall we say, softer! With care you can avoid drowning your socks, although the line of the path is quite vague at times. On arriving at a gate in a downward fence, don't go through but gingerly turn right (north) through the rushes. A gill offers an early obstacle, after which you climb with growing hope of firm ground. Coming alongside the point in the fence where walkers evidently cross from the Floutern Pass approach (Route **5**), break uphill right and, crossing the girdling sheepwalk, ascend on a thin but nonetheless clear path leading north-north-west to the summit.

Hen Comb from the drove-track above Whiteoak Beck

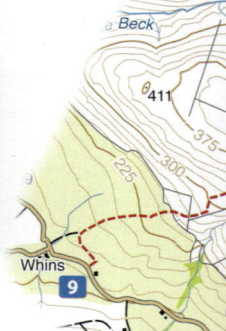

14 Hen Comb

Ascent from Maggie's Bridge 15

Via Whiteoak Beck →4.8km/3 miles ↑440m/1445ft ⏱2hr 20min

A straightforward route and a good partner for Route 1

4 Follow the open farm track to **High Nook Farm**. From the gate out of the yard by the farmhouse

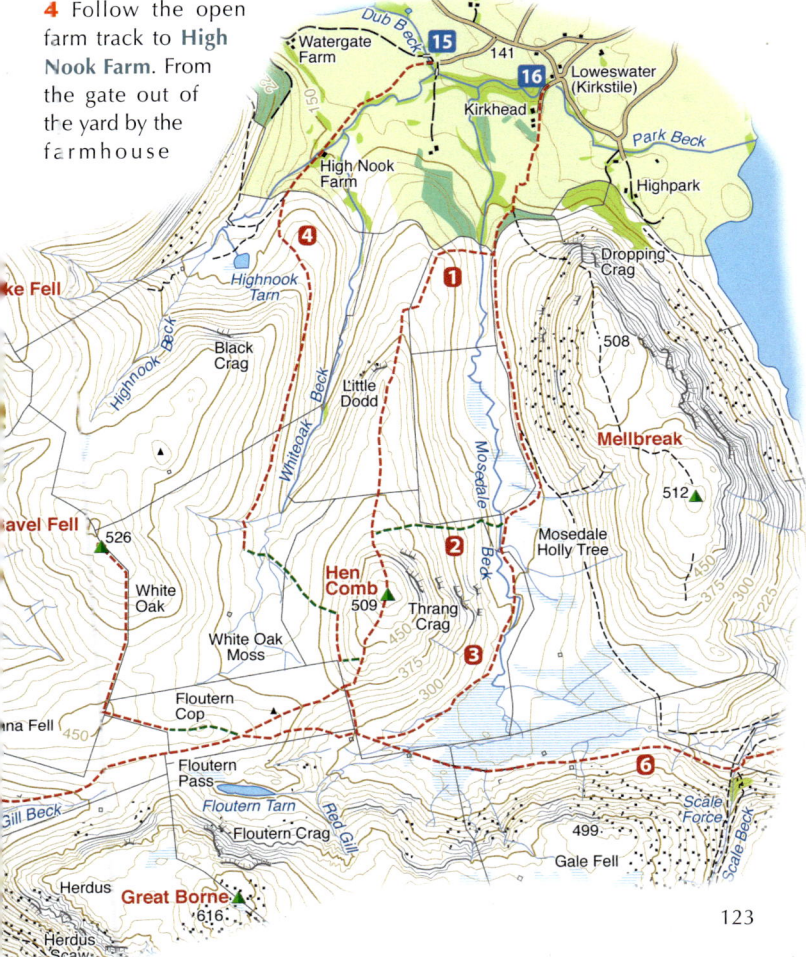

bear up left with the track to the gate in the intake wall. Go through and walk on to an obvious fork in the track. Bear up left, rising easily over the shoulder to gain views into the depths of the Whiteoak Beck valley. March on, imperceptibly rising, to pass through a fence-gate, all the time with attention focused on Hen Comb ahead. Some 100 metres after a re-entrant ford, look to break off the green-way down the bank in order to negotiate twin crossings of the feeder streams of **Whiteoak Beck**, and the subsequent plain fence. Aim southeast, up by a sheepfold, to come onto the lateral sheep-walk running south along the slope of Hen Comb. Coming to the fence-corner break directly up the slope east, with the odd remnant metal fence stake, to link to the narrow path climbing north-northeast to the summit.

Ascent from Whins 9

Via Floutern Pass →*4.5km/2¾ miles* ↑*440m/1445ft* ⏲*1hr 50min*

A natural line of ascent from the west on good paths, largely dodging the bog

5 From the parking area a bridleway signpost 'Buttermere 4.5 miles' directs along a confined hedged lane. Ford a small gill, and a second lane joins from

Fork in the path from Floutern Pass

14 Hen Comb

the left. From here follow the obvious part-walled, part-fenced track through gates. From the third gate the track runs up a pasture, coming to a fence and gate with a notice warning walkers not to attempt to reach Herdus's west ridge over non-access land through the adjacent fence-gate. So switch left up with the green-way to a further gate, from where the track enters rough pasture on the south slope of **Banna Fell**. Keep faithfully to the track to reach a gate/stile in the fence marking the top of **Floutern Pass**.

Follow on, and where you come to a fork, with stones ushering bridle-way-users right, take the left-hand option. This leads down by a stone ring feature, a Bronze Age cairn, which, unusually, has survived the ages. The path does its best to avoid the worst of the marsh by keeping to the right-hand lip of the slope, climbing to reach the rising fence. Cross and head straight up the fellside to the summit.

Ascent from Buttermere 30 *off map SE*

Via Scale Force →6.4km/4 miles ↑410m/1345ft ⏲2hr 20min

A long walk-in on good paths and full of interest

6 Leave the village by the Fish Hotel. The lane veers left then, after a gate, take the lane right (southwest) at a kissing-gate. This leads to the gated Scale Bridge spanning Buttermere Dubs, the river that links Buttermere with Crummock Water. Cross and bear right. After the Far Ruddy Beck footbridge, keep left on a path that traverses rough ground. There are two paths running across this fellside that meet at the foot of Scale Force.

Follow the higher path, which has become more popular recently. This veers up after some 250 metres but is quite eroded during its upward step. This joins the lower path at a kissing-gate then descends a flight of pink-stoned steps to the foot of the **Scale Force** ravine. Cross the footbridge and follow the continuing path across the steep fellside well above Black Beck. This duly contours under **Gale Fell**, at the head of the very mossy Mosedale, to reach a stile/gate. Continue over damp terrain to a further gate/stile but do not go through. Instead bear right through the wet rushes. Climb through the bracken with the fence close left. Short of the fence's brow, watch right for a tangible path mounting the steepish grass slope, above a lateral sheep path. This leads, via a mossy shelf, irresistibly to the summit.

The summit

Summit cairn, looking to Gavel Fell

Marked by a modest cairn, the outlook amply rewards the climb. Fine is the view to Mellbreak overtopped by the Grasmoor group, and exciting the glimpse into the Buttermere vale with Robinson, Fleetwith Pike and the High Stile range. Pillar makes a guest appearance on the ridge between Starling Dodd and Red Pike above Little Dodd. Elsewhere the Loweswater fells quietly dominate.

Safe descents

Stick to tangible paths and you'll have no trouble – the only crags lie on the east side of the fell. The main hazard is marshy ground; Whiteoak Moss and the head of Mosedale are horrible but not life-threatening.

Ridge route

Gavel Fell →*3.2km/2 miles* ↓*175m/575ft* ↑*190m/625ft* ⏲*1hr 15min*
Leave the summit trending S on a clear grass path, with Great Borne dead ahead. The swift descent leads to a simple fence-stile; continue SW aiming to cross the crown of Floutern Cop (no cairn). The short descent leads across a spongy moss to a corner in a fence rising from the left (up from Floutern Pass). Continue with the fence WNW to a fence-junction. Cross and turn right (N). After a damp hollow, a steady dry climb leads over the oddly-named subsidiary top of White Oak to reach the summit cairn (on the left side of the fence).

15 HIGH CRAG 744M/2441FT

Climb it from	Buttermere **30**, Gatesgarth **6**, Black Sail Hut **7** or Bowness Knott **8**
Character	Eastern component of an imperious trio of summits to the south of Buttermere
Fell-friendly route	3
Summit grid ref	NY 180 140
Link it with	Haystacks or High Stile
Part of	The Buttermere Round

High Crag, the easternmost component of the High Stile range directly above the head of Buttermere, is a prow of rock and scree, facing north and exposed to the full fury of the elements. With neighbouring High Stile, it harbours the wild corrie of Birkness Comb, within which lurks Eagle Crag, much-loved by climbers. The eager glacier that etched the combe left only the narrowest of connecting ridges between the two summits. To the southeast sits the rocky knuckle of Seat, a foretaste of Haystacks across the hause. In complete and utter contrast, the Ennerdale aspect is steep, barren and quite without distinguishing features.

    The fell's precipitous slopes seem to attract more than their fair share of rainwater, which rushes down the flanks with great gusto – on occasion too enthusiastically. This causes unusual erosion to watercourses and paths, and work for the path-fixers whose recent labours on the popular lakeshore trail have made it more durable.

↑ *High Crag's craggy northern aspect*

The dramatically sculpted northern slopes give scope for many varied approaches, four of which are offered here from either end of the lake (1–4). Visitors from Black Sail Youth Hostel, however, have one obvious approach (5) and there is only one clear route through the forestry from Ennerdale (6). And there's always the magical Buttermere Round to consider, a version of which is described in the Ridge Route section of this guide.

Ascent from Buttermere 30

Via Sheepbone Rake →4.1km/2½ miles ↑640m/2100ft ⏱2hr 15min

A rewarding if hard-won feather in the cap of any moderately proficient fellwanderer, this high tilted shelf beckons all the way from Buttermere.

1 Leading off from the village past the Fish Hotel, follow the gated lane signed to the lake. Cross the outflow footbridge and bear left via a hand-gate onto the popular pedestrian lakeshore pathway. At the first fork take the upper right-hand path. Walking on through **Burtness Wood**, watch for a path that forks right some 120 metres after passing over a ruined wall in the woodland. This grass trod leads up to a high fence-stile over the forest-bounding fence.

The continuing path leading southwest runs on comfortably above the wall (outside bracken season at least). The path rises, as too the wall, becoming less apparent on the ground once the wall is left behind. Keep up the right-hand side of the combe to minimise rocky terrain. Keep your eye on the left-hand side

Sheepbone Rake from across Birkness Comb

15 High Crag

of the combe, and spot the beginnings of an untidy rake leading up after the first major outcropping – only one possible gap exists. Once committed, a lot of stumbling among the rocks is needed to gain height – fortunately Sheepbone Rake becomes far more certain higher up. You'll huff and puff but as the rake ends you will, with relief, find even, easier ground.

Fleetwith Pike from the path above Burtness Wood

Veer right up a shallow gully to reach the bilberry and grassy slope leading to the ridge-top.

Ascent from Buttermere 30 or Gatesgarth 6

Via Scarth Gap or Birkness Comb →*4.8km/3 miles* ↑*640m/2100ft*
⏲*2hr 30min*

A free-flowing start along the shore leads to the popular path to the pass (Route 3) or a more subtle approach up Sheepbone Rake.

2 Leave the village centre heading west, passing the Fish Hotel, and follow the gated lane signed to the lake. Cross the outflow footbridge and bear left via a hand-gate onto the popular pedestrian lakeshore pathway. Nearing the end of the lake watch for the fork and bear up right to the copse corner, where you have two options, Routes **3** and **4**. (You can also reach this point from Gatesgarth by crossing the valley from the farm by the gated lane, crossing Peggy's Bridge and heading on up the pitched path.)

15 High Crag

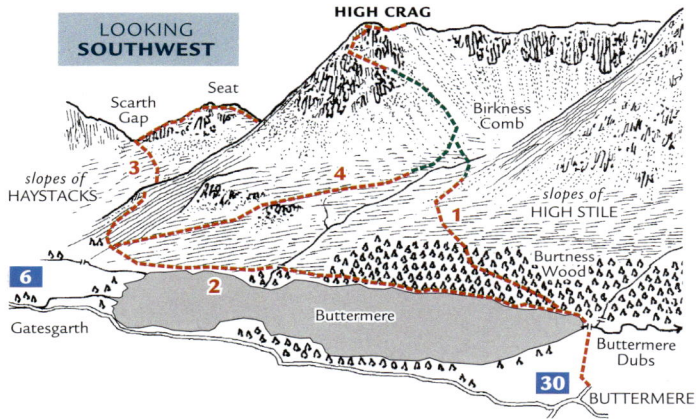

Via Scarth Gap →2.8km/1¾ miles ↑640m/2100ft ⏲1hr 40min

Gamlin End from Seat

3 Veer naturally left at the copse corner and complete the full ascent to **Scarth Gap**. Where the wall and beck intersect the path above **Wax Knott**, resist the temptation to short-cut right up the stony travail by the wall to the depression west of Seat. Keep resolutely to task and reach the cairn in the pass. Turn right (west) and climb the pitched path mounting the rocky headland, a beautiful heather garden. Make a point of visiting the summit cairn of **Seat**, a scenic seat indeed for your first break of the day! The path drifts down to the damp depression then sets to work on a new course climbing **Gamlin End**. The path has received commendable repair, although it remains quite loose near the top. It leads assuredly to the summit.

Via Birkness Comb →*2.4km/1½ miles* ↑*640m/2100ft* ⏱*2hr 15min*

4 From the copse corner, a distinct path runs up northwest across the slope. Watch for the vague fork, a lower path contouring more confidently across the scree towards **Comb Beck**, where you can ford and ascend on a grass strip through the bracken to a ladder-stile. The 'proper' (and recommended) climbers' route takes the less obvious course up from the fork to sneak over the brow between and above the outcrops to reach another wall ladder-stile situated south of Comb Beck. Here turn left to tackle **Sheepbone Rake**, in harmony with Route **1**.

Ascent from Black Sail Hut 7

Via Scarth Gap →*2.8km/1¾ miles* ↑*455m/1495ft* ⏱*1hr 30min*

5 Scarth Gap is perhaps the most commonly used pedestrian link with the outside world from this divine location. The open access track leads west to a gate at the entrance to the forest land. Ignore this and instead ascend right with the pitched path beside the fence, which climbs unwaveringly into the hause, then turn left to follow Route **3**.

Ascent from Bowness Knott 8 *off map W*

Via Scarth Gap →*11.2km/7 miles* ↑*655m/2150ft* ⏱*3hr 45min*

A useful ascent or descent route for a day on Ennerdale's northern skyline

6 The long dale approach is almost 8km (5 miles) from the car park at Bowness Knott to the point of divergence from the forest track above the Memorial Footbridge. The path starts through young conifers and quickly shakes clear of them, climbing on a diagonal line to a high-stepped fence-stile. It then maintains its easterly course via two further fences-stiles before slipping over a shoulder to arrive at Scarth Gap. From this point follow Route **3** to the summit.

The summit

An untidy cairn rests in a sublime situation which simply begs you to stay. Revel in the wide eastern arc from Fleetwith Pike round to Pillar Rock. Looking to upper Ennerdale, it is a peach of a prospect, centred upon Great Gable.

Haystacks from Seat

Safe descents

Your choice is limited to the steep descent SE to Seat and Scarth Gap (**3**) for Buttermere and upper Ennerdale. Sheepbone Rake is not suitable as a way down.

Ridge routes

Haystacks →*2km/1¼ miles* ↓*325m/1065ft* ↑*175m/575ft* ⏲*1hr 10min*
Follow the regular path SE. This angles right before resuming the SE course during the steeper part of the descent of Gamlin End. The ridge path is held over the lower ridge-summit of Seat and down pitched steps to Scarth Gap. Continue E, via sweeping zig-zags, onto the summit, but do not waver from the strong path.

High Stile →*1.6km/1 mile* ↓*25m/80ft* ↑*90m/300ft* ⏲*35min*
Follow the metal stacks from a former estate boundary, which give extra confidence in mist, along the narrow ridge W, following the clear route all the way to the summit.

16 HIGH STILE 807M/2648FT

Climb it from	Buttermere **30** or Gatesgarth **6**
Character	Central and most elevated summit rising direct from the southern shore of Buttermere
Fell-friendly route	2 or 3
Summit grid ref	NY 170 148
Link it with	High Crag or Red Pike
Part of	The Buttermere Round

While most of Lakeland's fells stand reasonably well back, High Stile shows no such reticence. Supported by two armed guards, High Crag and Red Pike, it stands as the centrepiece of a mighty mountain facade dominating Buttermere. Visitors driving over Newlands Hause descend to the village mesmerised by this great expression of fell architecture.

On either side of this wall of heather and rock nestle two hanging valleys, spilling white cascades, with all the drama of Glencoe. The Ennerdale face, as a complete contrast, is quite blank although no less huge.

Direct assaults for sure-footed fellwalkers do exist, exploiting the fact that most of the daunting rock lies well back at the head of the combes. Two ascents from Buttermere (1–2) and a variant from Gatesgarth (3) are described here.

↑ *Chapel Crags from Red Pike*

16 HIGH STILE

Ascent from Buttermere 30

Two steep but steady assaults on the northern slopes

Via Bleaberry Comb →*3.7km/2¼ miles* ↑*715m/2345ft* ⏲*2hr 30min*

1 Leave Buttermere village by the Fish Hotel and follow the gated lane to the outflow of Buttermere lake. Cross the footbridge and either go left via the hand-gate or step up via a hand-gate to stand on the footbridge spanning the base of the lower cascades of powerful **Sour Milk Gill**. Step back off the Sour Milk Gill footbridge (do not cross) and go through the gate on the level track in the wood. A matter of 40 metres beyond the gate, find a flight of stone steps climbing right, rising into **Burtness Wood**. Take it steady – it can be hellish on unaccustomed thighs and lungs!

After a hand-gate in the fence bounding the top of the wood, the pitching continues up the open fellside. Where the modern pitching levels and ends, come below ragged pines and take a path switching uphill to cross the broken wall. This is an older part of the regular way into Bleaberry Comb. As this also levels, break left into the thick heather without the benefit of a consistent path, heading south-southeast onto the shallow ridge. As you step through a wall-gap on the crest of the ridge, a path is apparent, and this continues as you keep on up the steep, rocky, scree-streaked northern slope ahead. There are no obstacles beside steepness and loose stones, and a few random cairns coax you to high skyline elation. Proceed to the summit.

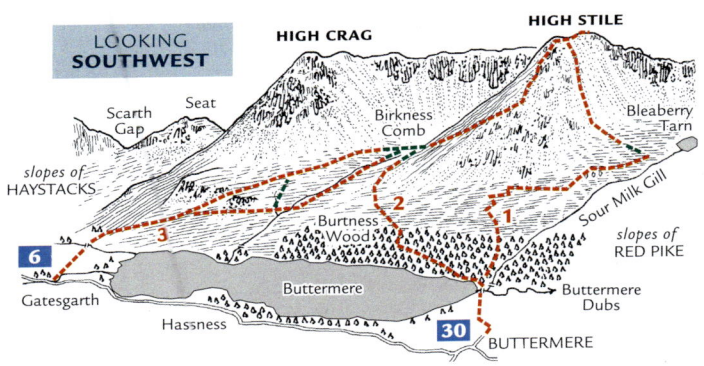

Red Pike from the top of Chapel Crags

Via Birkness Comb → 3.2km/2 miles ↑700m/2300ft ⏲2hr 20min

2 Set off on the gated lane beside the Fish Hotel, signed to the lake. Cross the outflow footbridge and bear left via a hand-gate onto the popular pedestrian lakeshore pathway. At the first fork take the upper right-hand path. Walking on through **Burtness Wood**, watch for a path that forks right some 120 metres after passing over a ruined wall in the woodland. This grass trod leads up to a high fence-stile over the forest-bounding fence. The continuing path leading southwest runs on comfortably above the wall. The path rises, as too the wall, becoming less apparent on the ground once the wall is left behind. As you come above the wall to enter the combe the path is less certain for a while, but if you keep up above the knoll with its fenced debris, slant right and join a worn path which comes onto a definite shelf mounting northwest up the bulky fellside, there is only one path. It bends slowly round west, making steady upward progress. As the ridge becomes narrower and rocks intervene, the path is clearly marked, offering a few incidental hands-on-rock moments and ever-improving views en route to the summit.

16 High Stile

Ascent from Gatesgarth 6

Via Birkness Comb →2.4km/1½ miles ↑700m/2300ft ⏱2hr

Choose your way into scenic Birkness Comb before joining Route 2.

3 Traverse the valley from the farm by the gated lane, crossing Peggy's Bridge and heading on up the pitched path to the corner of the copse. From here a distinct path runs up northwest across the slope. The map shows the three variations available on the first rise into the combe. The old climbers' path came into existence to avoid fording Comb Beck in spate.

It bends up to the left through a brow weakness in the scarp of rock defending the lower combe. The more obvious path contours to **Comb Beck**, where – if you don't fancy fording – you can at least switch up left on grass to reconnect with the climbers' path and reach a ladder-stile. If you do ford Comb Beck then a grass path can be followed immediately up to a second ladder-stile. Above this join forces with Route **2** and follow it to the summit.

The summit

It is only natural to reach the top of Chapel Crags and think the climb complete but the summit lies on the northeast spur ridge, spaced-out cairns vying for the crown. From here you can gaze over Bleaberry Tarn to Red Pike and the Crummock Water vale beyond, cross over to the east side to a jumble of white rocks at the top of Grey Crag to marvel at Birkness Comb, then wander a little further north for a breathtaking view over Buttermere and the facing fells to the north.

Looking across the head of Birkness Comb to Grey Crag, with Eagle Crag in shadow

Safe descents

For all the staggering scale of High Stile when viewed from Buttermere village, it is not outrageously dangerous, but in mist stick with the main spine ridge path, going E via High Crag to Scarth Gap for either Black Sail or Gatesgarth, or W via Red Pike for Buttermere. Dismiss any thought of using the two routes of ascent depicted here. In mist, high wind or lashing rain they would be no fun at all.

Ridge routes

High Crag →*1.6km/1 mile* ↓*90m/300ft* ↑*25m/80ft* ⏱*30min*
The line of old metal stakes is a rough guide although the wear of a million walking boots gives the better clue. Head S, then, as the ridge narrows, keep SE to the summit.

Red Pike →*1.2km/¾ mile* ↓*105m/345ft* ↑*60m/200ft* ⏱*25min*
From the top of Chapel Crags the common route heads E, although it is more stony than necessary so find easier ground a little to the left. Resume the natural NW run of the ridge after this initial loose trail. A cairn and small shelter indicate your arrival at Red Pike.

Looking east across Birkness Comb to Fleetwith Pike

WALKING THE LAKE DISTRICT FELLS – BUTTERMERE

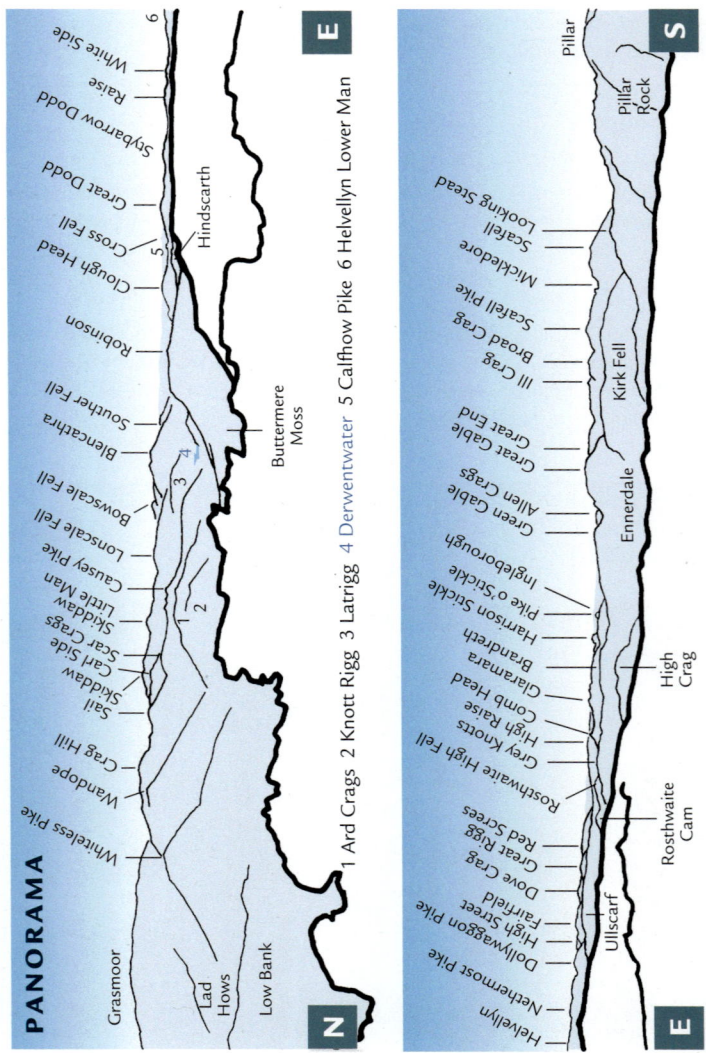

16 High Stile

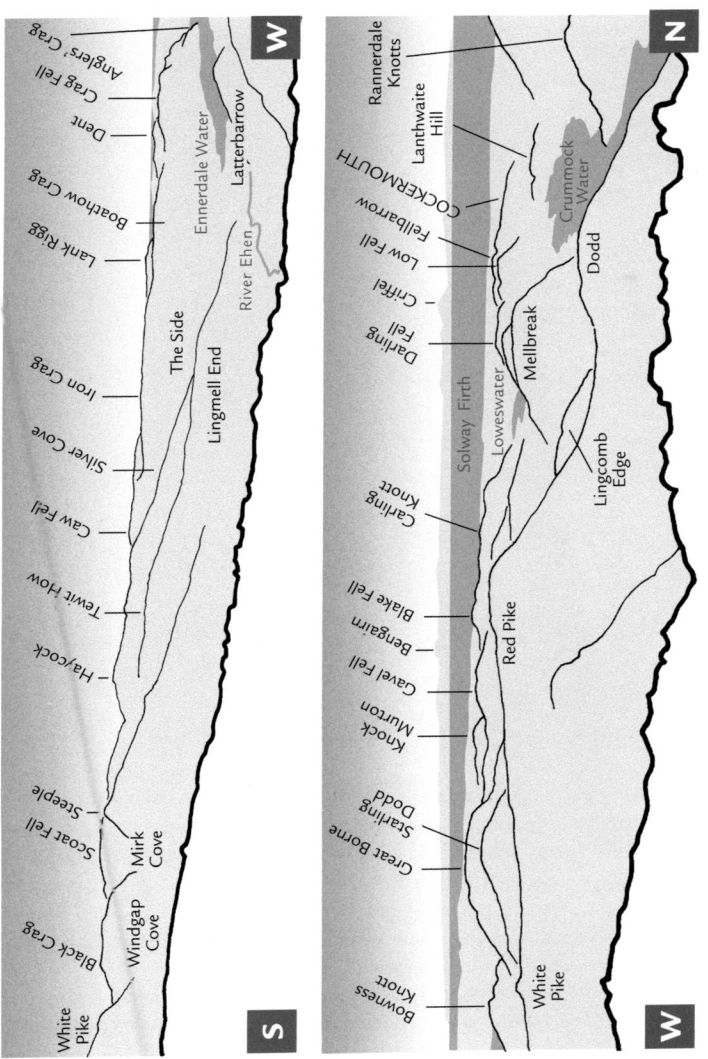

17 HINDSCARTH 727M/2385FT

Climb it from	Chapel Bridge **27** or Gatesgarthdale **5**
Character	Domed bulk that reserves its finest qualities for its northern aspect from Newlands, with the Scope End ridge a special treat
Fell-friendly route	1
Summit grid ref	NY 216 165
Link it with	Dale Head or Robinson
Part of	The Newlands Round

In some respects Hindscarth is a natural sibling to Robinson, but there is little family resemblance here. Hindscarth is a real individualist, full of character, and a fell you will never tire of climbing. Ridge walkers travelling between Dale Head and Robinson pass by little knowing what they are missing but the same cannot be said for anyone seeing the fell from Newlands. This handsome stand-alone fell – and particularly the heather-clad, sharply chiselled ridge running down north to Scope End – just begs to be climbed.

The principal point of interest on the fell is the Goldscope Mine, which was opened in 1564 and worked by German miners. They were invited by Elizabeth I to exploit the mineral riches of the Cumberland mountains, winning considerable

↑ *Hindscarth and High Crags from Scope End*

17 HINDSCARTH

quantities of copper and lead (no gold) to underpin her personal treasury. All activity ceased at the end of the 19th century because of flooding, and the site is now protected by English Heritage. And just to the north lies Newlands Church where the trim little white-washed chapel and old school-room certainly deserve a moment's contemplative admiration.

The fell offers one obvious ridge approach (1), with a roving scrambling alternative high up. To this is added here a side-door line out of Little Dale (2–3) and a two-pronged climb out of Gatesgarthdale – one a plod (4), the other an engrossing engagement with a heathery gill (5).

Ascent from Chapel Bridge 27

Three ways to reach High Crags and the Hindscarth ridge – all full of interest

Via Scope End →4km/2½ miles ↑610m/2000ft ⏲2hr 15min

1 Follow the road to **Newlands Church** and bear left onto the facing track (private road – permissive path). This duly leads to and through the gated yard of **Low Snab Farm** – an authentic Cumbrian fell farm, alive with hens. Pass through the end-gate and bear up right following the green-way, with the great spoil banks of the **Goldscope Mine** strikingly apparent. The path comes up beside the intake wall. Take a well-worn ever-popular path that breaks left, climbing step by step onto the heather ridge of **Scope End** and passing the upper rift of Pan Holes. The ridge path keeps below the crest of **High Crags**,

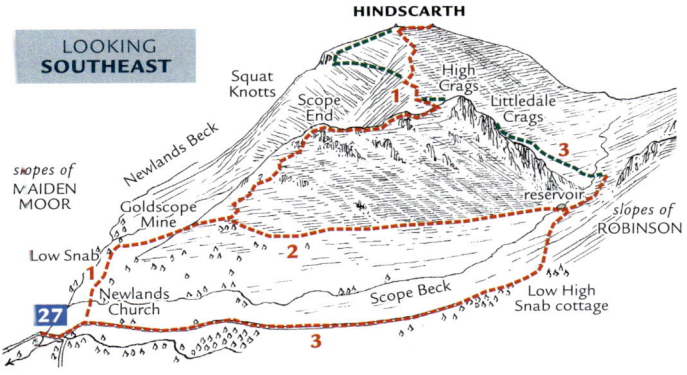

WALKING THE LAKE DISTRICT FELLS – BUTTERMERE

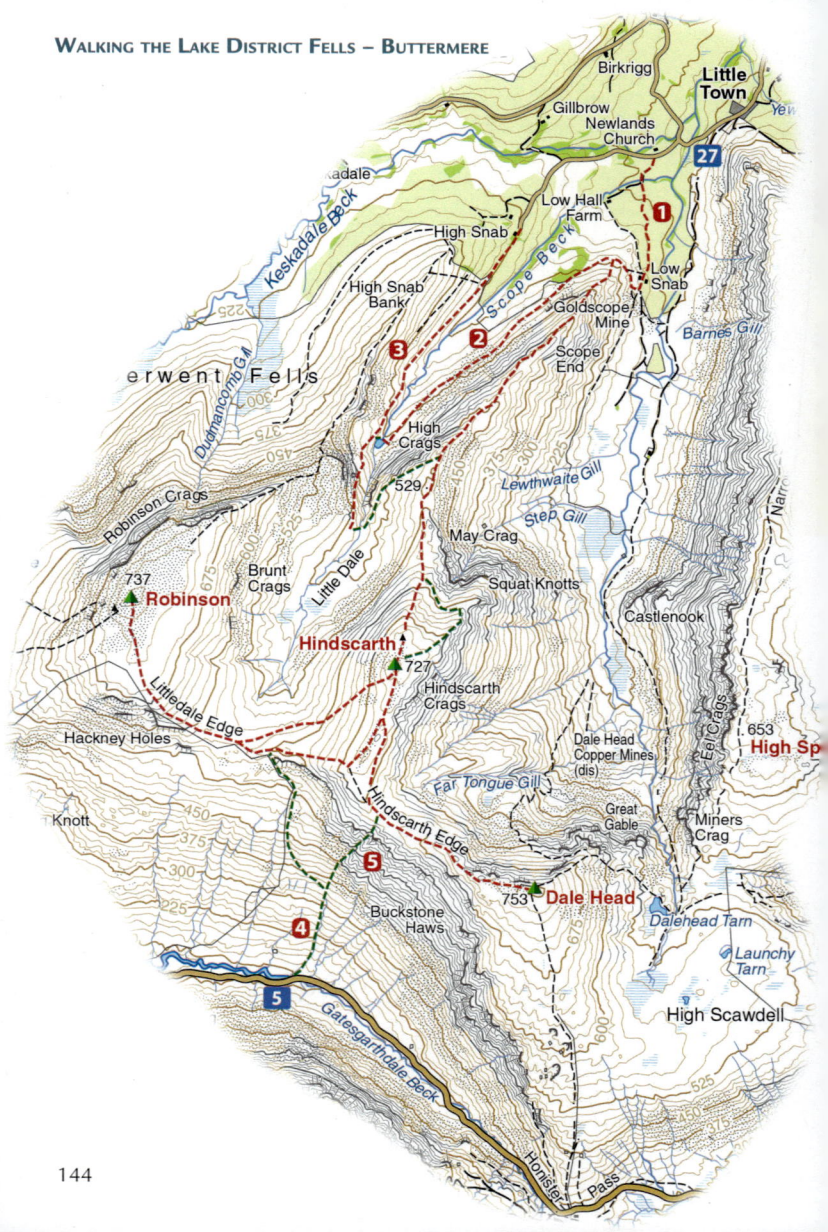

Scope End from High Crags

although you could easily take it in your stride. The main path keeps east of the crest of the ridge until the considerable final climb is met and completed without obstacle. For excellent views to enjoy in splendid isolation, bear left above the head of Step Gill to follow the knife edge above Squat Knotts before heading southwest to the summit.

Via the old aqueduct →*5.2km/3¼ miles* ↑*630m/2065ft* ⏲*2hr 40min*
2 Set off with Route **1** and stay with the green-way, countouring round Scope End to reach some spoil debris associated with a level and quarried portion of the **Goldscope Mine**. Step up here to join the line of the old aqueduct, which once carried water from the reservoir to the mine. As you come close to the **reservoir** bear up right over the boulders to cross the footbridge and the walled dam, clambering up the bank to join the valley drove-way. This mounts the bouldery ground, passing below an old holding fold to come above the turbulent ravine with its quartz-streaked boulders.

Ford Littledale Beck where you can and swing pathless up the rising pasture shelf. Here you can choose to take in **High Crags** or just drift onto the ridge path to face the stern task of climbing the regular way due south to the skyline cairn with Route **1**, and so to the summit.

Maiden Moor from above High Crags

Via Little Dale and High Crags →5.2km/3¼ miles ↑630m/2065ft ⏱2hr 45min
3 Follow the no-through-road, passing Newlands Church. Continue with the tarmac road rising up to Low High Snab Cottage, passing through the charming environs by gates. The green lane opens at a gate. Keep company with it as it gradually becomes more of a drove-path and leads above the reservoir, joining with Route **2**.

Ascent from Gatesgarthdale 5

Two no-nonsense routes to the top, best enjoyed in August when the heather is in full bloom

Via Littledale Edge →2.4km/1½ miles ↑680m/2230ft ⏱2hr
4 Cross the road-bridge and ascend left from the solitary boulder. Follow the gill flowing directly into the valley

Scope Beck valley

17 Hindscarth

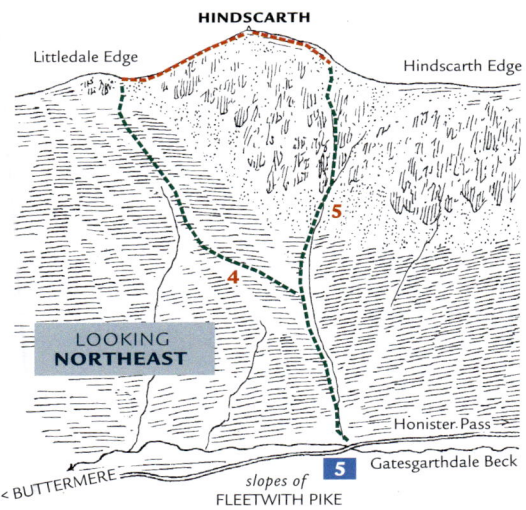

beck at the bridge. A line avoiding the bracken is easy to achieve. Follow the tongue and, two-thirds of the way towards the heather slopes, find a sheep trod veering left through the bracken to join and accompany the wall/fence. Clamber onto **Littledale Edge**, bear right with the ridge path and then turn left (north) to reach the summit. **5** Alternatively, for a little more adventure, keep faith with the gill as it tumbles through the steeper heather-clad ground, where the rocks are well broken and encourage a steady climb. On reaching the skyline turn left then quickly right again to follow the ridge path north to the summit.

The summit

North-top viewpoint shelter-cairn

The cairn marks a brilliant outlook, although the slightly domed top may tempt the occasional visitor to wander east for a better sense of the upper Newlands valley, taking in the craggy facade of High Spy and Dale Head to best effect. The large cairn some 150 metres north, where the north ridge meets the plateau, makes a better viewpoint for Keswick and the Skiddaw massif.

Safe descents

In poor weather stick resolutely N on the path to Newlands (**1**). Alternatively, for Honister, continue S along the summit ridge, finding a shortcut path curving round from S to SE on the east side of the ridge. The route leads along Hindscarth Edge, continuing via modest outcropping to the tall cairn on Dale Head, from where it heads S for the security of the pass.

Ridge route

Dale Head →*2km/1¼ miles ↓70m/230ft ↑95m/310ft ⏱35min*
Begin by following the summit ridge S, finding a shortcut path on the east side of the ridge which curves round from S to SE along Hindscarth Edge. Rise by modest outcropping (keep an eye open to avoid stumbling on the remnant metal fence posts underfoot) and continue to reach the unmistakable summit cairn.

Robinson →*2.4km/1½ miles ↓155m/510ft ↑165m/540ft ⏱50min*
Head S, but after some 50 metres find a path breaking half-right SW off the ridge down the grass slope. This is a shortcut to the head of Little Dale, otherwise known as Littledale Edge. Follow the obvious ridge path by the fence, and on the final rise veer away from the fence NW to the summit.

18 HOPEGILL HEAD 770M/2526FT

Climb it from	Lanthwaite Green 33, Hopebeck 19, Swinside 20, Hobcarton 21 or Braithwaite 24
Character	Impressive summit above a craggy facade, at the convergence of ridges
Fell-friendly route	4
Summit grid ref	NY 186 222
Link it with	Grisedale Pike or Whiteside
Part of	The Grasmoor Fell-gather and the Coledale Horseshoe

A high-running ridge leads east from Whiteside and angles up to form the shapely peak of Hopegill Head. Thereafter, this high divide curves around the head of the great U-shaped glacial hollow of Hobcarton to peak again, after a similar distance, on Grisedale Pike. On either side of the considerable trench of Hobcarton Gill, both major fells have steep valleys splaying to the northeast and northwest. Hopegill Head presides over the Hope Gill valley to the northwest.

For all Grisedale Pike dominates from Keswick perspectives, Hopegill Head equals it from northern perspectives and is much loved by Cockermouth folk. Two elements mark the fell out – a stupendous crag, Hobcarton, where rare alpine plant species survive beyond the nibbling teeth of Herdwick and careless tread of walkers; and the northern approach over Ladyside Pike, an airy fellwalking adventure culminating in an ascent of the notch and slabs at the brink of the great crag.

↑ *Approaching Ladyside Pike from Swinside, with Hopegill Head behind*

WALKING THE LAKE DISTRICT FELLS – BUTTERMERE

Routes to the top include the Hope Beck and Hope Gill approach itself (2) and the lovely heather-clad Swinside ridge up to Ladyside Pike, which offers three lines of attack (3–5). There are two further natural valley routes up Liza Beck (Gasgale Gill) (1) and Coledale Beck (6), with both routes coming together on the broad saddle of Coledale Hause to head north over Sand Hill.

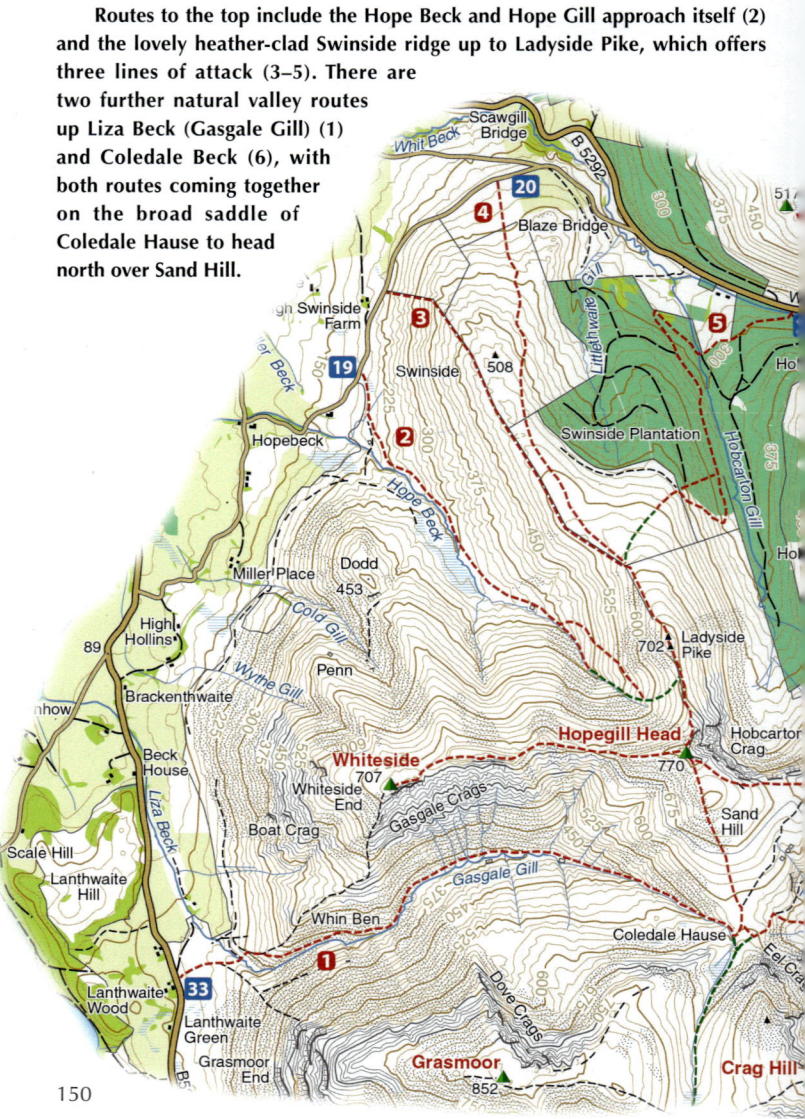

18 Hopegill Head

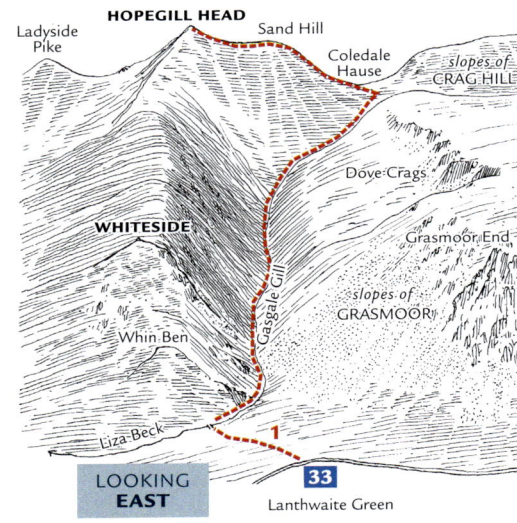

LOOKING EAST

Ascent from Lanthwaite Green 33

Via Gasgale Gill →4.8km/3 miles ↑720m/2360ft
⏲2hr 30min

Subtle and scenic up the ravine

1 Cross the open common to the footbridge spanning **Liza Beck** and then you have a choice. Follow the beck upstream, coping with an entertaining rock-step beside a handsome waterfall. (Or, to avoid this – not marked on the map – clamber up the fell, taking the right-hand branch off the ascending path to **Whin Ben** to avoid the outcrop above the gorge and walk on to join the lower path.) Head easily upstream. With increasing evidence of flood damage to the path, enjoy the succession of small waterslides en route to the dalehead level pasture of **Coledale Hause**, at which point join the obvious path that leads half-left to join the main spinal ridge path leading north, climbing the loose slope of **Sand Hill**. From the bare top the going eases to the summit – although **be watchful** of the profound edge of **Hobcarton Crag**.

Ascent from Hopebeck 19 and Swinside 20

These three routes could also be tackled from High Lorton. A narrow lane signed 'Boonbeck and Scales' leads off from the road bend by Yew Tree Hall. Follow this up to the farm to take the green lane from Scales to High Swinside Farm and walk up through the farm to the fell-road.

Via Hope Gill →*4km/2½ miles* ↑*710m/2330ft* ⏱*2hr*

The least-frequented option

2 From just beside the lower parking area at Hopebeck, a green drove-way leads up the valley, keeping to the northern bank of the beck. After the second sheepfold (and about 1.5km) there are two options. You can keep company with the tumbling gill – although the scope for a path diminishes as height

Hobcarton Crag rising to the summit from the notch

18 HOPEGILL HEAD

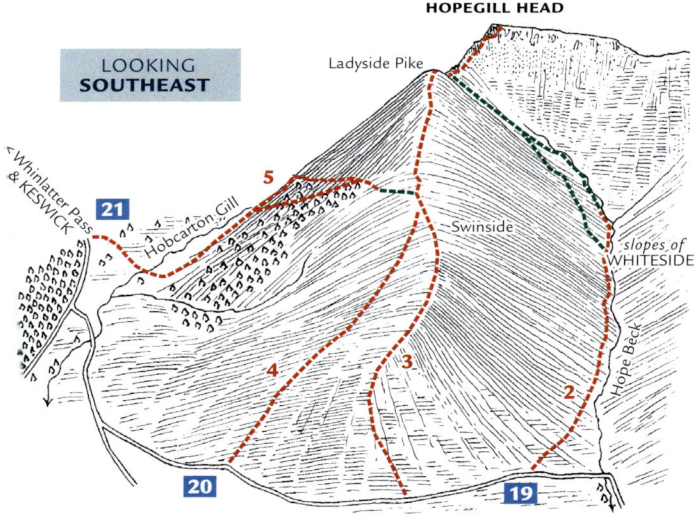

is gained, especially at a rocky nook – and shortly after bear away from the progressively stony and dry gill, as the heather is lost, to gain the ridge at the dip between **Ladyside Pike** and the pointed ridge-top outcrop. Alternatively, some 30 metres after a landslipped patch step up onto the heather and find a path that angles up and across the dense heather, becoming more apparent with each stride. Climb out of the heather and make up the pathless slope (with the gill-side variant). Ultimately, cross over the broken ridge wall and turn right, following the ridge path. Skirt round to the west side of the sharp knuckle of rock to come up to the most exciting part of the climb, the slabs and notch, from where there is the most amazing view down Hobcarton Crag. A rock groove provides the obvious and secure scramble to the top.

Via Swinside →4.4km/2¾ miles ↑715m/2345ft ⏲2hr 20min

The route of highest elation

3 Follow the road from either parking spot to an intermediate road-gate and smartly step up the bank, climbing beside the rising wall onto the ridge-top of Swinside. Continue beside the wall on grass, a pace or two from the fringing heather, with the lure of Ladyside Pike dead ahead. After a rise, the wall is defended by fencing and, where the dilapidated wall falters, at a fence-junction (and hand-gate on the far side), begin the ascent proper of **Ladyside Pike**. Follow the broken wall up to the twin-cairned summit. The broken wall continues through the narrow saddle, with the path holding a left-hand bias, leading to an awkward arête. Keep to the right, advancing over the rock-steps to mount to the notch at the brink of **Hobcarton Crag**. **Be watchful**, but do make the effort to

Looking back down to Ladyside Pike

enjoy the excellent view over the edge if you can. Follow the groove in the slabs, slanting half-right direct to the summit.

Direct →4km/2½ miles ↑690m/2270ft ⏲2hr

The most comfortable approach to the Swinside ridge

4 From the verge parking at Swinside go through the gate and follow the open track up to a gate and through the sheep-handling pens onto an obvious green track which continues due south, climbing into the heather banks. The track continues consistently to a hand-gate, after which it dwindles to a conventional path. This leads onto the ridge and arrives at the gate, uniting with Route **3** where the broken wall and fence converge.

18 Hopegill Head

Ascent from Hobcarton 21

Via Swinside Plantation →4km/2½ miles ↑715m/2345ft ⊕2hr 15min

Take the ridge by surprise from the shelter of the forestry.

5 Follow the forest track west, keeping right at the first open track junction. Descend to cross the broad Hobcarton Bridge. The track swings right then makes a sharp hairpin left at the forest edge, heading south. Advance unwaveringly to a gate at the end of **Swinside Plantation**. Keep forward through the rushy pasture on a green-way to cross a stile beside a gate in a downward-trending fence. Pass the old sheepfold filled with rushes and bear up smartly right to join a narrow path which runs up the steep slope in harmony with the fence to cross the hurdle at the top. The adjacent stile at the top edge of the plantation can also be reached by a more direct – and therefore steeper – route off the forest track just before the gate at the edge of the conifers. The onwards path dissolves into the moor grass as it rises onto the ridge. Slant southwest to reach the hand-gate in the fence-corner where Routes **3** and **4** come together. Proceed with them to the summit.

Ascent from Braithwaite 24 *off map NE*

Via Coledale Hause →6.8km/4¼ miles ↑730m/2395ft ⊕3hr

The miners' way to the pass

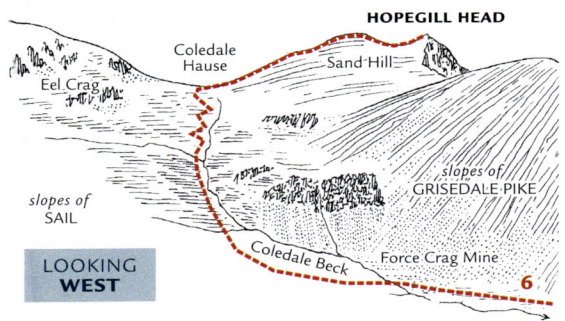

6 Follow the old mine track up Coledale. Where the track forks, short of the derelict buildings associated with the old **Force Crag Mine**, turn down left to ford **Coledale Beck**. Stick firmly to the rough trail leading west and climbing above the side-ravine with a fine view of Low Force. Higher up, the reinforced path snakes up the steeper slope and comes under **Eel Crag** to reach **Coledale Hause**. Bear right (north), following the strong path up the scree bank onto and over **Sand Hill**, drawn irresistibly to the summit.

The summit

Rarely does a cairn survive on this raw rock top, and the splintered nature of the available stones makes them all redundant. The summit is sufficient exultation in itself. It is the ultimate point of both the Hopegill valley and Hobcarton Crag – a quite thrilling place to stand, if the breeze allows. To the west lies the inviting ridge to Whiteside, and to the east Grisedale Pike stands aloof beyond a craggy, curved cirque edge.

The inviting ridge to Whiteside

Safe descents

In poor conditions, the safest plan is to head S over Sand Hill and down to Coledale Hause, with secure dale paths leading E to Braithwaite (**6**) and W to Lanthwaite Green (**1**).

Eastern aspect from the nameless knoll on the way to Grisedale Pike

Ridge routes

Grisedale Pike →*2km/1¼ miles* ↓*95m/310ft* ↑*115m/375ft* ⏱*45min*
Leave the summit, moving from SE to E – either hugging the edge or taking the more regular, set-back path. Ahead rises a nameless knoll, and on the rise a path from Coledale Hause joins from the right. Cross the top, now with evidence of a remnant ridge wall underfoot. The ridge mounts easily NE to the summit.

Whiteside →*2km/1¼ miles* ↓*110m/360ft* ↑*45m/150ft* ⏱*40min*
This popular path heads W upon a sharp edge, declining, with some rocky sections, to step onto a long heather crest. En route it strides over the east top of Whiteside (higher ground than the acknowledged summit) to land on the summit. All the way the views down the serried gullies into the Gasgale Gill ravine and across to Dove Crags on Grasmoor are tremendous.

19 KNOCK MURTON 447M/1467FT

Climb it from	Cross Rigg **10** or Felldyke **11**
Character	Western end of the Blake Fell group, overtopping Cogra Moss reservoir
Fell-friendly route	2
Summit grid ref	NY 094 191

In the company of great heights, many quite sprawling in character, it is fun to find one fell where the summit can be reached in 40 minutes from the road and offers a lovely outlook in reward. Fell-runners take evening exercise over the fell, their ascent and descent times measured in minutes and seconds. Sitting on the far side of Blake Fell from delightful Loweswater, this little knob marks the western limit of fell country hereabouts.

Within its tiny scope, Knock Murton was a centre of Victorian iron mining, and spoil, quarry hollows and extraction-railway embankments remain as reminders of its former industrial life. The re-landscaping of the Cogra Moss basin has brought out the best in the whole setting and it shows off Knock Murton as a hill of distinction. Tackle it from the south (1–2) or north (3), or combine it with an exploration of the plantation on a variety of forestry tracks.

↑ *Knock Murton across Ennerdale*

19 Knock Murton

Ascent from Cross Rigg 10

Direct →1.6km/1 mile ↑200m/655ft ⏱45min

1 From the recessed gate follow the track to a further gate, then divert up left, rising with the fence. As the slope eases, bear off right on an emergent path which crosses the shallow ridge to climb the final upthrust slope to the summit.

2 Alternatively, from where Route **1** heads up left, continue with the track to the next gate at the entrance into Cogra Moss forestry. Do not go through the gate. Instead step up left beside the fence. Pass evidence of iron mining, which runs down into the plantation, and either divert left to pass up by the little crag or continue to where the fence levels by a redundant stile. Turn up to make your way steeply through the rank heather. Go over the intermediate cairnless top to reach the true summit.

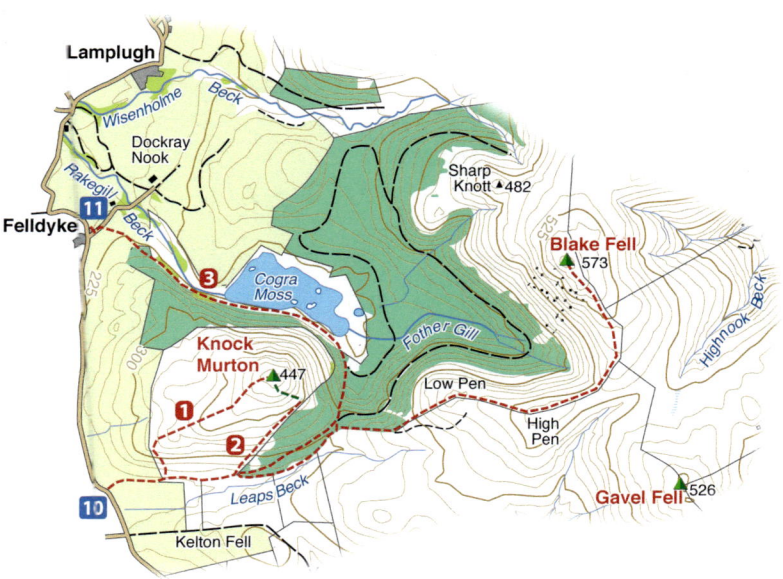

WALKING THE LAKE DISTRICT FELLS – BUTTERMERE

Ascent from Felldyke 11

Direct →3.7km/2¼ miles ↑270m/885ft ⏲1hr

Swing right round the fell to make the most of your hill day.

3 From the car park follow the waymarked path into the lane, then go left then right through the kissing-gate. Stride along the open track to a kissing-gate gaining entry into the Cogra Moss reservoir and forestry enclosure (Forestry Commission information panel). The track leads on, rock-cut into the flanks of Knock Murton, passing a handsome line of mature beech to arrive at the dam on **Cogra Moss**. Continue along the southern shore. (Watch out for fly-fishermen back-casting their lines.) The right-hand climb begins where a path branches from the shore track at the water's end. This narrow path, known as the Donkey Trod, ascends the felled bank to meet the forest track from Cross Rigg. Turn right, following this path back through the dark forest to the entrance gate. Pass through. Turn immediately right, and continue with Route **2** to the summit.

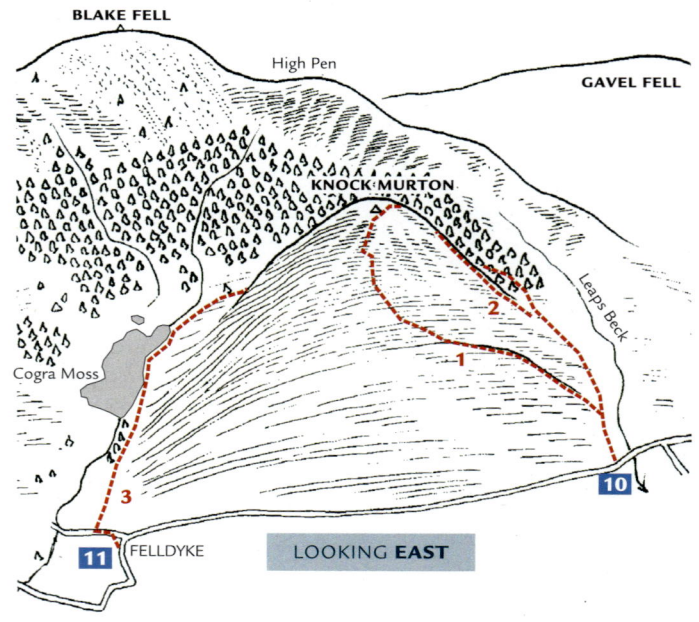

Cogra Moss from the foot of the Donkey Trod

The summit

Beside the substantial summit cairn stands a large, rather complex shelter, cosy no matter where the wind is coming from and a place to relax and enjoy the Lake District's long, low maritime horizon.

Safe descent

Follow the obvious ridge-top path SW (**1**). This leads assuredly down to a fence marking the top of enclosures. Angle left down to the forest access track and go right via the gates.

Ridge route

Blake Fell →*4km/2½ miles* ↓*175m/575ft* ↑*300m/985ft* ⏲ *1hr 20min*

Swing down SE to find a tangible path by the fence heading SW, with some gorse and rough ground to avoid. At the foot, step onto the track and go through the gate into the Cogra Moss forestry. Bear right, keeping beside the forest-edge fence then climbing via Low and High Pen, each a lovely viewpoint, enjoying grand prospects back onto the shapely knob of Knock Murton. Keep by the fence. Only after the ridge path from Fothergill Head has joined at a stile does the principal path waver from its fence-side duty to reach the summit.

20 KNOTT RIGG 556M/1824FT

Climb it from	Buttermere **30**, Newlands Hause **29** or Keskadale **28**
Character	Southern summit of an enticing little curved, grassy ridge, north of Newlands Hause
Fell-friendly route	2
Summit grid ref	NY 197 188
Link it with	Ard Crags
Part of	The Newlands Round

If there can be such a thing, this is the perfect 'nursery' fell (although inclement weather can prevent any fell from being mere child's play). Motorists arrive at Newlands Hause, ease their cars onto the wide verge, and, having gazed amazed at Moss Force, are tempted to take a leg-stretching walk. Knott Rigg beckons to the north, an unthreatening grassy slope rising to a pronounced peak – how could they resist?

The elegant arc of the fell, akin to the upturned hull of a long ship, combined with its situation among such great peaks, makes this a worthy objective. Three lines of ascent are available – from Buttermere (1), the route direct from the hause (2) and, most exciting of all, Keskadale Edge (3), climbing southwestwards from the farm of that name. Most visitors will want to complete the expedition by following the ridge to its summit at Ard Crags, with little further effort necessary.

↑ *Knott Rigg from above Newlands Hause*

20 KNOTT RIGG

Ascent from Buttermere 30

Via Sail Beck →*3.6m/2¼ miles* ↑*460m/1510ft* ⏱*1hr 30min*

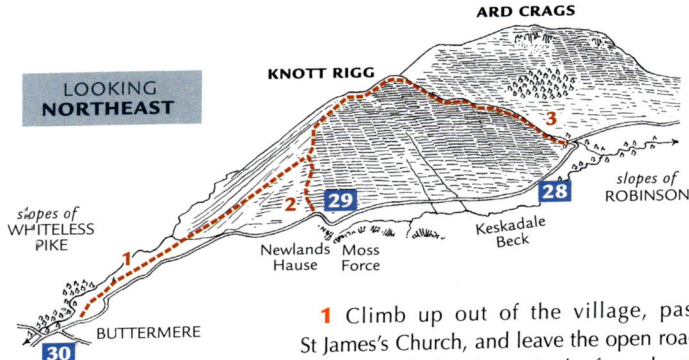

1 Climb up out of the village, past St James's Church, and leave the open road quickly after the last barn. As the fence bears down find a path, little more than a sheep trod, running just below the road, well above **Sail Beck**. After fording **Swinside Gill** the climb proper begins, mounting a broad green carpet. The path fades but the way is never in doubt. Come over the first top-knot and shake off the immediate disappointment that this is not the summit. There is further to go and, despite the small area of marsh, it is a pleasant walk to the cairn on the summit.

Ascent from Newlands Hause 29

Via the south ridge →*1.6km/1 mile* ↑*230m/755ft* ⏱*45min*
2 Several paths set out from the hause to come together as the slope steepens. Stick to the carefully repaired path and join Route **1** to claim your felltop.

Ascent from Keskadale 28

Via Keskadale Edge →*2km/1¼ miles* ↑*330m/1080ft* ⏱*1hr 15min*
3 Walk northeast to **Keskadale Farm**. Descend the road from the farmhouse, down from the first left-hand hairpin. Find traces of a path stepping off the road on the left, clamber up the untidy slope, pass the noisy kennels and cross a fence-stile. The path rises beside a fence to cross a second fence-stile.

Looking towards Ard Crags from the summit

Follow the path forwards, ascending the steep ridge of Keskadale Edge with a fence close right, above the secretive depths of Ill Gill, no longer accessible for casual entry. It is a sanctuary, protected as part of the Keskadale Oakwood Special Area of Conservation. The ridge has no physical obstacles. Pass on by two fenced bogs to reach the summit.

The summit

No fanfares or great edifices greet walkers, just a pile of stones set on a grassy pillow, befitting a modest felltop. The view is not as grand as those from its loftier neighbours. But the intimacy of the view into the Newlands valley and east to the Helvellyn range, and the sense of scale engendered by the surround of great fell ridges, are more than ample compensation.

Safe descents

In mist, keep to ridges and avoid descending to the N or W into the Sail Beck valley, where the declivity is abrupt. The best route

20 KNOTT RIGG

is S to Newlands Hause (**1**), while that E then NE down Keskadale Edge (**3**) is steep but the path should never be in doubt.

Ridge route

Ard Crags →*1.6km/1 mile* ↓*50m/165ft* ↑*75m/245ft* ⏲*30min*
Head NE, with the ground falling gently to a depression, still on a comparatively narrow ridge. The path is all too apparent on the steady rise to the summit, with heather the attractive accompaniment.

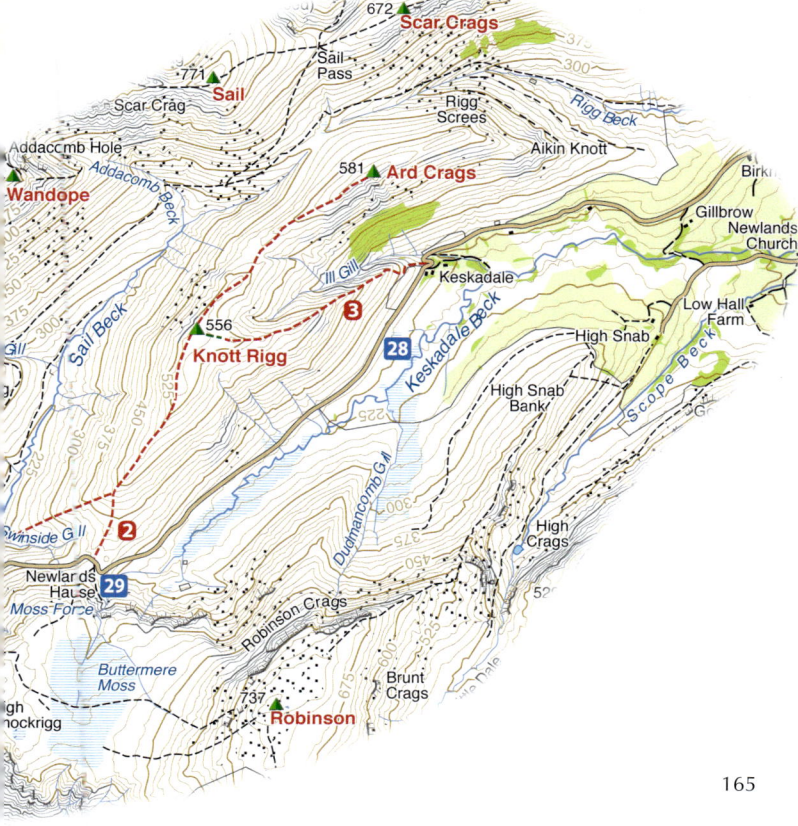

21 LOW FELL 423M/1388FT

Climb it from	Thackthwaite **18**, Church Bridge **16** or Waterend **13**
Character	Popular local viewpoint offering views over Loweswater and the grand parade of fells above Crummock Water
Fell-friendly route	3
Summit grid ref	NY 137 226
Link it with	Fellbarrow

Many fells build their reputation on their stature. A select few have pride of place as sensational viewpoints. All who stand on the modest crest of Low Fell know at once in which aspect it excels, and excel it does. From several situations along the ridge, and also from neighbouring Darling (traditionally pronounced 'dirlin') Fell, you will enjoy outlooks that will live long in the heart and memory. They are so widely appreciated that the opening sequence of the film *Miss Potter* famously featured the classic view of Mellbreak from Low Fell, even while alluding to a very different Hilltop about 40km to the southeast.

Four approaches are described from all around the fell, candidates for a good circuit. However, beware the footpath straddling the fell from east to west, marked on Harvey and OS maps. It does exist but is excessively steep. If you must use it at all do not use it in descent.

↑ *Low Fell from above High Nook Farm*

21 LOW FELL

Ascent from Thackthwaite 18

Via Watching Crag →*3.2km/2 miles* ↑*340m/1120ft* ⏲*1hr 15min*

1 Leave the road via the narrow lane signed 'footpath to Low Fell' beside Thackthwaite Farm. The lane goes by a hand-gate and up a field-edge to a second hand-gate onto a green drove-way. This lovely track sweeps easily north then west through a gate up the **Meregill Beck** combe and zig-zags generously to arrive on the level felltop. Go through the facing kissing-gate, passing a sheepfold. A casual diversion left allows you to stand on top of **Watching Crag**, a neat little viewpoint, before rejoining the ridge path and crossing a fence-stile to complete the ascent.

WALKING THE LAKE DISTRICT FELLS – BUTTERMERE

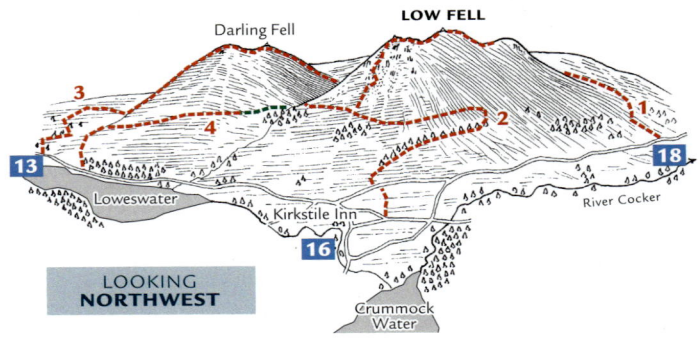

Ascent from Church Bridge 16

Via Whinny Ridding →4.1km/2½ miles ↑375m/1230ft ⏲1hr 30 min

The craggy southern aspect of the fell is the most dramatic, but parking is limited.

2 Walk back up to the minor crossroads by the **Kirkstile Inn** and keep right of the church, heading along the road to the junction with the kiosk. Find a signposted footpath opposite the cottage, which heads north along field-edges via stiles to the road at **Foulsyke**. Turn left then first right up the access lane passing Woodend. From the wall-stile beside the gate follow the open track which sweeps up to a gate and into the woodland fringe. The tree-sheltered path runs north through Whinny Ridding. From the hand-gate at the far end, a clear path accompanies the wall, fords a gill, then bears up to a hand-gate in the fell-bounding wall.

Switch back south on the shelf path. When you encounter a fence ignore the very evident path that climbs up the steepest of slopes beside the fence. Cross the fence-stile and continue along the slope, curving from south to west. Pass a lonesome pine and cross another fence-stile. You have two options here. Continue, to find a large shapely stone on the terrace, and climb up the steep rocky fellside by a fang of quartz to arrive at the southernmost 'viewpoint' cairn – there is evidence of a path all the way up. Alternatively, contour on and skirt by the conifer copse. Keep up through the gorse on a path rising beside the juvenile **Crabtree Beck**. When you reach the fence climb east up through the heather to gain the ridge, then turn left via the fence-stile to reach the summit.

Ascent from Waterend 13

Via Darling Fell →3.7km/2¼ miles ↑420m/1380ft ⏲1hr 30min

Take in the peerless felltop view from Darling Fell.

3 From the verge parking take the metalled lane signed 'Askill B&B/bridleway' directly opposite. As the tarmac switches to concrete, bear left then smartly right into the green lane, rising by gates to meet the Mosser Fell Road. Turn right and follow the gently descending lane, which in early summer is lined with vivid blooms of yellow broom. Come to some steps and a stile up the bank to the left. Aim left and walk up, avoiding the light scree, joining a path that rises by the fence. The fence is lost but not so the path, which mounts over the brow to cross a fence-stile and reach the summit of **Darling Fell**. The path leads

Pastoral scene at Loweswater

on down in harmony with the new-found fence, crossing the **Crabtree Beck** depression, to join Route **2** on the heather climb to the summit ridge.

Via Crabtree Beck →*3.7km/2¼ miles* ↑*375m/1230ft* ⏲*1hr 15min*

The terrace route

4 Start out with Route **3** but continue down the Mosser Fell Road until you reach a seat beside a padlocked gate. Here cross the stile and follow the level turf track. This passes an old shallow quarry and continues as a narrow path which gently rises to an intervening fence. A stile has been placed in the fence below the scree and gorse bank, but there is no need to use it. Pass through the gap to continue with your chosen path. This ascends across the slope, passing two cairns, and slips over a brow. Now on a slightly declining line through the bracken, pass beneath the bank of gorse to ford **Crabtree Beck**. At this point turn left and ascend with Route **2** to reach the summit.

Crummock Water from the forward cairn

The summit

A rag-tag cairn does little justice to this spellbindingly beautiful spot. It is a place to stand and stare if ever there was one. The view from east to south is out of this world, but its most complete expression lies at the southern tip of the ridge. Walk on south with the ridge path, crossing a fence-stile. Pass a crest cairn, and a little further on down the rocky slope find another – aim to be the first to arrive at and the last to leave this supreme viewpoint.

Safe descents

In contrast to many other fells, all routes can be reversed. However, in mist the surest options are either to head N for Thackthwaite (**1**), or S for Loweswater (**3**), crossing the fence-stile and turning right (W) over Darling Fell.

Ridge route

Fellbarrow →*2km/1¼ mile* ↓*90m/295ft* ↑*85m/280ft* ⏲*40min*

Head N along the ridge, crossing a fence-stile and advancing to a kissing-gate left of an old sheepfold. Immediately E of this spot find the scarp top of Watching Crag – a particularly fine viewpoint across the Lorton vale to the great company of fells centred around Whiteside and Grasmoor. From the kissing-gate either follow the fence left over Sourfoot Fell, being guided by the fence down into the marshy 'sour foot', or contour NW to reach the hollow. From here the ridge fence is your guide over Smithy Fell. In the next dip cross the fence-stile, left, and the ensuing fence-stile, and climb the grass slope to the summit pillar.

22 MELLBREAK 512M/1680FT

Climb it from	Church Bridge 16, Lanthwaite Wood 17 or Buttermere 30
Character	A handsome, heather-clad saddleback fell to the west of Crummock Water
Fell-friendly route	4
Summit grid ref	NY 148 186

Forming a noble and invariably dark backdrop to the glistening waters of Crummock, Mellbreak is an inseparable partner of the lake, looming over its western shore, a striking, stand-alone saddleback ridge. Rather like an oddly asymmetric upturned boat, the fell has four strikingly different aspects: a seemingly inaccessible eastern slope and great, rocky northern gable end and a much more hospitable western slope and even easier access from the gentle southern slopes.

    Although closely associated with Loweswater thanks to that dramatic northern face, Mellbreak makes a splendid objective from Buttermere, with Scale Force adding spice to the expedition. Archaeologists have found the area downstream from the ravine to be particularly rich in evidence of Viking settlement. Although not clear to the inexpert eye, this serves to remind us that, while the modern road runs along the east shore of Crummock, both shores were

↑ *The north top of Mellbreak from Black Crag*

once alive with agricultural settlement. Another interesting feature hereabouts is the Mosedale Holly Tree. In a dale otherwise devoid of trees thanks to the inveterate sheep, this sturdy tree makes a striking feature worthy of mention on the maps.

No less than eight routes or route sections, from all angles, are described here, including the popular scramble up the northern face (1); the lesser-known and trickier challenge of Pillar Rake (5), the only line of access to the midriff from the east; and Todd's Trod (2) from the west – a little gem, named by your author after the farmer at Kirkgate who introduced him to it.

Ascent from Church Bridge 16

Via Kirkhead →3.7km/2¼ miles ↑395m/1295ft ⊕1hr 40min

The head-on route contemplated from the Kirkstile Inn

1 From the parking area follow on south down the road by **Kirkhead** and **Kirkgate Farm**. Pass on through into the walled lane. At the second right-angled turn in the lane notice a large, low square earthwork over to the right. Arriving at a gate, step off the continuing track and head straight up the

Kirkstile Inn backed by the north face of Mellbreak

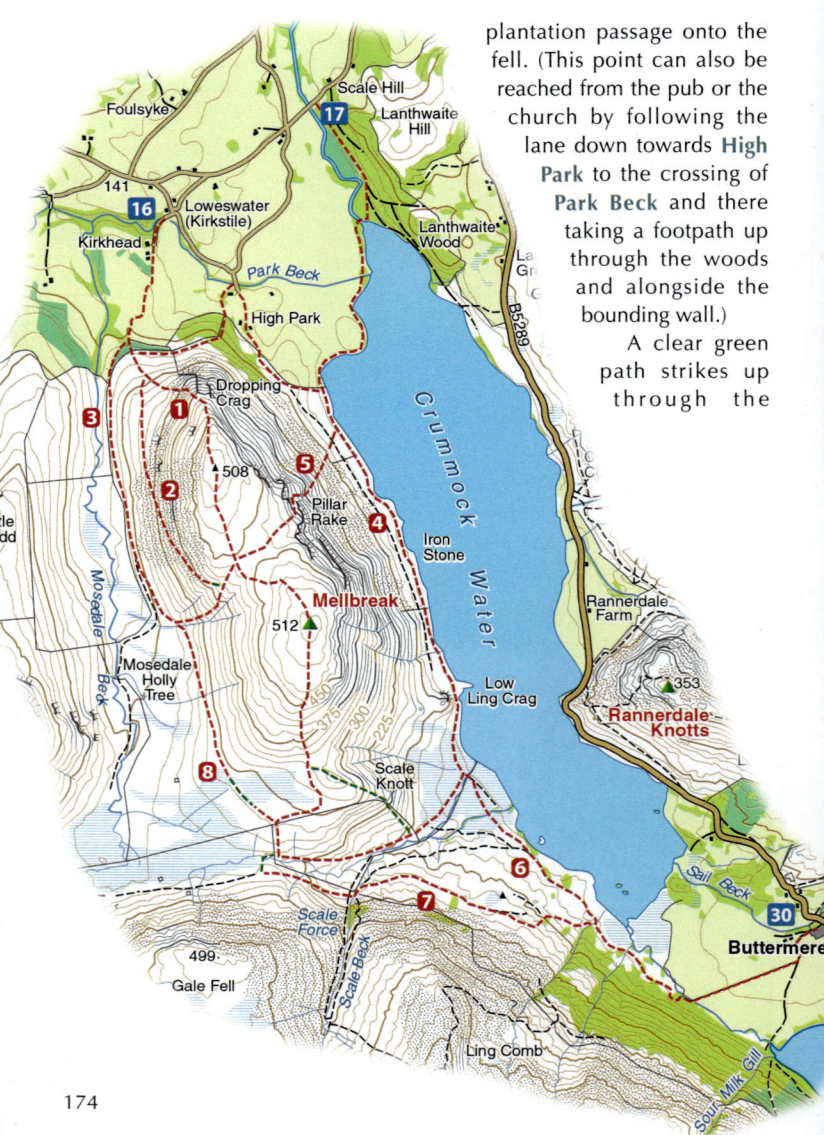

plantation passage onto the fell. (This point can also be reached from the pub or the church by following the lane down towards **High Park** to the crossing of **Park Beck** and there taking a footpath up through the woods and alongside the bounding wall.)

A clear green path strikes up through the

22 MELLBREAK

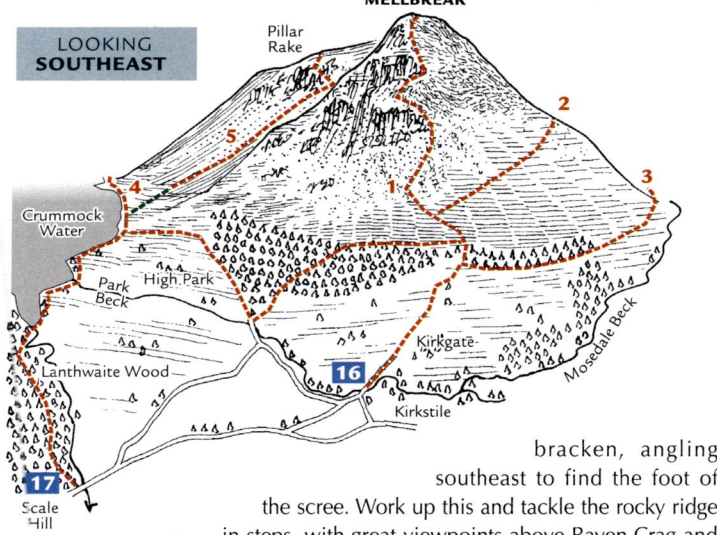

bracken, angling southeast to find the foot of the scree. Work up this and tackle the rocky ridge in steps, with great viewpoints above Raven Crag and then **Dropping Crag**, where you can sneak a peek round to the left towards Buttermere. The ridge narrows, and the path slants to the right to gain the northern summit cairn. A clear path heads on south through a lovely bed of heather and crosses the saddle to the south top and then the summit of the fell.

Via Todd's Trod →*3.2km/2 miles* ↑*395m/1295ft* ⏲*1hr 30min*

The ('shepherds') path of least resistance

2 Follow Route **1** to the point where it sets off towards the scree. Sense the shoulder to the right. Here a sheep-path moves effortlessly across and up the steep western slope. As the upper reaches of a gill are met the route heads more earnestly up with a grassy path onto the heather in the saddle, and the ridge path is quickly joined. Proceed southeast to the summit.

Via the Mosedale Holly Tree →*4.1km/2½ miles* ↑*410m/1345ft* ⏲*1hr 50min*

3 Walk south from the parking area and, from the gate at the head of the **Kirkgate Farm** lane, keep company with the wide comfortable track heading

Mosedale Holly Tree

on into Mosedale. Where the track splits, keep to the left-hand track along the foot of the fell until you reach the gill. Here consider visiting the **Mosedale Holly Tree**, a little further on and just down from the track. Having done so, return to the gill, crossing to take the abrupt turn uphill to join Todd's Trod (Route **2**) to the summit.

Ascent from Lanthwaite Wood 17

Via Low Ling Crag →*7.2km/4½ miles* ↑*400m/1320ft* ⏲*2hr 45min*

The long way round, savouring the Crummock shoreline

4 Follow the woodland track, which leads close above the River Cocker to the shore of **Crummock Water**. Bear right and cross two bridges at the lake's outflow to wander along beside the modest dam parapet. Keep to the shore path, passing through hand-gates. Sweeping round a shingle beach go through a hand-gate in a wall. From here the path runs open beneath Mellbreak. (You can reach this point from the Kirkstile area by following the road south from the crossroads to pass through **High Park** by gates and over the wall-stile, right. Follow the wall beneath Green Wood faithfully on down to the shoreline path beside the hand-gate.) Hold to the lower path, enjoying close contact with the shore and passing the solitary **Iron Stone** bathing its feet in the lake. Take a moment to wander out onto the tiny **Low Ling Crag** peninsula. Continue south. Come to a footbridge and gate.

Turn right with the grass path through the bracken, passing a large sheepfold. Go through the gate and step over the fence-stile, right, amid much marshiness. Ascend the steep ridge, alongside evidence of a wall, and cross the fence at the top of the rise. Coming over **Scale Knott** onto the ridge, bear left to join the popular path leading to the right up the southern slope towards the summit. Alternatively, instead of heading steeply and pathlessly up the fellside, continue up the **Black Beck** valley on the rough path to encounter a metal hand-gate in a fence. Do not go through. Follow the fence up to another hand-gate. Go through and bear right (east) to minimise contact with an extensive area of rush marsh ahead. Follow the light fence in skirting round and seek the continuity of the path leading north up the south ridge to the summit.

Via Pillar Rake →4.1km/2½ miles ↑445m/1460ft ⊕1hr 40min

This route will not be to everyone's taste – most walkers would do well to explore Pillar Rake from above and backtrack – but it's great fun.

5 Follow Route **4** to the base of the crags. Spot the one obvious ribbon of scree and work your way up the bracken, across the lateral path from High Park, towards it. Follow the edge of the line of scree up, hauling yourself up by the heather. (It's clear why more walkers descend this way than ascend it.) The key issue lies just short of the top of this slithering race of stones. Watch to break up **right** of the outcropping. (The wear of the scree implies a leftward slant, and this is totally wrong and hugely problematic.) The only way

The narrow grass trod of Pillar Rake

up is round the north side of the mass of pinnacles and gullies, keeping to the heather. Reach the narrow rake hugging the cliff base and find a sequence of exciting crags and gullies to admire. At the top follow a sheep path southwest through the heather, traversing the saddle to link up with Route **1** on the west side and turn left for the summit.

Ascent from Buttermere 30

Mellbreak makes a splendid objective from the village, with Scale Force adding spice to Route 7.

Via Scale Knott →6.4km/4 miles ↑435m/1425ft ⏲2hr 25min

6 Follow the lane to cross Scale Bridge, and from the gate turn right to follow on with the path towards the lake. Cross a small footbridge over Far Ruddy Beck and keep to the lower path, traversing the damp pasture to a gate and a footbridge over **Scale Beck**. Here turn left to carry on with one or the other variant of Route **4**.

Via Scale Force →6km/3¾ miles ↑440m/1445ft ⏲2hr 10min

7 Start out with Route **6** but at the Far Ruddy Beck plank-bridge bend left to follow the popular path, taking either of two variants that lead across the slopes (beside thorn bushes in their lower reaches) to a kissing-gate, and continuing down steps to cross the footbridge beneath the **Scale Force** ravine. You cannot get far into the ravine itself, but it's worth a glance to see the pencil-thin fall – the

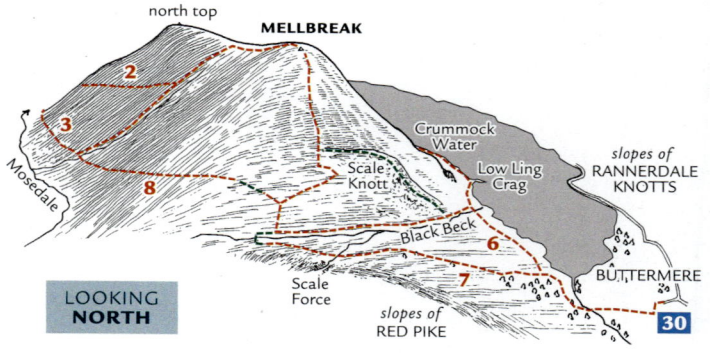

22 MELLBREAK

Herdwick ewes on Scale Knott

tallest single drop in Lakeland at 37m/120ft – crashing within the chasm. Continuing west, a great landslip has swept part of the path away, necessitating a deviation up the bank through the bracken. Watch for the fence-corner and, when you can, turn down to ford the beck and turn back to the hand-gate. Go through it, rising with the fence to your left, following Route **4**.

8 From the hand-gate across the beck on Route **7**, the footpath continues northwest into Mosedale. It has to cross an area of rush marsh but you'll not drown, and it eventually finds firm turf and continues as a lovely drove-way. It leads first to the **Mosedale Holly Tree** and then, a little further on, to the steep ascent to the ridge with Route **2**.

The summit

Mellbreak has two summits. The south top is the higher by 3m/10ft and is marked by a very modest cairn, but the scenic setting has everything to commend it. For the best views head southeast as the ground breaks away and enjoy a fantastic view over the head of Crummock Water to Buttermere and its spellbinding surround of fells. Directly below is Low Ling Crag, projecting into the lake like an arrow pointing towards Hause Point on Rannerdale Knotts, with the majestic Grasmoor group brilliantly displayed.

Two cairns grace the north top, but that to the west is the higher by a whisker. The key highlights here are Crummock Water and the mighty Grasmoor, best seen from a little way east of the fell crown.

Safe descents

The safest ways are S (**6**) for Buttermere or the lakeside path, and W from the saddle (**3**) down into Mosedale for Loweswater.

23 OUTERSIDE 568M/1863FT

Climb it from	Braithwaite **24** or Uzzicar **25**
Character	Midpoint step-aside crest above Coledale, connected to Barrow, north of the main Causey Pike ridge
Fell-friendly route	3
Summit grid ref	NY 211 214
Link it with	Barrow
Part of	The Coledale Horseshoe

Viewed from the miners' track leading into Coledale, Outerside rises like the inverted fin of a yacht. The highest of the little group of perfectly pyramidal, lesser heights just north of Causey Pike, it offers a handsome mid-height view of this majestic valley even when the tops are wreathed in cloud and, on clearer days, with Stile End and Barrow, long views of the massif of the Northern Fells.

Starting from Braithwaite, you can savour Outerside's shapely profile as you approach from the Force Crag Mine track (1) or trek up to Barrow Door and under or over Stile End as you prefer (2). Another good line follows the scenic Stonycroft Gill valley track to High Moss and doubles back (3). All these offer a sense of the fell's situation among lofty mountains. Routes 1 and 2 can be used to make a low-level, three-peak mini-Coledale Round when time or conditions are limiting factors.

↑ *Outerside from Coledale*

Ascent from Braithwaite 24

Via Coledale Beck →4.8km/3 miles ↑500m/1640ft ⏲2hr

The ideal approach for anyone wishing to make a round-trip

1 From the car park simply follow the Coledale track beyond the barrier. As you near the mine buildings fork down left with the track to ford **Coledale Beck**. Continue beyond, ascending to where, at a cairn, a path veers sharply left. This fords **Birkthwaite Beck** and sweeps up to join the regular path south of High Moss. Turn northeast on what quickly becomes a track, coming onto the plain, and bend half-left to traverse the marshy hollow of **High Moss**. Regain dry ground on the simple climb and curve from north to northeast to reach the summit.

Via Stile End →4km/2½ miles ↑500m/1640ft ⏲1hr 45min

The direct route up two little ridges

The distinctive profile of Causey Pike from Stile End

WALKING THE LAKE DISTRICT FELLS – BUTTERMERE

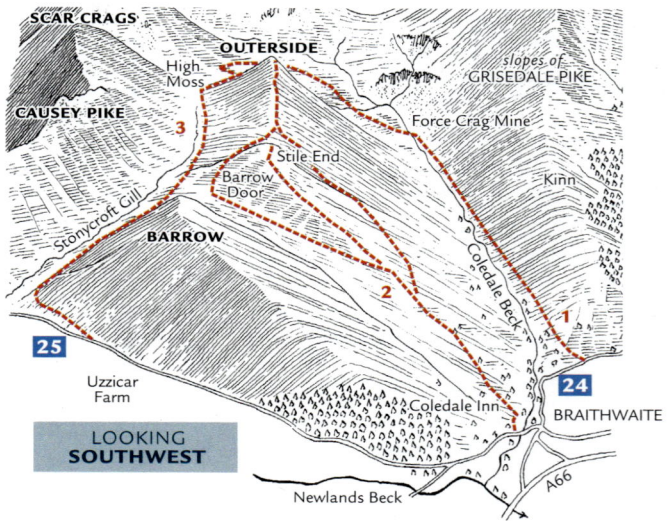

2 From the parking area walk down the bottom of the pass, turning off right at the bend and, a little further on, right again to reach the village shop at the heart of Braithwaite. From here follow the street south, rising by Moss Garth and winding up the succeeding track to meet the road, with the **Coledale Inn** behind a large hedge 100 metres to the right. Turn left and follow this road up to a kissing-gate, and take the open track leading on, passing the copse sheltering the ruined **High Coledale**. At this point the track reverts to a turf path leading through bracken, which opens up as the ridge of Stile End approaches. You may either keep to the path slanting up the eastern flank to Barrow Door, from where you can also ascend the inviting ridge onto **Stile End**, or hold to the more regular course on the western side to meet the ridge-top at the

23 Outerside

pool on **Low Moss**. However you get there, head west across the marsh to embark on the heathery northeast ridge. The path is deeply eroded in parts but leads confidently to the summit.

Ascent from Uzzicar 25

Via Stonycroft Gill →3.6km/2¼ miles ↑475m//1560ft ⏱1hr 40min

3 The old miners' track leads off from opposite the broad verge parking at a gentle gradient, and heads up the **Stonycroft Gill** valley. As the track eases towards the saddle bend right

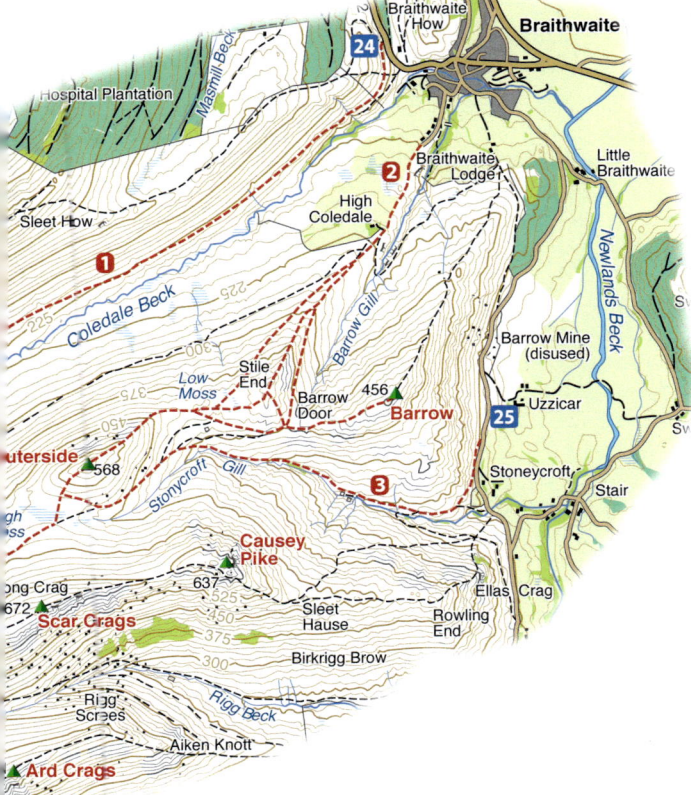

WALKING THE LAKE DISTRICT FELLS – BUTTERMERE

Outerside from the old mine track at High Moss

to contour, initially with a dyke feature, in order to avoid the marsh in the hollow of **High Moss**. Soon meet the ridge path leading up the west ridge to the summit and turn right to join the final stretch of Route **1**.

The summit

A few stones occasionally survive on the rock-bed of this little peak. Grisedale Pike towers above you but this is no reason to diminish the achievement of your ascent. Outerside has its pride, and an excellent view of Coledale, in most conditions, is your reward.

Safe descents

The easiest walking is found off the west ridge, curving S onto High Moss (**1** and **3**), from where all ports are accessible. The Stonycroft mine track gives immediate security either directly E down towards Stair (**3**), or via Barrow Door N to Braithwaite (joining **2**).

Ridge route

Barrow →*2km/1¼ miles* ↓*245m/805ft* ↑*130m/430ft* ⏲*45min*

The natural ridge NE is fine, but water and walker erosion have made some deep grooves in the path through the rank heather. Descend to the low saddle, passing the shy reedy pool in Low Moss, to either skirt along the southern flanks of Stile End or make a positive left turn to include this lovely little top. By either course come down by Barrow Door and march on upon the rising ridge path to the summit of Barrow.

24 RANNERDALE KNOTTS 355M/1165FT

Climb it from	Buttermere **30**, Hause Point **31** or Cinderdale Common **32**
Character	A rugged little terrier of a ridge, sheltering the famous Rannerdale bluebells from Crummock Water
Fell-friendly route	1
Summit grid ref	NY 167 182
Link it with	Whiteless Pike
Part of	The Grasmoor Fell-gather

Since the Romantic period, Rannerdale Knotts has provided the perfect foreground for myriad paintings, setting off the majesty of the surrounding fells with its rugged mountain-in-miniature profile. Balancing another distinctive loner, Mellbreak, across Crummock Water, what it lacks in height it more than compensates for in rocky appeal. At not very much over 1000 feet, it packs a surprising punch.

Rannerdale valley, headed by a low connection with Whiteless Breast and drained by Squat and Rannerdale Becks, has evidence of Viking settlement close to where these becks meet. Rannerdale Beck flows on into Crummock Water, flanked to the left by the pastures of Rannerdale Farm and to the right by the mighty slopes of Grasmoor. In late May, Rannerdale Wood draws visitors from

↑ *Rannerdale Knotts from Robinson*

far and near to enjoy a breathtaking carpet of bluebells. To the southwest of the summit, the path over the Buttermere Hause saddle was the main valley thoroughfare not so long ago.

There are three basic lines of ascent and five routes described here, all ideal for the construction of circular walks. Routes 1 and 5 unite to parade along the spine of the ridge, Routes 2 and 3 come up the steep western edge and Route 4 climbs directly out of Rannerdale.

Ascent from Buttermere 30

Via Low Bank →2.4km/1½ miles ↑260m/850ft ⏲50min

All the ingredients of a classic ridge walk without a big ascent or descent to face

1 Start from the National Trust car park on the northern edge of the village. Walk down right (towards the village) to find a double footpath sign directing left alongside cottages to a hand-gate. Continue with the fence close right until you get a first glimpse of Whiteless Pike and a path breaks left. Here two inviting paths climb Low Bank towards the head of Rannerdale. The turf carpets that wind up the bracken slopes are a sheer joy, and the views back give ample excuse to pause. Bend left onto the emergent ridge, which

Looking along the Low Bank ridge to Robinson

24 RANNERDALE KNOTTS

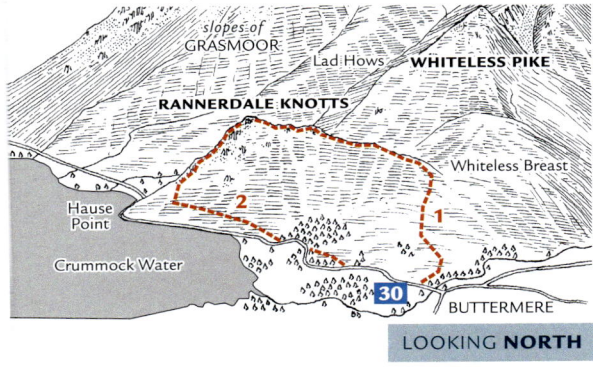

LOOKING **NORTH**

roller-coasters over **Low Bank**, rounding rocky knotts at the far end to reach the ultimate craggy top.

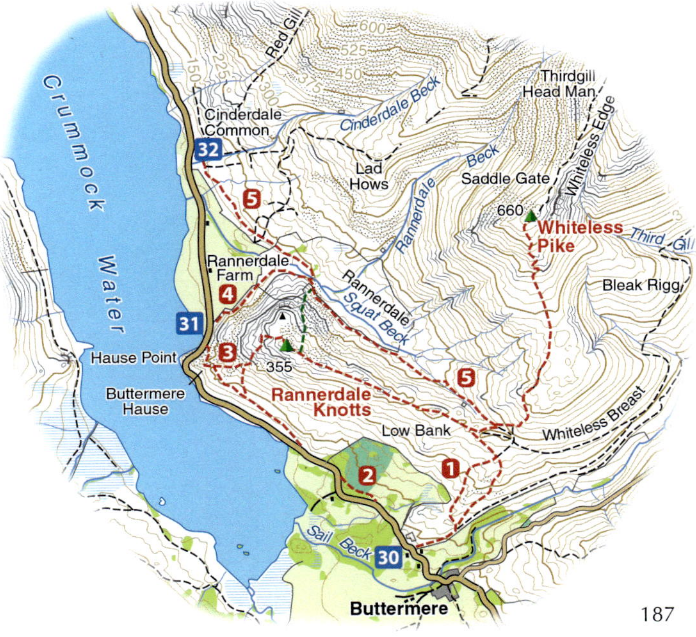

Via the old road terrace →*2.4km/1½ miles* ↑*270m/885ft* ⏱*50min*

A good return route for Route 1, or vice versa

2 From the National Trust car park, turn left and follow the road as it dips and metal railings replace stone walls. Fork right to follow the parallel lane in the conifers, re-emerging onto the road opposite the entrance to the exquisitely located guesthouse Wood House. Keep with the road after the woodland ends to find a green path stepping off from a small layby on the right – the old road to **Buttermere Hause**. Watch for the next path-fork and take the rising path. This meets up with a path from the left to continue onto a pitched section hugging the right-hand outcrop. The path is clear, later bearing right to come up to the final short climb. Just before this, you can cut left to enjoy the peerless views from the isolated cairn at the top of the main craggy headland. Return to the main path for the final pull to the summit.

Ascent From Hause Point 31

Via Buttermere Hause →*0.8km/½ mile* ↑*255m/835ft* ⏱*40min*

3 Head southwest along the road from the parking area. Turn off the road at the footpath/bridleway sign. The pitched footpath climbs to reach

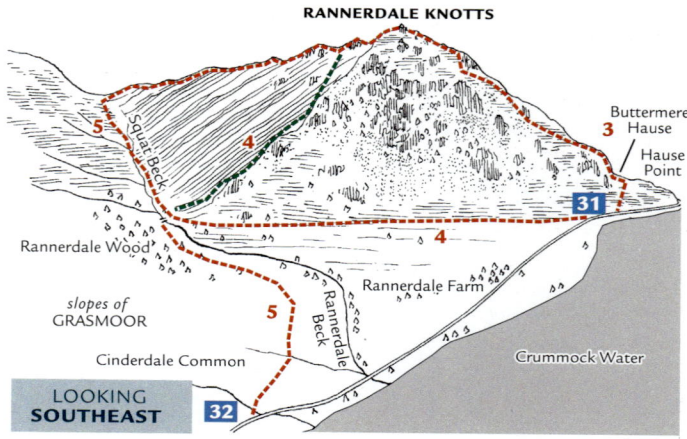

24 Rannerdale Knotts

Pitched path above Buttermere Hause

Buttermere Hause, where low rock-cut grooves mark the course of wagons of old. Bear up left, with the path irresistibly climbing to a flight of pitching which hugs an outcrop with scree spilling left. The path unites with Route **2** to bear right and climb on to the highest ground, with its characterful outcropping.

Via the north ridge →*1.2km/ ¾ mile* ↑*255m/835ft* ⏲*50min*

Lose the crowds for a moment on this shady direct ascent.

4 Follow the path beside the wall leading northeast from the parking area. This leads, via a kissing-gate, past the remains of the Viking homesteads of Rannerdale and skirts a looming outcrop to reach the footbridge. Do not cross but instead bear right to go through the kissing-gate and walk on, passing under the outcropping to switch up right on the steep grass bank. Take your time – there's no hurry, and no path either! This line brings you to the wall-end at the abrupt lip of outcropping. Bear half-left and keep just above the scree. This southerly line has sheep trods but no hint of boots. Press on up to gain the ridge simply enough, avoiding all hint of rock obstacle, and come back right to reach the summit.

Ascent from Cinderdale Common 32

Via Rannerdale Wood →*3.6km/2¼ miles* ↑*270m/885ft* ⏲*1hr*

5 From the large parking area follow the signposted turf track heading southeast, fording **Cinderdale Beck** and advancing to a gate where you enter **Rannerdale Wood**. The green-way leads on into the wood – in May a joyous tramp between swards covered with fragrant bluebells. The track comes down to a footbridge. Cross it and bear left, going through the gate and following the ensuing path as it winds up the dale in harmony with **Squat Beck** to reach the saddle at the dalehead. Switch right and follow the undulating skyline with Route **1**, a merry roller-coaster ride leading on to the summit.

The summit

A neat cairn rests on a rock stand surrounded by other scenic outcropping. The view is out of this world. Mellbreak lies to the west, the High Stile range and Haystacks to the south and southeast, and the great partnership of Grasmoor and Whiteless Pike fill the eastern view, with High Snockrigg and Robinson to the southeast.

Safe descents

The best descent is along the ridge SE (**1**). At the end turn left for Rannerdale (**5**) or right for Buttermere (**1**). Otherwise, go W and SW down the pitched path to Buttermere Hause, switching right down further pitching to the road.

Ridge route

Whiteless Pike →*2.8km/1¾ miles* ↓*65m/215ft* ↑*370m/1215ft* ⏲*1hr*
Follow the inviting ridge E via one minor rock-step to the shallow saddle at the top of Squat Beck (Rannerdale) where the fell merges with the broad slope above Buttermere village. Go left, quickly switching right to ascend the path, with the odd pitched step, keeping to the left-hand side of the slope. Higher up reach rocky terrain as you scramble up to this exciting summit.

25 RED PIKE 755M/2477FT

Climb it from	Buttermere **30** or Bowness Knott **8**
Character	Glorious scarp top immediately south of Buttermere village, connected to High Stile
Fell-friendly route	5
Summit grid ref	NY 160 154
Link it with	High Stile or Starling Dodd

This fell, at the heart of mountain Lakeland, has the best high-altitude outlook imaginable. No wonder fellwalkers visiting Buttermere set their heart on this eye-catching fell – one of a trio of commanding summits forming the famous High Stile range. Flanked by Bleaberry Tarn and Ling Comb, Red Pike is the westernmost peak, its distinctive summit hidden from the village by the little dome of Dodd to its northeast.

Traverse the range east to west and you will notice a sudden change in the rock colour from grey to red. From Red Pike to Great Borne the rocks have a definite pink hue and the scree is a vivid burnt-ochre tone. This is due to the presence of the mineral haematite, vividly displayed on the scree-scarred northern flanks of Red Pike itself and elsewhere, such as in the vicinity of Scale Force, and referenced in names such as 'Far Ruddy Beck'.

↑ *Lingcomb Edge leading to the summit*

Bleaberry Tarn (photo: Maggie Allan)

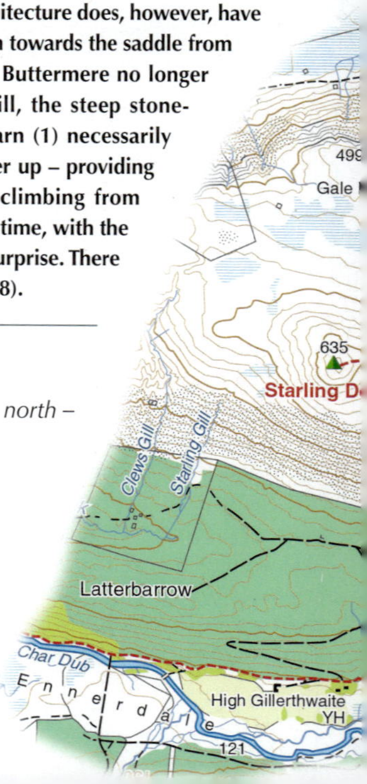

This near-perfect example of mountain architecture does, however, have a flaw, and it is those torrid screes spilling north towards the saddle from the summit. While the modern highway from Buttermere no longer clambers awkwardly up beside Sour Milk Gill, the steep stone-pitched ascent securely reaching Bleaberry Tarn (1) necessarily falls apart and becomes quite unpleasant higher up – providing challenging work for Fix the Fells. Walkers climbing from Ennerdale (9) have an altogether more pleasant time, with the excitement of coming upon the scarp edge by surprise. There are also many other options to choose from (2–8).

Ascent from Buttermere 30

Myriad paths converge on Red Pike from the north – why not try them all?

Via Bleaberry Tarn →3.2km/2 miles
↑655m/2150ft ⏱2hr

The most popular but by no means the most comfortable ascent

25 Red Pike

1 Leave Buttermere village by the Fish Hotel and follow the gated lane to the outflow of Buttermere lake. Cross the footbridge and either go left via the hand-gate or step up via a hand-gate to stand on the footbridge spanning the base of the lower cascades of powerful **Sour Milk Gill**. Step back off the footbridge (do not cross) and go through the gate on the level track in the wood. A matter of 40 metres beyond the gate find a flight of stone steps climbing right, rising into **Burtness Wood**. Take it steady – it can be hellish on unaccustomed thighs and lungs!

After a hand-gate in the fence bounding the top of the wood, the pitching continues up the open fellside. Higher up, the path duly winds and elbows right, largely bereft of pitching as it comes closer to the upper cascades of Sour Milk Gill. It runs on to ford the gill short of **Bleaberry Tarn**. The obvious path begins the steady 300m climb west of the tarn outflow. It is pitched much of the way until the

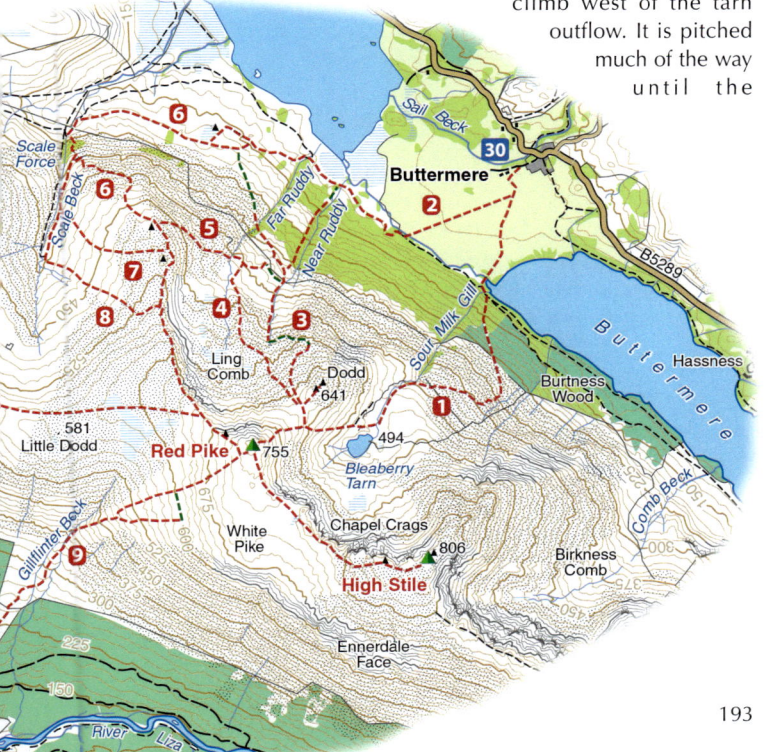

WALKING THE LAKE DISTRICT FELLS – BUTTERMERE

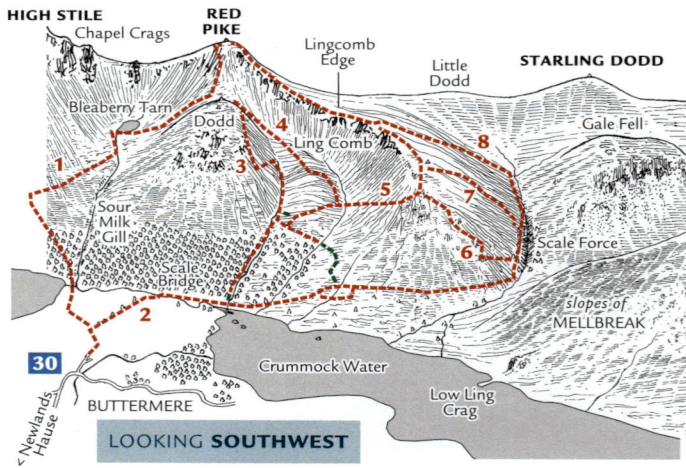

screes are met, from where matters deteriorate badly on your final pull to the summit.

Via Ling Comb → 5.2km/3¼ miles ↑665m/2180ft ⏱2hr 45min

2 Head west from the village on the popular track to Sour Milk Gill, and after the first hand-gate take the right-hand lane from a kissing-gate at the right-hand bend. This lane leads to Scale Bridge. Turn right from Scale Bridge and, immediately after fording **Near Ruddy Beck**, just short of the head of Crummock Water, break up left through the bracken and quickly enter birchwood. A regular path leads straight up through the wood, with its understorey of mossy boulders and slippery roots. The path emerges from the wood and climbs to a gap in the high fell wall where Near Ruddy Beck drains underground.

Shelter on the summit looking to High Stile and Pillar

From here there are two choices. **3** Head straight on up through the dense heather with the dwindling gill. The path eventually gives up the ghost in a tediously tiny watercourse. Turn left to mount the broken slope and bear left to reach a right-hand elbow, and from here the trail becomes more certain as it rises to the saddle to join Route **1** to the summit. Before turning to the final climb, you could take the opportunity to visit the cairns on **Dodd**. The path up left allows easy access to the top. For the best view, descend the short way north to the large viewpoint cairn and then backtrack to the saddle.

4 The altogether more worthy choice is to turn right by the wall to meet up with a path coming through the wall at a gap after some 70 metres. (This point can be reached by a more circuitous route which avoids the woodland roots and rocks of Near Ruddy Beck. Continue along the low path from Scale Bridge to cross the footbridge over **Far Ruddy Beck**. Where the path forks bear left, and after the worn rise bear left again up the narrower path. Where this, in turn, levels, immediately break left (southeast), with no hint of a path, to pass a solitary holly tree. Next bear up the bracken-free patch, angle left and find a thin path aiming up to the top of the main body of woodland. Ford Far Ruddy Beck and continue, passing a solitary larch tree, to reach the wall-gap.) Follow the wall right. A tangible path leads up left from the wall through the heather into the combe. As this drifts right (Route **5**), and before fording Far Ruddy Beck, encounter a minor path-junction. Turn up left through the dense heather. Climb easily, keeping to the natural swell of the ridge in the middle of **Ling Comb**. Where the path levels notice an eroded path dropping left (erroneously marked as a right of way on maps). The ridge path curves right then takes its leave of the heather to climb a shallow gully, reach the saddle and head up with Route **1**.

Via Lingcomb Edge → 6km/3¾ miles ↑670m/2200ft ⏲3hr

The best route of all

5 Keep to the main path, fording the upper section of **Far Ruddy Beck** where it leaves the combe. This mounts northwest, crossing the ridge-end prow of **Lingcomb Edge** with its inviting view over Crummock Water. The path arrives at a minor path-junction on level ground. Here turn left to accompany the rising ridge. Complete a wonderful ascent along the crag-rimmed edge overlooking Ling Comb to reach the summit. Keep right, off the worst of the loose stones, on the final rise.

Red Pike and Dodd from Lingcomb Edge

Via Scale Force →6.4km/4 miles ↑675m/2215ft ⏲3hr 10min

The minor path-junction on the ridge-end (see Route 7) can also be reached from Scale Beck.

6 Set out with Route **2** but keep with the higher contouring path from the **Far Ruddy Beck** footbridge – either keep up left after the eroded gully or, beyond the bracken, turn up left by a large cairn in open grass and rise to the path contouring west to a hand-gate and down to the footbridge spanning **Scale Force**. There is not much scope to venture into its ravine but make sure you catch a glimpse of the pencil-thin principal 37m/120ft fall. Step back and up the flight of pitched steps on the east bank, among birch trees. As the path levels, watch for an unheralded path branching left. This quickly veers right, coming below a rock, and works up the steep rocky fellside with one or two minor rock-steps. It then turns south above Blea Crag onto the heather-decked

Scale Force (photo: Maggie Allan)

25 RED PIKE

slopes leading to the minor path-junction at the ridge-end. Follow Route **5** to the summit.

7 Alternatively, stick with the Scale Force gorge, with one notable rock-step above the rushing beck, and turn left with the main path. This winds up the fellside, generally on a southeast line, although there is an early minor path that forks left (northeast) to join the path to the ridge-end. Hold to the principal path to arrive at a prominent ridge-top cairn and follow **Lingcomb Edge**, right, to the summit.

8 The more usual option continues close to **Scale Beck**, taking a sharp turn and climbing on a very worn trail east-southeast to the Lingcomb Edge ridge. Overuse by descending walkers has done this path no favours.

Ascent from Bowness Knott 8 *off map W*

Via Gillflinter Beck →*6.8km/4¼ miles* ↑*635m/2085ft* ⏱*3hr 30min*

The one corridor of ascent through the Ennerdale forestry

9 Follow the attractive dale access track, continuing on from the youth hostel to reach the first track-gate after 3.2km (2 miles). Immediately to its left find a stile at the forest corner. Cross this, ford the gill, and follow the one path. This eases up the bracken slopes in a widening forest gangway, then crosses a fence-stile and remains at an easy angle until the double-stranded ford of **Gillflinter Beck**. The clear path onwards then sets to work on the southwestern slopes of Red Pike. Watch for a fork – the less obvious left-hand path is the

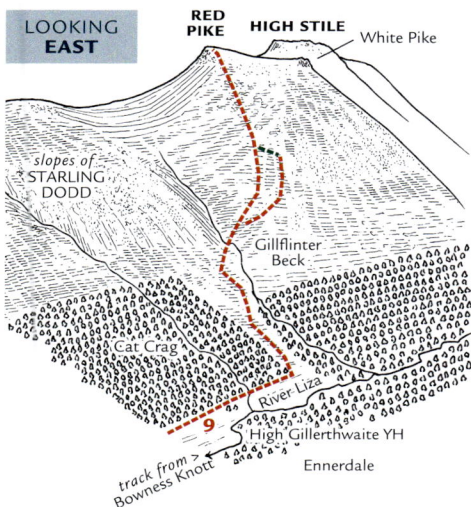

main cairned route. If you are lured onto the right-hand way you will climb up by a bield and rise to a boulder patch, where you need to bend left, passing a second bield, to meet up with the cairned path. Follow on up grassy slopes to the summit.

The summit

A small stone wind-break and cairn mark the summit. The north lip provides ample scope for visitors to sit and soak up a most satisfying northward view. The felltop is otherwise uncomplicated, although the fall of the scarp is profound enough to require caution in misty conditions.

Safe descents

Resist the temptation to simply step off the northern edge bound for Bleaberry Tarn (**1**). A cairn marks the start of this path, to the east of the summit cairn. The longer route is by far the better option. Follow Lingcomb Edge NW (**5**), breaking down into the Scale Beck gorge (**7**) for a secure path bound for Buttermere (5km/3 miles). The route SW down into Ennerdale (**9**) is uncomplicated and secure but leads only to the youth hostel and a long trudge back to Bowness Knott.

Ridge routes

High Stile →*1.2km/¾ mile ↓60m/200ft ↑105m/345ft ⏲30min*
Walk S, thereby skirting the edge of Bleaberry Comb. In mist it is important to be aware of this deep hollow. There are several really fine situations that lend themselves to the camera, with gullies and crag-faces to admire as the path comes by Chapel Crags, although there is easier, less commonly trod ground over to the right.

Starling Dodd →*2km/1¼ mile ↓200m/655ft ↑75m/245ft ⏲45min*
Head down W. Never was a ridge walk more predictable and simple to follow, entirely on grass. The regular trail side-steps the stony top of Little Dodd but it merits a visit nonetheless, being more entertaining than the target fell. Continue to the summit of Starling Dodd.

26 ROBINSON 737M/2418FT

Climb it from	Chapel Bridge **27**, Keskadale **28**, Newlands Hause **29** or Buttermere **30**
Character	Bold mass of fine fell rising east of Newlands Hause and High Snockrigg
Fell-friendly route	4
Summit grid ref	NY 202 168
Link it with	Hindscarth
Part of	The Newlands Round

With a commanding presence in two revered walking arenas, Buttermere and Newlands, Robinson's 'best side' is definitely its northwestern aspect. For those coming updale from Braithwaite, Robinson is the star attraction with its strong lines and striking profile. Ever more imposing the closer you get to Newlands Hause, it makes a splendid objective for a fellwalking day, with many natural lines of approach.

The leg-up provided by Newlands Hause will tempt many to make a there-and-back expedition (5) and from Newlands valley itself there are three options (1–3), Route 1 rightly the most popular. Higher up Keskadale, a rarely climbed ridge offers an interesting hands-on route (4). From Buttermere village the steep drove-way onto High Snockrigg provides a sure, uncomplicated line (6) and the contrasting Hassness and Goat Gills route (7) combines the pleasure of the lakeshore with a stiff pull in an amazing situation.

↑ *Robinson from Knott Rigg*

WALKING THE LAKE DISTRICT FELLS – BUTTERMERE

26 Robinson

Ascent from Chapel Bridge 27

Via High Snab Bank →*4.8km/3 miles* ↑*625m/2050ft* ⏲*2hr 10min*

1 Follow the no-through-road passing **Newlands Church**. Continue with the tarmac road, rising up to **Low High Snab Cottage**, passing through the charming environs by gates. The green lane opens at a gate, after some 120 metres, and as the wall on the right veers uphill follow suit, climbing the bracken bank on a clear path. Brushing through the gorse near the top, come onto the roof-like grassy ridge of **High Snab Bank**.

The rock-steps on the northeast ridge, from High Crags

Head along the ridge and climb over the knoll of **Blea Crag**, with the old mine reservoir directly below. The ridge dips then encounters two definite rock-steps (a little tricky in descent). Thereafter the ridge mounts impressively, but without hazard, to the summit plateau.

Via the old aqueduct →6.4km/4 miles ↑625m/2050ft ⏲2hr 45min
2 Follow the road to **Newlands Church** and bear left onto the facing track (private road, permissive path). This duly leads to and through the gated yard of **Low Snab Farm** – an authentic Cumbrian fell farm, alive with hens. Pass through the end-gate and bear up right following the green-way, with the great spoil banks of the **Goldscope Mine** strikingly apparent. The path runs on to come upon spoil debris. Step up here to join the line of the old aqueduct which once carried water from the reservoir to the mine. As you come close to the reservoir bear up right over the boulders to cross the footbridge and the walled dam, clambering up the bank to join the valley drove-way. This mounts the bouldery ground, passing below an old holding fold to come above the turbulent ravine with its quartz-streaked boulders. Advance towards a sheepfold and bear up right, a rock band up to the right acting as a shield to the craggy ground. Climb above this onto the shoulder and join the northeast ridge path (Route **1**) above the early rock-steps.

26 ROBINSON

Via Little Dale →6.4km/4 miles ↑625m/2050ft ⏲2hr 45min

3 Follow the no-through-road passing **Newlands Church**. Continue with the road as it rises up to **Low High Snab Cottage**, passing through its charming environs by gates. The green lane opens at a gate. Keep company with it as it gradually becomes more of a drove-path and leads above the reservoir. Follow on with the valley path to the sheepfold where, amid a great mass of rushes, the path disappears. Skirt the worst of the damp ground to the right, advancing up the peaceful pasture of **Little Dale** and mounting the dalehead slopes, in the later stages following a strong sheep path, to the skyline. Here join the popular ridge path beside the fence. Higher up you may be tempted to cross the fence to inspect **Hackney Holes**, an irregular fault fracture. Gain the highest ground and bear up right to reach the summit.

High Snab Cottage

Hackney Holes

WALKING THE LAKE DISTRICT FELLS – BUTTERMERE

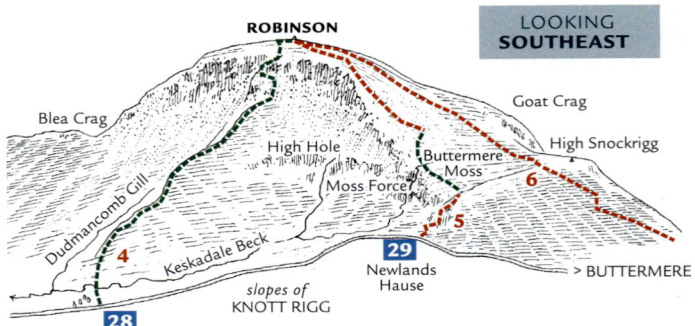

Ascent from Keskadale 28

Via Dudmancomb Edge →*2km/1¼ miles* ↑*500m/1640ft* ⏱*1hr 30min*

This northern ridge, prominent from Keskadale, is a simple scramble in fair weather but is not suitable for descent or wet weather.

4 Descend directly from the verge parking to ford the sinuous marshy beck. Set to work clambering up the predominantly grassy slope and find the skyline edge that peers into Dudman Comb. There is no path. The grass ridge ultimately merges with the scree apron of the upper fell, above which the ground is slightly steeper, with simple rock-steps. Easing up among the outcropping, climb until the rock band looms. Now veer left to round a corner where the upper gully of Red Gill opens onto a green ramp leading easily onto the domed plateau. Keep along the brink for some breathtaking views down into High Hole as you continue to the summit.

Ascent from Newlands Hause 29

Direct →*2km/1¼ miles* ↑*430m/1410ft* ⏱*1hr*

The popular option

5 The path towards **Moss Force** is only for viewing the falls. Follow the clear trail mounting the edge southwest from the pass. As the fell-slope eases, leave the ridge path bound for High Snockrigg, slanting left onto pathless terrain to ford the outflow of **Buttermere Moss**. Even in dry conditions this is an unpleasant morass. Avoid it by cutting across pathlessly to connect to the regular path on the rising slope of Robinson, keeping to firm turf all the way. The final pull up to the skyline, while in no way problematic, is certainly better in ascent.

Ascent from Buttermere 30

Via High Snockrigg →4km/2½ miles ↑655m/2150ft ⏲2hr

The old shepherds' drove

6 Leave the open road at a small layby on a left-hand rising curve. The signed turf path winds up and has the odd delicate moment, especially where it comes above a steep ravine. Come up the groove to cross the skyline edge. A detour to savour the view from the summit of **High Snockrigg** is recommended. The continuing route heads southeast to traverse the upper edge of **Buttermere Moss**, although it is difficult to avoid wet feet on the peaty sponge. With firm ground regained on the eastern side, climb the steady slope on a strong path to the brink cairn, on the way to the summit.

Via Goat Gills →4.4km/2¾ miles ↑670m/2200ft ⏲2hr 15min

A stiff but scenic climb, useful as the 'out route' for a circuit with Route 6

7 Join the merry band of casual walkers, many engaged in walking around the lake. Leave Buttermere village through the yard of Syke Farm (with its tearoom and tempting home-made ice cream). A gated bridleway leads on along the initial lane to become an open pasture-way, and comes to a handgate with 'shoreline path' notice. The confined path leads down via a further hand-gate to steps beside a big glaciated slab. Ushered on by a light fence, it continues via further hand and kissing-gates and a short pedestrian tunnel, revelling in the tree-shaded shore of Buttermere.

Emerging from the tunnel clamber over the root-covered rock-step and come down to the shore. Ignore the kissing-gate and instead turn away from the shore, left, beside the wall, and come by a small footbridge to a hand-gate onto the road. Cross straight over to go through the facing hand-gate, with a

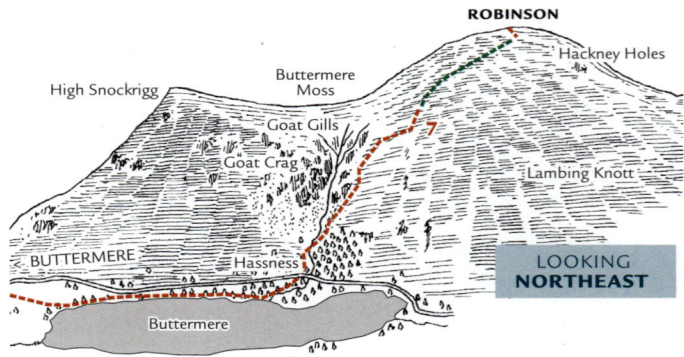

footpath sign to 'Robinson'. Follow up beside the wall in woodland to a fence-stile and continue to where the gill constricts. Here step up to the fence-stile in the wall. The path ascends the obvious ridge, with a fine view of the little dam created to capture water for Hassness. Climbing higher, the path negotiates a flight of steps to reach a wall-stile. The steep path, now lined with bilberry and heather, works up to accompany the light fence. The one really steep section is tight between the fence and some outcropping and is uncomfortable underfoot. But this soon relents, and the path climbs on to reach a fence-stile. Cross and ascend the open pasture, with the fence to the right, to gain the ridge-top and summit.

The Goat Gills ravine

The summit

A conspicuous cairn rests on a low outcrop, with a parallel outcrop a carriageway distant. The view is wide and comprehensive. For the best outlook onto the Grasmoor/Crag Hill group you should wander down the slope a little way north, as the plateau takes away all depth from the panorama.

Safe descents

If heading for Newlands, consider descending Little Dale rather than the north ridge, which has some awkward rock-steps in its latter stages. Head S (**3**) to accompany the ridge fence SE down to Littledale Edge, where you turn into the pastoral bowl of Little Dale itself and exit into the Scope Beck valley leading down by High Snab. Alternatively, for Buttermere trend SW (**6**), descend to cross spongy Buttermere Moss, rise over High Snockrigg and follow the steep drove-path direct to the village. You can also veer right down the ridge of High Snockrigg to reach Newlands Hause as the quickest route to a road.

Ridge route

Hindscarth →2.4km/1½ miles ↓165m/540ft ↑155m/510ft ⏱45min

Walk S to come by the ridge fence and follow this SSE, entirely upon a well-worn ridge path. This leads along Littledale Edge. Take the branch-path half-left and climb diagonally across the west slope of Hindscarth to gain the summit ridge some 100 metres south of the cairn.

The Scafells from the summit

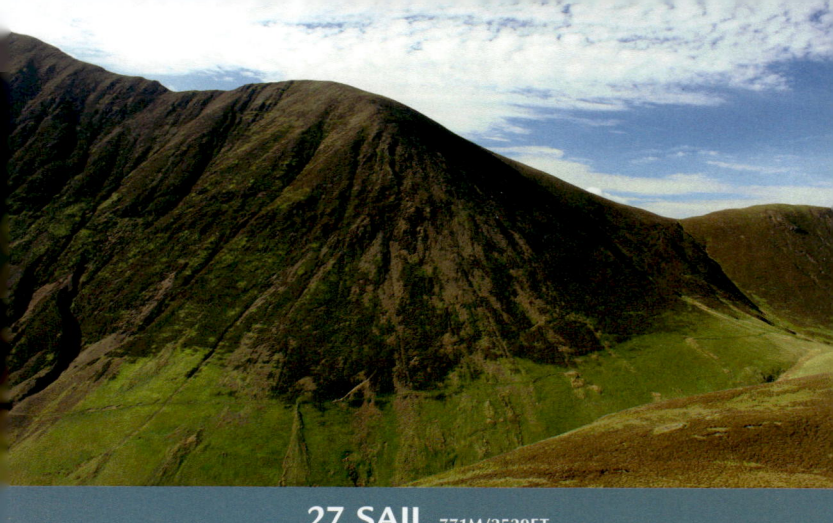

27 SAIL 771M/2529FT

Climb it from	Braithwaite **24** or Buttermere **30**
Character	Sleek and curvaceous top, one step down to the east of Crag Hill
Fell-friendly route	2 or 3
Summit grid ref	NY 198 203
Link it with	Crag Hill or Scar Crags
Part of	The Coledale Horseshoe

Its sheer stature, the precipitous nature of its northern and southern slopes and the elegance of its domed summit ought to make Sail a flagship. However, sitting as it does among the craggy Northwesterns it counts as a mere companion fell, performing a supporting role in the greater scheme of things. A splendid stepping-stone along the handsome rising ridge from Causey Pike and Scar Crags bound for Crag Hill, ridge walkers with a following wind may indeed 'sail' up it.

Seldom climbed alone, Sail is an integral part of the marvellous skyline-round known as the Coledale Horseshoe, but is far from one-dimensional. Routes 1 and 2 make use of the pass, with many thanks to Fix the Fells for their extensive work on the northeasterly climb, to get you onto the fell from north or south to customise your own fell-round. Route 3 is for the explorer, whom this landscape richly rewards.

↑ *Sail from Knott Rigg*

27 SAIL

Ascent from Braithwaite 24 *off map NE*

Pick your way on Route 1 or follow the paths with Route 2.

Via the north ridge →*5.6km/3½ miles* ↑*675m/2215ft* ⏱*2hr 30min*

1 From the car park simply follow the Coledale track beyond the barrier. As you near the mine buildings fork down left with the track to ford **Coledale Beck**. Keep with the popular if rough trail and come up above the cascades to the south of Force Crag. As the metal culvert pipe is reached, bear off left onto pathless fell. Climb the easy mossy bank to confront the steeper north slope, locate the one green strip between scree fans, and ascend to the northeast shoulder of the fell, all with no hint of a fellow walker's footsteps. From here the ridge eases to a gentle swell which rises to the summit.

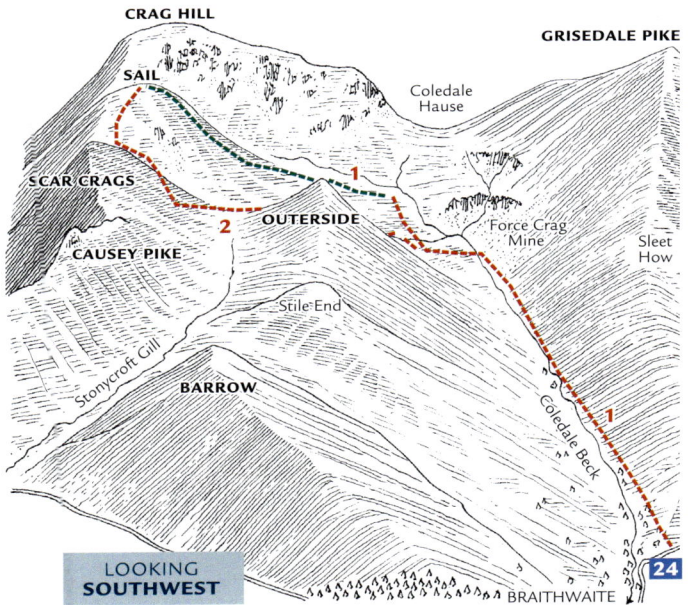

Eastward ridge to Scar Crags and Causey Pike across Sail Pass

Via Sail Pass →*5.6km/3½ miles* ↑*715m/2345ft* ⏲*2hr 40min*

2 Start out on Route **1**, but from the **Coledale Beck** ford below Force Crag Mine follow the trail up to an early cairn, where a clear path breaks left heading south towards **Long Crag**. Fording **Birkthwaite Beck**, the path climbs the pasture and curves right to unite with the regular path from High Moss as the outcropping begins on the northwestern flank of Scar Crags. Follow this regular path, the top secured by pitching, to reach **Sail Pass**. Ascend west with the zig-zagging ridge trail to reach the felltop.

Ascent from Buttermere 30

Via Sail Beck →*6.4km/4 miles* ↑*780m/2560ft* ⏲*3hr*

A delightful valley approach via Sail Pass on surprisingly good paths

3 From the National Trust car park at the northern approach to the village either walk straight over the road and, from the stile, cross the High House Crag brow, or go right with the road and bear off left, guided by the footpath sign, past the cottages to a gate, and follow the field boundary to meet up with the path from the wooded

27 Sail

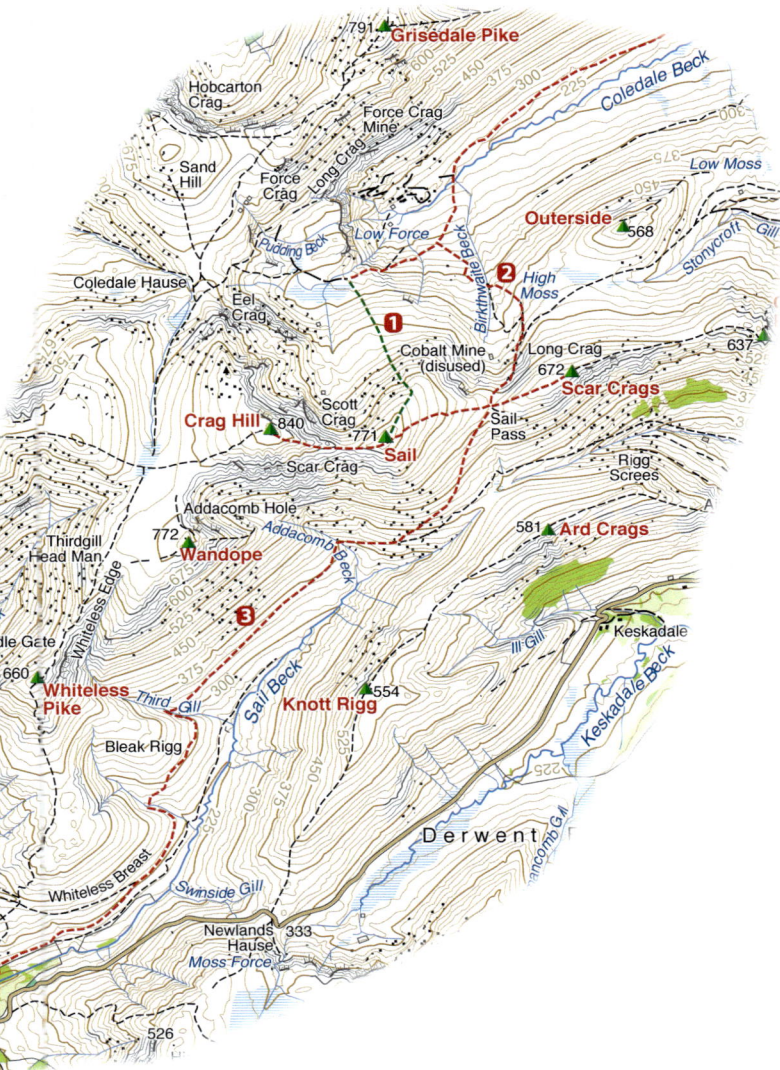

dell. At this point there are two routes up the **Sail Beck** valley. The more common path, a shepherds' drove, makes a deliberate break up left, just where the fence ends and before the final length of wall. Take this and move comfortably through the bracken on **Whiteless Breast**. It swings into the re-entrant valley, then up and across **Bleak Rigg** bank to enter and ascend from the **Third Gill** valley before it embarks on a long traverse across the slopes of Wandope. This leads over **Addacomb Beck** and across a gullied section of path, and climbs beside heather to an obvious cairn and path-fork. Bear

Intense zig-zags above Sail Pass

up left with the path, climbing handsomely to **Sail Pass**, the saddle with Scar Crags, and then bear up left again on the re-engineered trail to the summit.

The summit

Only a tiny proportion of those who cross the felltop actually trouble to visit the summit – an excuse for a cairn beside a summer-dry puddle – especially when the best of the view would seem to be from the southern edge. However, many a sandwich has been enjoyed on the northern edge, away from the general flow of walkers, a quiet situation looking across the nameless combe to Crag Hill.

Safe descents

The southern slopes, decorated with heather and scree, are excessively steep, and the northern slopes fall away quite smartly too, with outcropping on the northeastern flank. Stick carefully to the uncomfortably skiddy trail down to Sail Pass (**2**) to find the secure paths to either Braithwaite (**2**) or Buttermere (**3**).

Ridge routes

Crag Hill →*0.8km/½ mile* ↓*30m/100ft* ↑*100m/330ft* ⏱*25min*
The ridge path leading W is straightforward in mist, but has a few rocky moments that may cause you to watch your footing in wet or icy conditions. The short descent along a narrow ridge is followed by an exciting climb onto the crowning plateau – great fun.

Scar Crags →*1.2km/¾ mile* ↓*150m/490ft* ↑*50m/165ft* ⏱*35min*
The long, loose gravel travail E down to Sail Pass is followed by a soothing rise onto the plateau, which leads to the summit cairn on the scarp brink.

28 SCAR CRAGS 672M/2205FT

Climb it from	Braithwaite 24, Uzzicar 25 or Rigg Beck 26
Character	A simple ridge connection at the heart of the magnificent Northwestern Fells
Fell-friendly route	2
Summit grid ref	NY 208 207
Link it with	Causey Pike or Sail
Part of	The Coledale Horseshoe

But for the attention-stealing position of Causey Pike, Scar Crags might be more widely appreciated. Viewed close up from the east it is a striking ridge and an inviting climb. From Ard Crags to the south the well-weathered southern aspect is broken into an almost regular pattern of arêtes and gullies. The short western slopes are rocky and were once the site of the only cobalt mine in the district, although there is little to show for it today. Only the northern slopes are unremarkable.

The Rigg Beck valley is one of the unsung heroes of inter-dale connection and it is plausible that the fell name might be a natural contraction of 'scarth', alluding to the passage of this path. The heathery flanks of Causey Pike and Ard

↑ *The ridge and top of the oak copse, from Ard Knott*

28 Scar Crags

Crags glower over the passage of the path (4) and the presence of the old coppice oakwood above the line of the path adds further interest before you come beneath the drama of the crags themselves.

To make a traverse of the range, taking in Sail and Causey Pike, you could start from Buttermere, follow Sail Beck, and branch up to Sail Pass to claim the summit en route to Braithwaite (and a bus back in season). Expeditions usually begin from the north or east – either Braithwaite (1–2), or the Newlands valley at the Uzzicar verge (3) or the hairpin at the foot of Rigg Beck (4).

Ascent from Braithwaite 24

Take the low route (1) or the high route (2), or combine them for a great Coledale fell day.

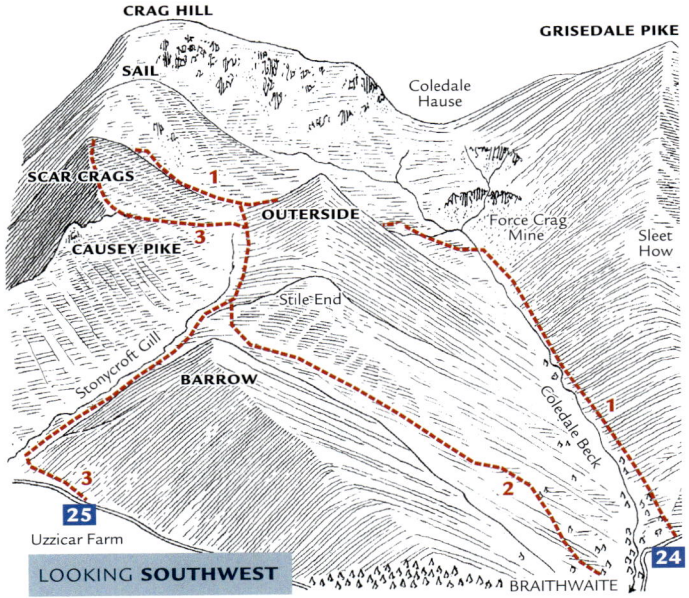

Via Coledale →5.6km/3½ miles ↑580m/1900ft ⏱2hr 40min
1 From the car park simply follow the Coledale track beyond the barrier. As you near the mine buildings, fork down left with the track to ford **Coledale Beck**. Continue, ascending to where, at a cairn, a path veers sharply left. This fords **Birkthwaite Beck** and sweeps up to join the regular path south of High Moss. Follow this path, secured by pitching, to reach the ridge saddle of **Sail Pass**. Bear up left onto the plateau to approach the prominent cairn.

Via Barrow Door →5.2km/3¼ miles ↑585m/1920ft ⏱2hr 20min
2 From the car park walk down the pass to the first bend, take the lane to the right and shortly turn right again to reach the centre of the village. From the shop over the bridge follow the lane climbing gently out of the village to the south. Rising and rounding a bend to meet a T-junction, turn left to continue south and follow the tarmac to its end at a gate. Now an open track, the way leads on uphill, passing a reservoir enclosure. As you pass the copse shielding the ruins of **High Coledale** head straight on, the track now a grassy drove. The path forking left here leads attractively to the ford over the gill but ignore it. Continue on towards the rising ridge of **Stile End**, but stay with the droveway along the eastern flank to reach the pass of **Barrow Door**. Here turn west, contouring under Outerside to join the old mine track up the **Stonycroft Gill** valley and passing on by **High Moss**. Continue as the track dwindles to a path which climbs up beneath Long Crag to **Sail Pass**, and here turn left (east-northeast) to the summit.

Paths leading up from High Moss by the old cobalt mine

28 SCAR CRAGS

Ascent from Uzzicar 25

Via Stonycroft Gill →4.8km/3 miles ↑565m/1855ft ⏱2hr 30min
3 From the broad road verge above **Uzzicar Farm** follow the old mine track up **Stonycroft Gill**, originally constructed as a mineral track-bed to the cobalt mine under Long Crag. After Route **2** merges from the right, continue for a kilometre and then switch left on the eastward-trending path, climbing to the

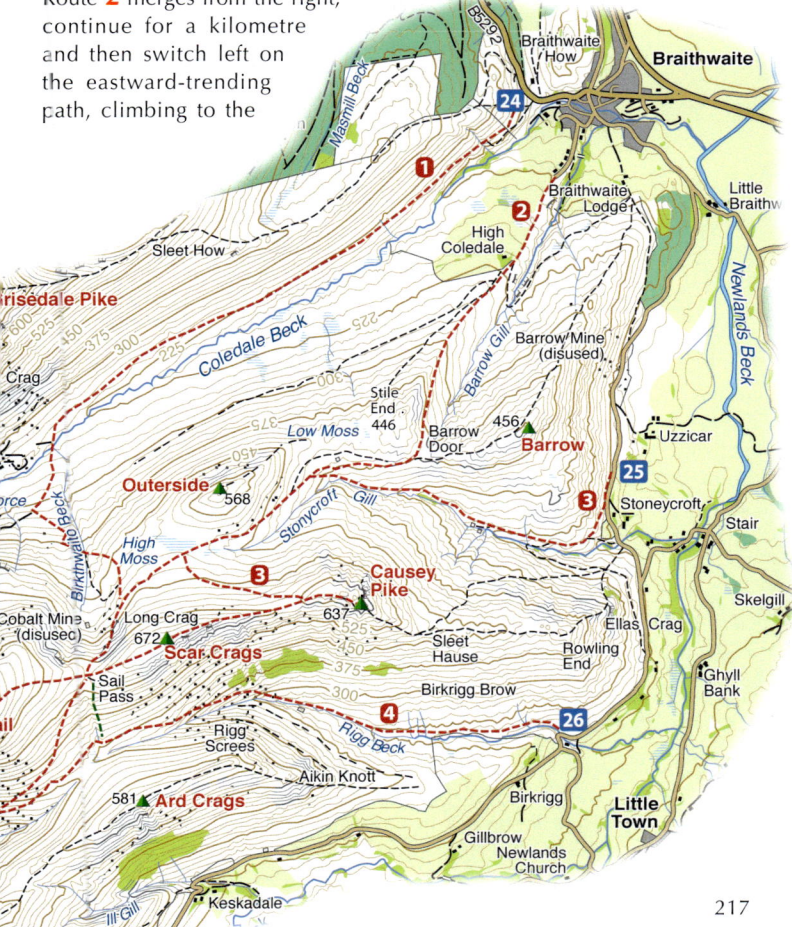

Ascent from Rigg Beck 26

Via Sail Pass →4.8km/3 miles ↑550m/1800ft ⏲2hr 25min

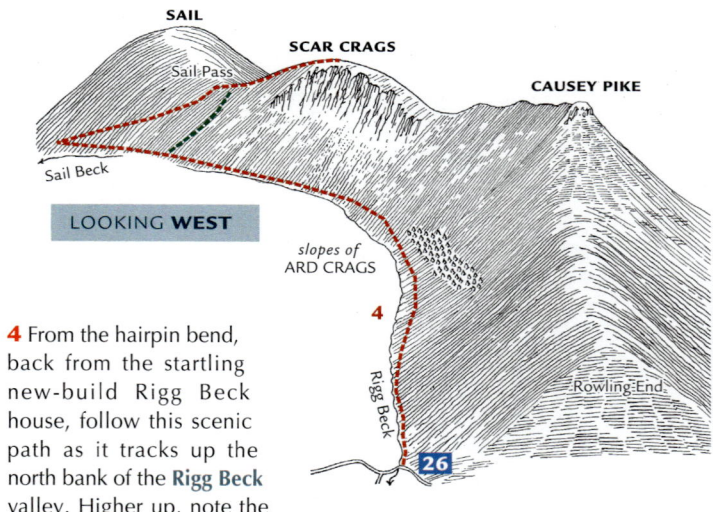

4 From the hairpin bend, back from the startling new-build Rigg Beck house, follow this scenic path as it tracks up the north bank of the **Rigg Beck** valley. Higher up, note the old coppice oakwood above the line of the path. At the watershed you can choose to break up the heather slope, right, beside a gill, to make a direct assault on **Sail Pass**, or continue down a short way further before turning acutely right, at a cairn, on a more measured path which cuts back up (northeast) to Sail Pass and continues east along the ridge to the summit.

The summit

Walkers plodding up the east ridge will blink to discover a plateau spread before them. A sizeable cairn marks the top spot, with another a little further to the east. The pleasure of sitting at the edge, looking down the heather-decked gullies into the Rigg Beck valley, is worth stopping for. Elsewhere there is

28 SCAR CRAGS

Looking to Causey Pike from the summit cairn

much on view, principally to the east, although your sights will most likely be trained northwest on the striking composition formed by Hopegill Head and Force Crag below.

Safe descents

Just follow the ridge paths. From Sail Pass you can safely descend the steep heather flanks to the head of Rigg Beck (**4**) or follow the initially pitched path NE under Long Crag to join the old mine track down to either the Stonycroft valley (**3**) or, via either Birkthwaite Beck (**1**) or Barrow Door (**2**), to return safely to Braithwaite.

Ridge routes

Causey Pike → *1.2km/¾ mile* ↓*90m/290ft* ↑*55m/180ft* ⏲*30min*
Savour an enjoyable walk that keeps strictly to the ridge, descending ENE to lead through the depression, surprisingly adorned with peat groughs, from where the continuing ridge weaves up over the four vertebra tops to the conclusive final knoll.

Sail → *1.2km/¾ mile* ↓*50m/165ft* ↑*150m/490ft* ⏲*45min*
Leave the plateau SW to Sail Pass from where the worn trail leads on W, drifting SW on the final rise. The path glances to the south of the summit cairn so watch you don't get caught out and miss it!

29 STARLING DODD 635M/2083FT

Climb it from	Buttermere **30** or Bowness Knott **8**
Character	A rounded top invariably enjoyed in concert with Great Borne and Red Pike
Fell-friendly route	6
Summit grid ref	NY 142 157
Link it with	Great Borne or Red Pike

This fell has a venerable history. A woodland boundary charter of 1230, associated with Loweswater, mentions the fell with Little Dodd and Gillflinter Beck. It fixes the boundary along the steep ridge path called 'Styalein' (a reference to a personal name, Alein). In this document, Little Dodd is termed 'the high Dod de Gillefinchor'.

From the south Starling Dodd holds little for the fellwalker – a rounded top above steep scree slopes and forestry (which will melt away as Ennerdale's natural ecosystem is re-established). To the north Gale Fell, a lower northern scarp to the fell, remains a seldom-visited outpost. Here you can survey the soggy hollow of Mosedale and the old bridle route between Buttermere and Ennerdale, Floutern Pass. From either side of this portion of fell spill amazing spouts. The open cascades of Gale Gill contrast with the secluded Scale Force, the highest free-fall in the Lakes, with its red-stained sub-soil and charming silver-birch-flanked ravine.

↑ *Starling Dodd from Floutern Cop*

29 Starling Dodd

That said, two exciting off-beat routes from Ennerdale are described here (5–6), taking advantage of the south-running gills, the first leading past what seems to be an example of Viking-era cavity-wall insulation using bracken. There are also four further interesting – albeit watery – options to explore from the north (1–4).

Ascent from Buttermere 30

There's not much chance of keeping your boots dry on these northerly approaches.

Via Scale Beck →5.8km/3½ miles ↑535m/1755ft ⏲2hr 45min

1 Walk down from the car park and through Buttermere village to leave by the lane leading from the Fish Hotel. This turns left and passes through a gate. At the next bend go through the kissing-gate to the right, following a sign to 'Scale Force'. Follow the rough lane, fenced to the right, southwest. This leads to and over the gated Scale Bridge spanning Buttermere Dubs. Turn right and follow the rough but popular low path to ford Near Ruddy Beck, then cross the **Far Ruddy Beck** footbridge and bear left. Follow on along the rising worn trail, and watch for the second left upward turn, on the narrower path, for a drier traverse across the stony slopes. This passes some random shrub thorns to reach and pass through a kissing-gate in a rising wall. Venture momentarily

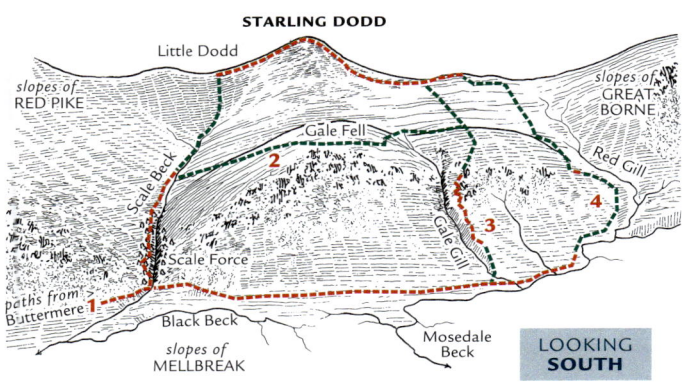

down to the Scale Beck footbridge and step a few paces into the ravine to gaze up into the dark recesses of **Scale Force** and spot the main pencil-thin waterfall, which crashes down an impressive 37m/120ft.

Backtrack to clamber up the stone-stepped path on the east side of the **Scale Beck** ravine. The way remains close above the beck and, apart from one notably awkward rock-step, remains quite level until the main trail breaks left – this is the popular path onto Lingcomb Edge for Red Pike. With little or no hint of a continuing path, keep alongside the diminishing beck, negotiating marshy patches and tough heather clumps. Where the gill forks, clamber up the right-hand section, which quickly turns subterranean, and cross a marshy patch to reach a large sheepfold (with three compartments!). Continue directly up the blank slope to reach the ridge path, adjacent to a pool in a dip. Turn right, due west, to ascend the open ridge to the summit.

29 Starling Dodd

Via Gale Fell →6.8km/4¼ miles ↑545m/1790ft ⏱3hr

Make your own way to a novel viewpoint.

2 Follow Route **1** up **Scale Beck** until roughly where the path onto Lingcomb Edge heads off to your left. Ford the beck to leave the valley and clamber pathlessly up the dense-heather-and-rock bank. Find an unlikely old fence-line on the rise to the scarp-top viewpoint of **Gale Fell**. Curve on southwest, passing a pool almost immediately and a shepherds' cairn further on on your left, to reach a fence running roughly south to the ridge. Follow this (left) to where the new fence cuts off the old ridge path (conservation notice) and bear left, climbing the obvious path mounting southeast to the summit.

Via Gale Gill →7.2km/4½ miles ↑545m/1790ft ⏱3hr 15min

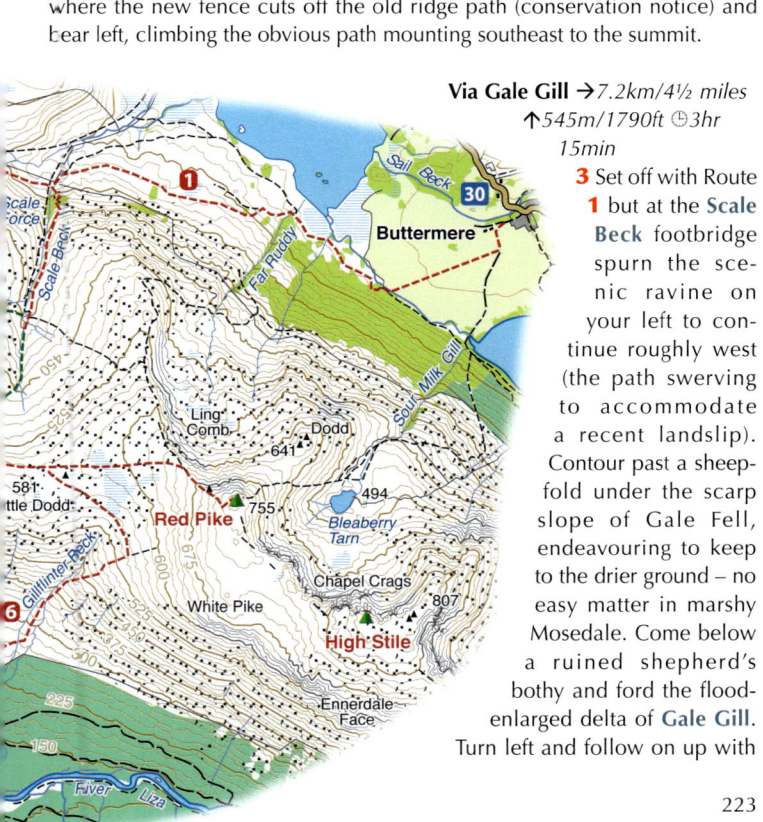

3 Set off with Route **1** but at the **Scale Beck** footbridge spurn the scenic ravine on your left to continue roughly west (the path swerving to accommodate a recent landslip). Contour past a sheepfold under the scarp slope of Gale Fell, endeavouring to keep to the drier ground – no easy matter in marshy Mosedale. Come below a ruined shepherd's bothy and ford the flood-enlarged delta of **Gale Gill**. Turn left and follow on up with the steepening ridge, an old seldom-trod shepherds' path zig-zagging up the west side of the ravine. Higher up, gain a grandstand view of the spout of water issuing from its cliffs. At the top, where the ravine is oddly dry, bend away right over the heather by a further shepherds' cairn to join Route **2** to the summit.

Juniper clinging to the steep flanks of Gale Gill

Via Red Gill →*8km/5 miles* ↑*550m/1805ft* ⏲*3hr 45min*

Extend your adventure to discover Red Gill and another cairned viewpoint.

4 Follow Route **3** as far as **Gale Gill**. Cross it to follow on with the bridleway, passing through a fence by a stile/gate. At the next fence ignore the stile and

Red Gill from the outflow of Floutern Tarn

Clews Gill sheepfold (photo: Maggie Allan)

turn left to follow its line up. Where it makes a right-angled turn to the right, continue forwards, curving up the east bank of Red Gill, gaining height on a sharply edged grass ridge. Take the opportunity to enjoy the view from the brink before rising past a small cairn to the ridge fence. Cross and join the ridge path leading left (southeast) to the summit.

Ascent from Bowness Knott 8

Via Clews Gill →5.2km/3¼ miles ↑560m/1840ft ⏲2hr 50min

An off-the-beaten-track ascent, laden with interest

5 Follow the opening strides of the Ennerdale access track down by the lakeside. Let yourself be lured left with the sign for the Smithy Beck Trail. This well-maintained woodland path leads to and over a footbridge in front of a picturesque little waterfall. When you reach a forest track go left and, at the crossing of Smithy Beck, take the second, slightly less confident path left. This leads by a cluster of Viking farmstead foundations with a curious double-wall feature. Sheltering beneath the pines, the path awkwardly fords Smithy Beck

WALKING THE LAKE DISTRICT FELLS – BUTTERMERE

and rises past sheepfolds to bend left and exit the forestry at a padlocked gate. Cross the adjacent plain fence.

A green path sets course up the fellside, well endowed with bracken. An obvious path heads straight up the fell, avoiding the worst of the bracken. As you shake clear, contour left and slip through **Clews Gill**. Bear left, trending back down the slope briefly towards the sheepfold. At the sheepfold climb pathlessly along the boulder-and-heather mid-ridge, rising between boulder hollows – a grand little passage culminating at rocks and a ruined goose bield. Descend into Clews Gill and keep up the main left-hand gill at the confluence, with the pink exposure apparent. The ravine has plenty of grass, which makes progress easy in comparison with the flanking heather moor. Passing a spring, the gully opens and leads easily up to the ridge path. Simply turn right (east) to follow the path past the pointed fence-junction and up the final cone to the top.

Via Gillflinter Beck →8km/5 miles ↑530m/1740ft ⏲3hr 20min

The one open avenue of ascent from Ennerdale

6 Follow the attractive dale access track that passes on from the youth hostel to reach the first track-gate after 3.2km (2 miles). Immediately to its left is a

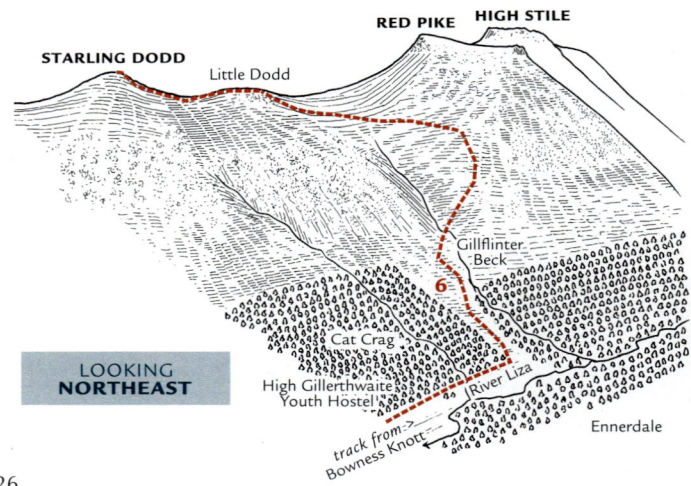

stile at the forest corner. Cross this, ford the gill, and follow the one path. This eases up the bracken slopes in a widening forest gangway, then crosses a fence-stile and remains at an easy angle until the double-stranded ford of **Gillflinter Beck**. Set to work on the southwestern slopes of Red Pike. Starling Dodd's adjacent slopes are smitten with boulders and ill-suited to sensible ascent. Watch for a fork. Here go left (on the less obvious path). Around 100 metres further on take an obvious sheep path curving up the shallow grassy combe to the boulder outcropping on **Little Dodd**. Cross the old fence-line to join the main ridge path, which misses the top of Little Dodd as it heads for the main summit.

The summit

Even in Wainwright's time, the rusting stakes here were a topic of conversation, and almost 60 years on they remain, forming a crazy tangled cairn beside the more usual stone pile. The domed summit is plain but the view is outstanding. From this situation Ennerdale Water dominates, with especially good views to the southern skyline of Ennerdale, where Pillar majestically rules the roost.

Summit cairn and tangle of old fencing (photo: Maggie Allan)

Safe descents

For Ennerdale either follow Route **6** (E then SE) over Little Dodd, or go W, bearing off the ridge soon after the pointed corner, and find easier ground – initially with Clews Gill then towards Starling Gill (**5**) – then gain the forest ride and Smithy Beck. For Buttermere head W then N to follow Route **1** down Scale Beck.

Ridge routes

Great Borne →*2.4km/1½ miles* ↓*135m/445ft* ↑*120m/395ft* ⏲*50min*
Begin NW, descending to the pointed fence-corner. Keep left of the fence, dipping through the headstream of Clews Gill to come back in union with the twin-stranded ridge fence, and climb naturally on to the top.

Red Pike →*2km/1¼ mile* ↓*75m/245ft* ↑*200m/655ft* ⏲*40min*
Descend E. A strong path is consistently evident, slicing through the angled course of the old metal ridge fence twice to complete the pull to the top. Keep right on the final rise for greatest underfoot comfort. Little Dodd provides mid-way interest on an otherwise featureless ridge, although the views are far from bland.

Looking back to Ennerdale Water (photo: Maggie Allan)

30 WANDOPE 772M/2533FT

Climb it from	Buttermere **30**
Character	Scarp top embracing Addacomb Hole, with an enthralling view
Fell-friendly route	3
Summit grid ref	NY 188 197
Link it with	Crag Hill, Grasmoor or Whiteless Pike
Part of	The Grasmoor Fell-gather

Wandope is a fell of considerable character. Whiteless Pike does its level best to outshine it to the south, while Crag Hill flaunts itself to the north, but from Newlands Hause and the Knott Rigg–Ard Crags ridge in particular, it reveals itself as a bold escarpment peak, even attracting intrepid paragliders and hang gliders on still summer days. It shares with Crag Hill custody of the hanging valley of Addacomb Hole, a seldom-visited wild place, and to the south is defined by the stony gully and ravine of inhospitable Third Gill.

Wandope is normally included as part of the ridge ascent from Whiteless Pike to Crag Hill, diverting at the cairn that stands on the western lip of the fell at Thirdgill Head Man. More intrepid fellwanderers will delight in the two little-known climbs described here, via Addacomb Beck (1–2) and Thirdgill Edge (3), the first with an optional variant along Sail Beck.

↑ *Wandope from Robinson*

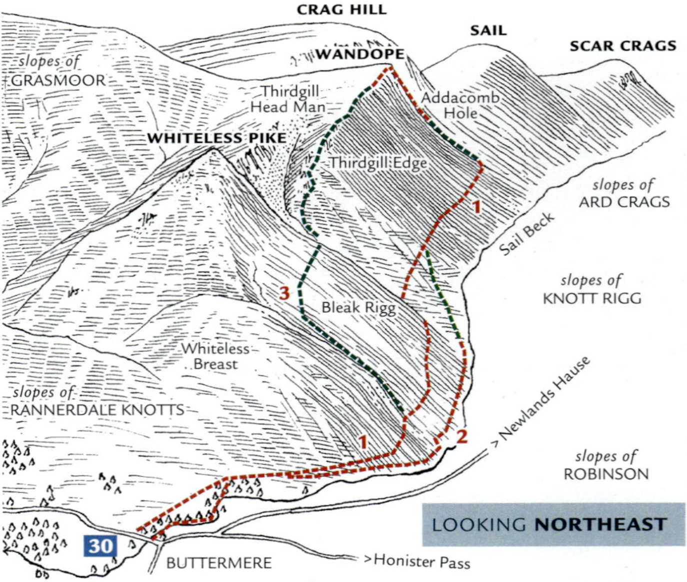

WALKING THE LAKE DISTRICT FELLS – BUTTERMERE

Ascent from Buttermere 30

Two routes contour round to the final assault on the summit, while Route 3 takes a more direct, pathless approach.

Via Bleak Rigg →5.6km/3½ miles ↑690m/2265ft ⏱2hr 20min

1 From the National Trust car park at the northern approach to the village, either walk straight over the road and, from the stile, cross the High House Crag brow, or go right with the road and bear off left, guided by the footpath sign, past the cottages to a gate, and

Walled bank on Bleak Rigg

230

30 Wandope

follow the field boundary to meet up with the path from the wooded dell. A little further on, just where the fence ends and before the final length of wall, the shepherds' drove makes a deliberate break up left. Progress comfortably through the bracken on **Whiteless Breast**, swinging into a nameless re-entrant valley, then up and across **Bleak Rigg** to enter and ascend from the **Third Gill** valley. Stay with the path as it breaks out of the valley to the right on a long traverse across the slopes of Wandope.

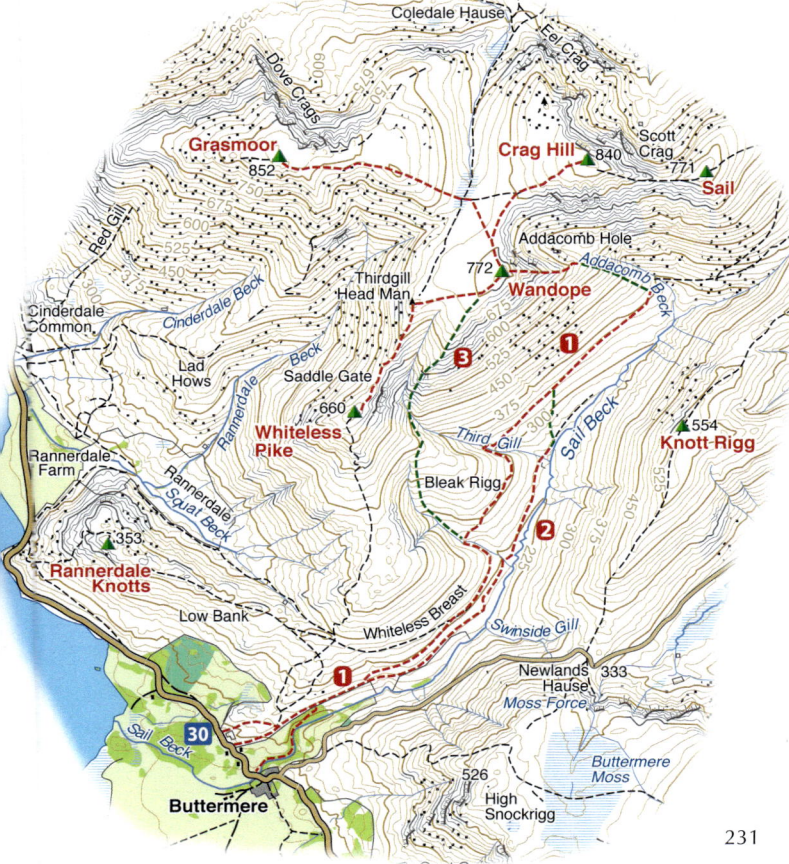

Just short of the ford of **Addacomb Beck** climb up the steep bracken-clad slope, avoiding the uninviting environs of the cascading beck. Admire the hanging valley of **Addacomb Hole** as you ascend its east ridge, there finding a narrow trod that winds easily and naturally to the summit.

Via Sail Beck →*5.6km/3½ miles* ↑*690m/2265ft* ⏲*2hr 30min*

2 Start out with Route **1**, but where it breaks up left keep to the natural line of the path from the wall-end up the valley. After fording **Third Gill**, above the old fold, the sheep-trod path dwindles and is quickly lost in the rushes. Here angle up the bank to what appears to be a ruined fold, then slant half-right to avoid the bracken and join the main path high on the slope. Turn right on this to follow Route **1** to the summit.

Via Thirdgill Edge →*4.4km/2¾ miles* ↑*690m/2265ft* ⏲*2hr 25min*

A little-used exploratory route directly out of Third Gill

3 Follow Route **1** as far as the first nameless re-entrant valley. Here break up left. If the bracken is up keep to the slightly steeper, left-hand grass slope until it is obvious that you can ford the gill and join the old wall-bank climbing up

The Sail Beck valley from High Snockrigg

30 Wandope

Ascent of Thirdgill Edge

Bleak Rigg. Follow this as it veers sharp right (northeast) to partition the better pasture from the headwall of Whiteless Pike. The wall-bank ends as it meets the steep slope falling into **Third Gill**. Follow the obvious sheep trod left. The path takes a delicate line above the steep slope via rock-steps to enter the gorge. Climb straight out and find your feet on the steep, pathless grass bank. Watch your hands on the gorse as you clamber higher, outmanoeuvring the outcropping, onto the ridge of **Thirdgill Edge**. As the slope eases a path is found, created by summit visitors from Whiteless Pike. Follow on to the summit.

The summit

A small cairn occupies a most pleasing perch overlooking the hanging valley of Addacomb Hole and offers a grandstand view of the massive scree-scarred escarpment of Crag Hill. The greatest excitement lies to the south-southeast over the shoulder of Robinson and above High Snockrigg, where Great Gable and the Scafells tantalise and Haystacks and High Stile complete the mountain collective.

Safe descents

The open prairie of grass to the west gives encouragement that an easy way is available. No such luck – steep ground of one sort of another lies in all directions. The safest option is to head WSW towards Thirdgill Head Man to find the popular ridge path S via Whiteless Pike. The sharp descent from the summit E (**1**) down the edge by Addacomb Hole is not problematic and gets you onto a good path down the Sail Beck valley to Buttermere quickest of all.

Across Addacomb Hole

Ridge routes

Crag Hill →*1.2km/¾ mile* ↓*35m/115ft* ↑*105m/345ft* ⏲*20min*
Head NNW, initially guided by the edge, to curve naturally around the combe-head and join the main ridge path NE up the plain back of Crag Hill.

Grasmoor →*1.6km/1 mile* ↓*30m/100ft* ↑*110m/360ft* ⏲*40min*
Head NNW, guided by the scarp edge, but continue straight ahead to the path cross-ways in the depression. Bear W up the bank on a regular path to a prominent cairn on the brow, from where a terrace path skirts the edge to reach the summit shelter.

Whiteless Pike →*1.6km/1 mile* ↓*145m/475ft* ↑*35m/115ft* ⏲*35min*
Aim SW to join the regular ridge path at Thirdgill Head Man (cairn), then trend SSW down the narrowing ridge through the dip of Saddle Gate to climb onto the summit.

31 WHITELESS PIKE 660M/2165FT

Climb it from	Buttermere **30**
Character	Abrupt ridge-end peak, a worthy first objective from the village of Buttermere
Fell-friendly route	1
Summit grid ref	NY 180 189
Link it with	Rannerdale Knotts or Wandope
Part of	The Grasmoor Fell-gather

As travellers come along the road by Rannerdale Farm their eyes are irresistibly drawn to Whiteless Pike. For sheer elegance of form this is a perfect peak. Seemingly standing alone, the narrow connecting ridge with the Grasmoor massif hidden from lowly stations, it adds greatly to the scenic abundance of this much-loved mountain vale.

Sharply defined to the west by Rannerdale Beck, the Pike is connected to Rannerdale Knotts by a low saddle at the head of Squat Beck. Two lower truncated ridges lie to the south and east, Whiteless Breast and Bleak Rigg, divided by gills draining into Sail Beck. The greatest and most deeply cutting of these ravines is Third Gill, which has so incised the northern slopes of the fell as to create a narrow ridge, Whiteless Edge, rising from the Saddle Gate col.

↑ *Whiteless Pike from Whiteless Edge, backed by High Stile and Red Pike (photo: Tim Thornton)*

As a ridge-end summit, with difficult slopes on either flank, the options for ascent are limited to the one direct climb up the southern slope. Most ascents begin from Buttermere village, although occasionally walkers begin from Cinderdale Common, wandering into the **Rannerdale Beck** and **Squat Beck** valley to join the primary ascent.

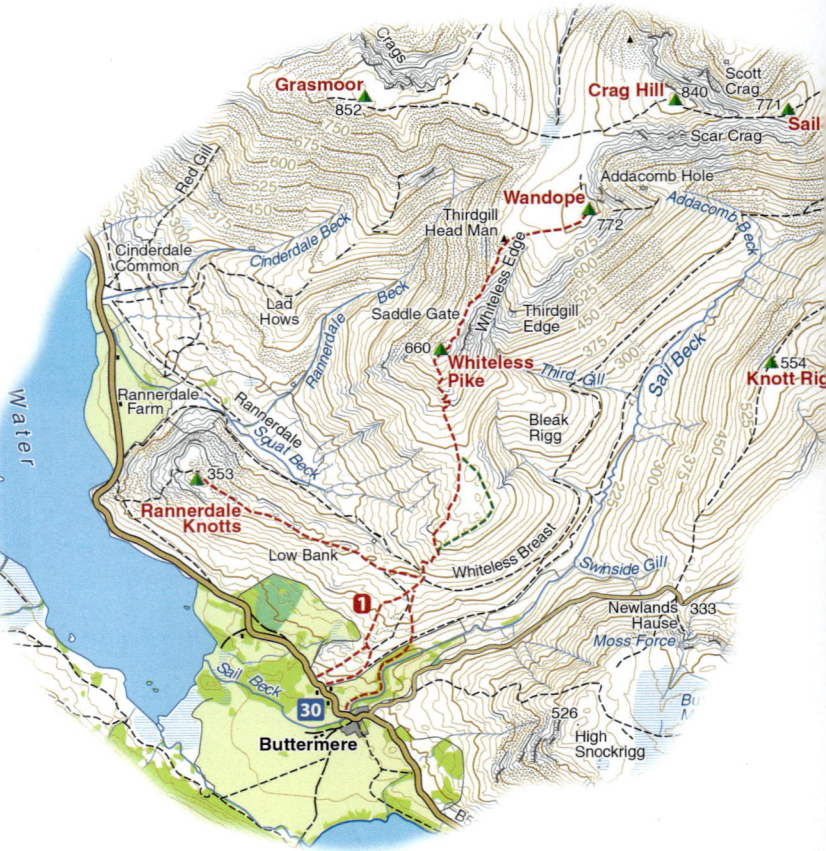

31 WHITELESS PIKE

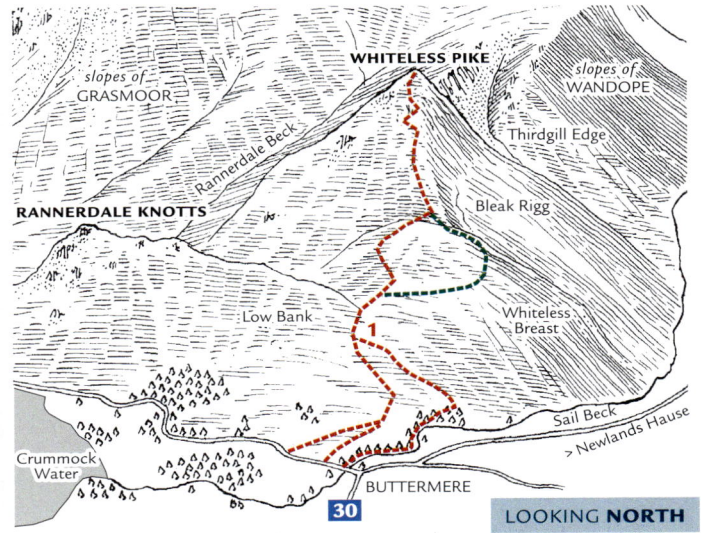

Ascent from Buttermere 30

Direct →*2.8km/1¾ miles* ↑*550m/1805ft* ⏱*1hr 50min*

A great climb from start to finish

1 Three options are available at the start. Pass to the right of the facing quarry, walk up the bank and, from the fence-stile, cross the High House Crag brow. Alternatively, step off the village road some 70 metres to the right of the car park entrance at the footpath sign, along the principal path up the Sail Beck valley. Walk on past the cottage garden to go through a hand-gate, taking the obvious path that shortly veers half-left up the fell in harmony with the High House Crag path to the saddle.

(Reach the same point from the National Park car park at the lower end of the village by walking back up the street and turning left in front of the Bridge Hotel to join the path on the left bank of Mill Beck. The path leads upstream in lovely woodland overlooking the dancing beck, and in its later

WALKING THE LAKE DISTRICT FELLS – BUTTERMERE

stages climbs a short flight of steps to a hand-gate. Head half-right up the fellside on a path which brushes aside the bracken. This is one of two turf-carpet paths clear of bracken that lead naturally up Low Bank to the saddle at the head of **Squat Beck**).

The only way is up (photo: Tim Thornton)

Look out for the winding path climbing north, coming onto the western shoulder on the reverse side of **Whiteless Breast**. Consider deviating on a pathless line around the upper eastern slopes for improved views into the Sail Beck valley, and then rejoining the main thoroughfare. After this point, set to work on the more earnest part of the climb. Apart from one minor rock-step high up, the climb is obvious, and with modern pitching supporting the heavy use, the way is never in doubt. Arrive at the summit with justified elation.

Looking north from the summit (photo: Tim Thornton)

The summit

Not quite the freestanding peak it seemed as you climbed, the summit still offers a wonderful sense of achievement and a magnificent view over the Crummock and Buttermere valley. Grasmoor still looks big but the climb no longer looks as daunting. There is a hint of a cairn but no need for one. If you intend to linger, a good place lies a short way down the western prow, overlooking Rannerdale, away from the regular passage of walkers.

Safe descent

Just as there is one way up, so there is just the one way down (S). Watch for an awkward rock-step quite early on. Take care. The path gets a real hammering from over-hasty walkers racing off the range so loose stones abound, and the ball-bearing effect can be disconcerting.

Ridge routes

Rannerdale Knotts →*2.8km/1¾ miles* ↓*370m/1215ft* ↑*65m/215ft* ⓒ*50min*
Take the regular path that leads S off the left edge of the summit. Watch for the rock-step and gully, below which there is pitching to secure the heavily burdened path. The path keeps to the right-hand side of the lower broader section of the ridge, and angles down to the saddle at the head of the Squat Beck valley. Move naturally W onto the emerging ridge of Low Bank which leads to the summit and follow it to its logical conclusion – a pleasure every step of the way.

Wandope →*1.6km/1 mile* ↓*35m/115ft* ↑*145m/475ft* ⓒ*35min*
Follow the ridge N down through Saddle Gate and up Whiteless Edge to Thirdgill Head Man (cairn). Here veer ENE over the grass to the cairn.

32 WHITESIDE 707M/2320FT

Climb it from	Lanthwaite Green 33, High Liza Bridge 34, Lanthwaite Wood 17 or Hopebeck 19
Character	Crag top, especially renowned for the fine ridge connection with Hopegill Head
Fell-friendly route	3
Summit grid ref	NY 170 219
Link it with	Hopegill Head
Part of	The Grasmoor Fell-gather

Whiteside is the abrupt western termination of a wonderful ridge, one of the simplest and most enjoyable airy strides in Lakeland. Many walkers visit the summit on a just-for-fun there-and-back excursion from Hopegill Head and the Coledale Horseshoe. Yet the fell makes a fine objective in itself, and from across the open common at Lanthwaite Green it rises handsomely, with Whin Ben the first inviting step. The fell name suggests the presence of quartz but the gullied east slope falling into the Gasgale Gill valley shows no characteristic white streaks.

↑ *Whiteside from above High Nook Tarn*

32 WHITESIDE

Two tough routes lead up from the west (1–2). The gentler northern ascent sets off from the Hopebeck fell-road (3) but an enchanting lead-in can be enjoyed from the village of High Lorton, via Boonbeck Lane, initially on a field-edge path to Scales and then along a lovely green lane with balcony views to High Swinside Farm.

Ascent from Lanthwaite Green 33

Via Whin Ben → 2.4km/1½ miles ↑565m/1855ft ⏱ 1hr 20min

Liza Beck tumbling out of the Gasgale Gill ravine

The swiftest and best way to the top

1 Go over the open road and traverse the common east to cross the **Liza Beck** footbridge. Embark on the steady upward climb through the heather.

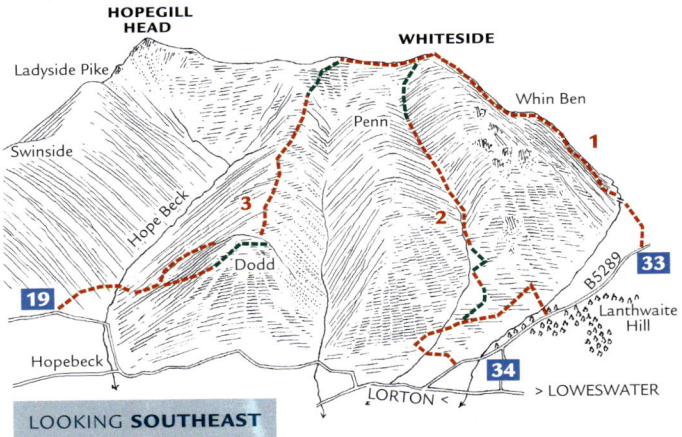

LOOKING **SOUTHEAST**

WALKING THE LAKE DISTRICT FELLS – BUTTERMERE

The pronounced step of **Whin Ben** provides fine views across the dale gulf. The climb is thereafter without incident as you gaze into the Gasgale Gill (Liza Beck) valley and along the ridge, with fine rock architecture in the foreground. Proceed to the summit.

Ascent from High Liza Bridge 34 or Lanthwaite Wood 17

Via Wythe Gill →*2km/1¼ miles* ↑*600m/1970ft* ⏲*1hr 30min*

A tough but quietly scenic way

Low Hollins backed by the Wythe Gill combe

2 (If the layby at High Liza Bridge is full use Lanthwaite Wood car park, walking up the road over Scale Hill to take the **Pickett Howe** footpath to High Liza Bridge.) Follow the road north, turning right opposite the 'give way 180yds' sign into the bridle-lane signed 'Millerplace'. This gravel track leads by Low Hollins to a hand-gate entering a confined lane. Coming to another hand-gate, with the handsome pink-toned **High Hollins** farmhouse glimpsed ahead, turn right through the adjacent gate into the field (permissive path notice). The path curves easily up and right onto a green-way by the wall corner and fords **Wythe Gill** to reach and go through a hurdle-gate in the intake wall. Quickly step onto the bracken-free footpath, which in its entirety runs from Lanthwaite Green to Hopebeck beside the intake wall. (Reach the same point by walking south from High Liza Bridge with the B5289, going through the gate on the left opposite Beck House, and crossing the new footbridge over **Liza Beck**. From the next gate keep close to the wall on the right and advance to the steps and the hand-gate in the intake wall. Bear left, rising briefly to join and follow the regular footpath in harmony with the wall. Some 300 metres on reach the path-junction.)

Go directly uphill without the aid of a path, coming up by low outcropping and towards the more general bracken slope. Moving up towards the scree, find a sheep path which drifts half-left to reach Wythe Gill, with some outcropping, and continue uphill with the gill. As the watercourse goes underground discover an unlikely path holding to the base of the rising valley. After passing a bield the path progressively falters but the way is no less clear – straight up the steep bank to the skyline. As the slope eventually eases the summit comes into view ahead.

Ascent from Hopebeck 19

Via the Dodd ridge →*3.6km/2¼ miles* ↑*600m/1970ft* ⏲*2hr*

A characterful climb – particularly to and through the heather

3 Follow the footpath sign south into the **Hope Beck** valley. Ford the beck beside the ruined sheep-wash fold and smartly branch half-left through bracken. Rise onto a shelf green-way slanting southeast along the slope of Dodd. Here you could choose to follow the walkers' trod directly up from the bield onto **Dodd** itself – a stiff prelude to the main climb – and then follow on pathless over the top to rejoin the main route. The more common option curves up into the slate-strewn gap south of the little outlier. The path mounts out of the gap south, climbing the heather ridge. Higher up the heather is replaced by grass, and the route becomes less certain underfoot as the ridge opens onto the nameless ridge-top crest. It is sometimes known as the East Top and is a bit higher than the accepted summit, which is reached by following the ridge right (west-southwest).

The summit

A modest cairn sits on top of a rock plinth. It is definitely a summit but not the summit. That accolade belongs to the next rise in the ridge, about 750 metres distant, known as the East Top. But this is the better spot to stand, with all the fun and excitement concentrated to the south. Standing on the profound craggy escarpment, savour sensational views into the Gasgale Gill valley and across the gulf to Dove Crags buttressing Grasmoor. To the east the twisting roof of a ridge directs attention tantalisingly towards the peak of Hopegill Head. The view from a little way down to the south offers the most impressive views along the craggy scarp.

Safe descents

The common path leading SSW down the edge to Whin Ben (**1**) is largely bereft of hazard, although it is quite steep as it makes for the Liza Beck footbridge. But there is a case in harsh conditions for heading NW (**2**), going steeply down into the embrace of the Wythe Gill valley to avoid all hint of outcropping and reach the intake wall. From there a path leads left to Lanthwaite Green and right to the Hopebeck fell-road.

Ridge route

Hopegill Head →*2km/1¼ miles* ↓*45m/150ft* ↑*110m/360ft* ⏱*40min*
The perennially popular, largely ridge-topping path runs almost due E, with the target peak a wonderful lure. Frequent stops to look over the heathery edge are recommended, and the final third of the journey is perhaps the very best as the crest narrows. Follow on to reach the summit.

Summit cairn

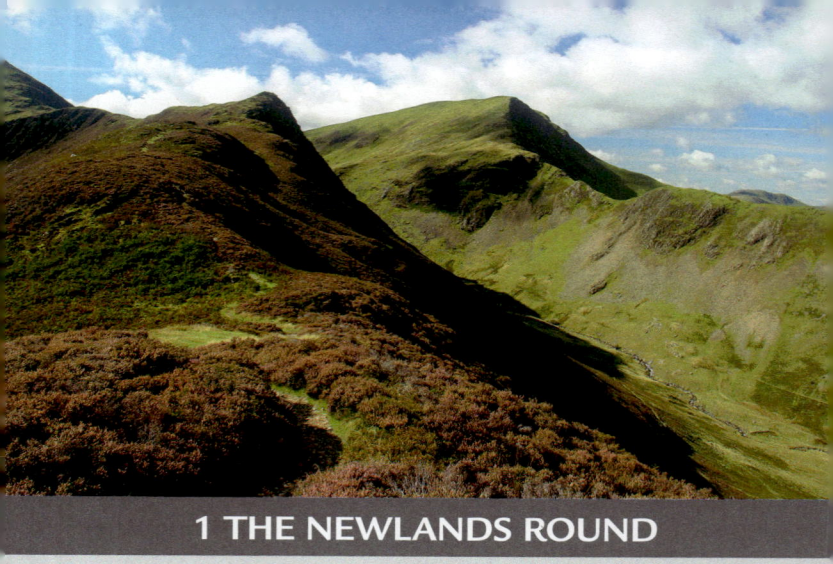

1 THE NEWLANDS ROUND

Start/Finish	Chapel Bridge **27**
Distance	16km (10 miles)
Ascent/Descent	1090m (3580ft)
Time	7hr
Terrain	Early minor scramble onto Scope End, followed by heather and free-flowing walking; a soggy crossing of Buttermere Moss, followed by grass and a quick descent to Rigg Beck
Summits	Hindscarth, Robinson, Knott Rigg and Ard Crags

A walk right at the heart of the Newlands fells, sweeping gloriously onto Hindscarth and over neighbouring Robinson, then crossing Newlands Hause to trip along the twin-topped ridge of Knott Rigg and Ard Crags.

The small parking area at Chapel Bridge fills rapidly so an early start is recommended on sunny weekends. Cross the road-bridge and then turn left at the T-junction to come to the white-washed **Newlands Church**. Here turn left, following the farm access lane to **Low Snab Bank**. Feast your eyes on Scope End ahead above the trees and the High Snab ridge on Robinson set back half-right, both ridges projecting as snouts (or 'snabs'). The track leads

↑ *High Crags, with Robinson rising beyond Little Dale*

1 THE NEWLANDS ROUND

over a cattle grid and later through gates, leading up through the farmyard by the whitewashed house. Beyond the barn go through a gate and swing right, slanting immediately up the bank, signposted to 'Hindscarth'.

Coming under the bulbous fans of spoil spilling from the **Goldscope Mine**, notice the Pan Holes (tilted fissures) above. Follow the green-way as it comes up by the intake wall to strike left up onto the fell as the ridge-end is reached. **Beware** that the ridge has several small rock-step hazards, uncomfortable when wet or icy, but all the steps are solid. This is a heavenly climb, especially once you reach the heather on the narrow crest. Ahead the peak of **High Crags** is a great lure above Littledale. Make a point of leaving the path briefly to stand on top for the splendid view. The path levels before the final pull up to the viewpoint wind-break on the northern rim of **Hindscarth**. Take time here to soak up the fabulous northward view to Skiddaw before advancing to the smaller summit shelter.

Follow the spine of the ridge. Some walkers opt to slant down half-right after 100 metres, but for the better views stay on the crown of the fell and admire Dale Head and the backdrop of the Buttermere fells. Keep to the right-hand fork further on to reach Hindscarth Edge. Joining the ridge path from Dale Head, descend right to the ridge-bridge of **Littledale Edge** and follow the fence climbing onto **Robinson**. The summit cairn, set on a low outcrop, is some distance north from the fence-line.

Looking northeast to Blencathra from Hindscarth

WALKING THE LAKE DISTRICT FELLS – BUTTERMERE

Your continuing journey now heads southwest, slanting down the steep though largely grassy slope. Lower down the path steps through a spring. It sweeps onto the spongy expanse of **Buttermere Moss** and you should be able to float your merry way directly across without difficulty. Easing onto the nose of **High Snockrigg** – a little way north of its highest point (though you might want to visit the higher spot for the commanding view of the Buttermere valley) – the path heads straight on down a groove, bound for Buttermere village. Don't follow this but instead bear down

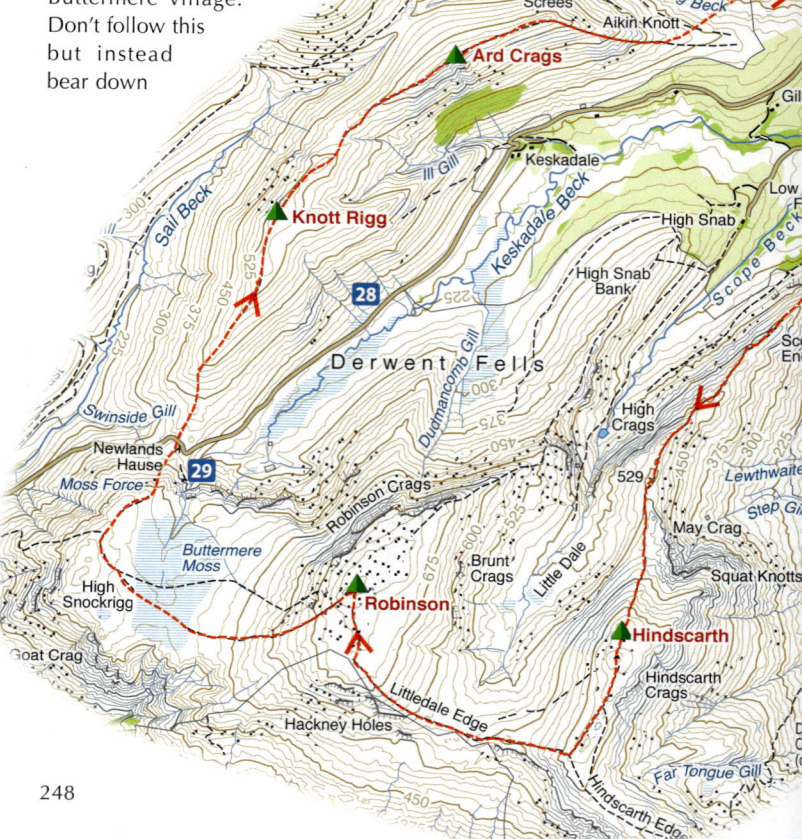

248

1 The Newlands Round

the ridge northeast, initially gently then, from an abrupt leftward cut, more steeply, with some stone steps lower down, to reach the popular parking area at **Newlands Hause**.

Cross diagonally and walk up the easy slope to the obvious rock headland. This is not a summit. The lovely grassy ridge leads on via a further outcrop to culminate on the modest swelling of **Knott Rigg**, where a tangent spur ridge draws up from the right. Follow on with the main ridge as it dips and climbs invitingly onto the crest of **Ard Crags**, all the way providing a sumptuous outlook on a gallery of handsome fells, Robinson especially well seen but more dramatically the high ridge to the west from Whiteless Pike round by Crag Hill to Causey Pike.

The heather ridge passes a feeble excuse for a cairn and then you embark on the headlong descent from **Aikin Knott**, which calls for steady footing. When the ridge eases and before the bracken ends, find a wooden waymark post (loose when the author passed) directing the path half-left. Follow this line down through the bracken, crossing a well-evidenced sheep track, to ford **Rigg Beck** (wet socks almost unavoidable), joining the valley path down to the road. Go right and then left down the minor road back to the start.

The Northwestern Fells from Robinson

2 THE BUTTERMERE ROUND

Start/Finish	Gatesgarth **6**
Distance	11km (7 miles)
Ascent/Descent	1250m (4100ft)
Time	7hr
Terrain	Rough going in parts, the opening leg steep but stepped, a winding heather trail to Haystacks concludes with a stiff rocky descent, then abruptly onto High Crag, the whole adventure ending with a long rough descent on a path of sorts.
Summits	Fleetwith Pike, Haystacks, High Crag and High Stile

A superb Lakeland mountain day with thrilling scenes from start to finish. Fleetwith is a rising crescendo, the Haystacks traverse is utterly absorbing and it is all completed by the mighty finale of High Stile. A walk that will linger long in your locker of happy memories.

From the Gatesgarth car park walk east with the road as if to Gatesgarthdale, stepping off right after the signposted bridle-track. Aim up the pasture towards the white cross on **Low Raven Crag** at the foot of **Fleetwith Pike**. A path

↑ *High Crag and High Stile from Fleetwith Pike*

2 THE BUTTERMERE ROUND

quickly appears, winding determinedly up onto Fleetwith Edge. This is a handsome climb punctuated by the odd minor rock-step and moments where a welcome breather can be taken. The ridge can be exposed to gusts so don't rush. A final scramble and you arrive at the summit cairn – a glorious moment of elation. Most attention during the climb is on Haystacks but beyond the summit the view opens up and the ridge-top remarkably takes on the character of a moor!

Leave the cairn on a path that takes an easy right-hand bias, as if heading towards Grey Knotts. Walk down gradually over the heather to a newly cut slate quarry and a slate-milling area. Here follow the track right, descending to the Dubs Mountain Shelter (old quarryman's shop). Below ford **Warnscale Beck** and join the ever-popular path skirting to the left of Green Crag on rough terrain. The path splits then re-unites before fording Black Beck, the outflow of the shy basin tarn. Pass up beneath a rockwall, with exciting views down the ravine into Warnscale Bottom. The rocky path comes by the shore of **Innominate Tarn** and above a second smaller pool adorned with bogbean, clambering onto the lateral spine that forms the summit of **Haystacks** with a cairn at either end. Beyond, held in the grip of the bedrock, a further pool sparkles. Seek the one sure line of descent to the right of the pool. A succession of awkward rock-steps inhibits hasty progress, giving you time to admire

Dubs Hut Mountain Shelter

WALKING THE LAKE DISTRICT FELLS – BUTTERMERE

some fabulous, flowing lava patterns high up in the rock. The grassy saddle of **Scarth Gap** comes with no little relief.

Head straight on from the cairn, following the scree path winding up onto Seat. The way is unambiguous and the ridge eases before the abrupt climb up Gamelin End. The old scree way has been sidelined by a major pitched zig-zag path which marshalls walkers and gives secure footing and cause for steady progress much of the way up. You will be surprised how much easier the climb is than it looks, thanks to the work of Fix the Fells. The highest section is, however, unavoidably loose, the mountain's geology having had the last say! Reach the summit cairn of **High Crag**, where an irregular line of metal stakes gives a clue to progress northwest along a long connecting ridge above Birkness Comb towards High Stile. You get no sense of Eagle Crag beneath your feet until, near the end, a sharp gully provides a brief glimpse into the cove below. The way mounts by boulders onto the top of **High Stile**, with three cairns vying for the crown of summit – a fabulously scenic station.

Seat and High Crag from Haystacks

Head northeast, following the path along the prow and avoiding the temptation to boulder-hop on the east side. The rock outcrops and steps are nowhere impassable. In due course the blunt ridge-end naturally ushers the path right (east), with some scree and heather easing the way down towards the lower lip of **Birkness Comb**. At **Comb Beck**, draining the hanging valley, take the traditional climbers' path. This keeps east via the right-hand ladder-stile (be warned: it is hanging in the air on the far side) and, after a plain stretch of grass, slips through a little shelf breach in Low Crag to keep its line through dense bracken. On emerging, meet a rough sheep trod beneath a rock wall, which leads to the Scarth Gap path at the corner of the thicket. Go left to round the head of Buttermere by Peggy's Bridge, crossing the meadow to return to Gatesgarth.

3 THE GRASMOOR FELL-GATHER

Start/Finish	Lanthwaite Green **33**
Distance	17km (10½ miles)
Ascent/Descent	1330m (4360ft)
Time	7hr 30min
Terrain	After the initial heathery climb, the route is largely on grass pasture paths and holds no shocks apart from startling views.
Summits	Whiteside, Hopegill Head, Grasmoor, Wandope, Whiteless Pike and Rannerdale Knotts

One of the most rewarding high-fell walks in the district. Two lovely ridges, compelling views from the summit of Grasmoor and, after the initial climb onto Whiteside, the going is easy.

From Lanthwaite Green cross the level open common east to the new footbridge spanning **Liza Beck**. Step over and begin the steady ascent of the heather slope. The path winds irresistibly onto **Whin Ben**. Be sure to take sideways glances into the Gasgale Gill gorge as you climb. The path then slips down through a saddle to start climbing steeply again. Higher up you reach some outcropping. The easier option here is to stick with the rock. As

↑ *Looking along the Whiteside ridge to Hopegill Head*

3 THE GRASMOOR FELL-GATHER

you near the summit the slope finally eases. The cairn on **Whiteside** is a great place to pause and take stock of a craggy scene, down the arêtes into the gorge, across to Dove Crags on Grasmoor and ahead towards Hopegill Head.

Approaching Hopegill Head

The ridge path onwards is never in doubt, offering many tempting places to stop and survey the scene. The peak of **Hopegill Head** looks so inviting and is reached without difficulty. This airy summit plinth has no cairn nor needs one. Enjoy the spacious view into the vast bowl at the head of the Hobcarton valley and across to Grisedale Pike. Turn south, passing the cairn on **Sand Hill** and descending on a loose trail into the wide col of **Coledale Hause**. As the path rises from the col on the other side, it is deflected by the scree of Crag Hill. Take an early half-right to ford the headstream of **Gasgale Gill** and begin an easy ascent west then southwest. Evidence of a path is thin to start with but soon becomes more pronounced as the scarp edge is gained. In due course the path comes dramatically above the great hanging valley above Gasgale Gill, rimmed by the soaring clefts and ribs of Dove Crags. In calm weather follow the sheep trod around the rim, avoiding losing height, before switching southwest over the domed pasture top of **Grasmoor** to the shelter. Talk about commanding a view!

A strong promenade path leads east, passing a prominent cairn marking the top of the Lad Hows route (the shortcut to the foot of Rannerdale). The path keeps just shy of the ridge-top before dipping to the pasture hause cross-paths. Here angle southeast with an obvious path direct to the summit cairn on **Wandope**, from where you can peer down into Addacomb Hole and

3 THE GRASMOOR FELL-GATHER

across to the Knott Rigg/Ard Crags ridge. Do not be lured by the natural edge but cut back west to descend **Whiteless Edge** via **Saddle Gate**, climbing onto the proud top of **Whiteless Pike**.

The southbound descent is not without rocky discomforts so take your time. The path keeps to the west side of **Whiteless Breast** and angles into the little sheep-path col at the head of Rannerdale. Turn up right to follow the ridge along **Low Bank**, coming over rocky ground to reach the end of the ridge and culminating point of **Rannerdale Knotts**. Set off again in the same direction to follow the heavily used path, never in doubt. Step down a short rock obstacle then angle left. Lower down the path becomes a stone staircase under gorse-clothed crags. Where it eases, keep to the right-hand path through the bracken to reach the road.

Rannerdale is a special pleasure, most assuredly when the bluebells are in full bloom in May. Therefore, rather than follow the road back to the starting point, bear off at the recessed parking area and follow the path beside the wall under the steep slope of the fell, coming round to a footbridge spanning **Squat Beck**, right at the bottom of this lovely valley. From this point join a turf track which leads through a gate onto **Cinderale Common** to reach the roadside verge. Follow the road north back to your parking spot.

Grasmoor and Hopegill Head from the east

4 THE COLEDALE HORSESHOE

Start/Finish	Braithwaite **24**
Distance	17km (10½ miles)
Ascent/Descent	1425m (4675ft)
Time	8hr
Terrain	The overly long climb to the first summit ends with easy scrambling, and thereafter the route is all unimpeded fell trails.
Summits	Grisedale Pike, Hopegill Head, Crag Hill, Sail, Scar Crags, Causey Pike, Outerside and Barrow

A hugely popular grand tour of the Northwestern Fells. Each of the eight summits has its own distinct character – a scenic triumph in its own right that draws you ever onwards.

From the footpath sign to 'Grisedale Pike' climb the inviting flight of steps, rising through light woodland. After passing through a hand-gate come onto the open fell, a grass path forging through the bracken (heavily used and in the process of careful restoration at the time of writing). After the path-side

↑ *Walker on the path from Coledale Hause*

4 THE COLEDALE HORSESHOE

fence is lost on Kinn, stride along the edge and savour the handsome views over Coledale. The very clear path levels, with fine views down onto the old Force Crag mine and the grand facade of fells at the dalehead. As you come across the head of the **Massmill Beck** valley climb up **Sleet How**. At the next dalehead, that of **Grisedale Gill**, with the forestry below, tackle the final stern challenge, the east ridge of **Grisedale Pike**. Some minor rocky moments are met and mastered with blessed relief before you step onto the cairnless summit to be rewarded with a magnificent panorama. A rock plinth provides a little shelter from the westerly winds.

Descend southwest beside the slumped ruin of a ridge wall, your open path offering fabulous views of the head of the Hobcarton valley and the shapely peak of Hopegill Head. From the brief depression climb again over an unnamed top. The ridge path descends once more to a fork in the way. The left-hand path leads directly down to Coledale Hause. However, **Hopegill Head** should not be omitted lightly and the next short pull is well rewarded as you reach a second cairnless summit with another triumph of a view and a slightly bigger bedrock block to provide eastern shelter.

Now head south through a very shallow dip and past a cairn on **Sand Hill** before sweeping down the gravelly trail on a long descent into the broad

Skiddaw from above the Grisedale Gill valley

WALKING THE LAKE DISTRICT FELLS – BUTTERMERE

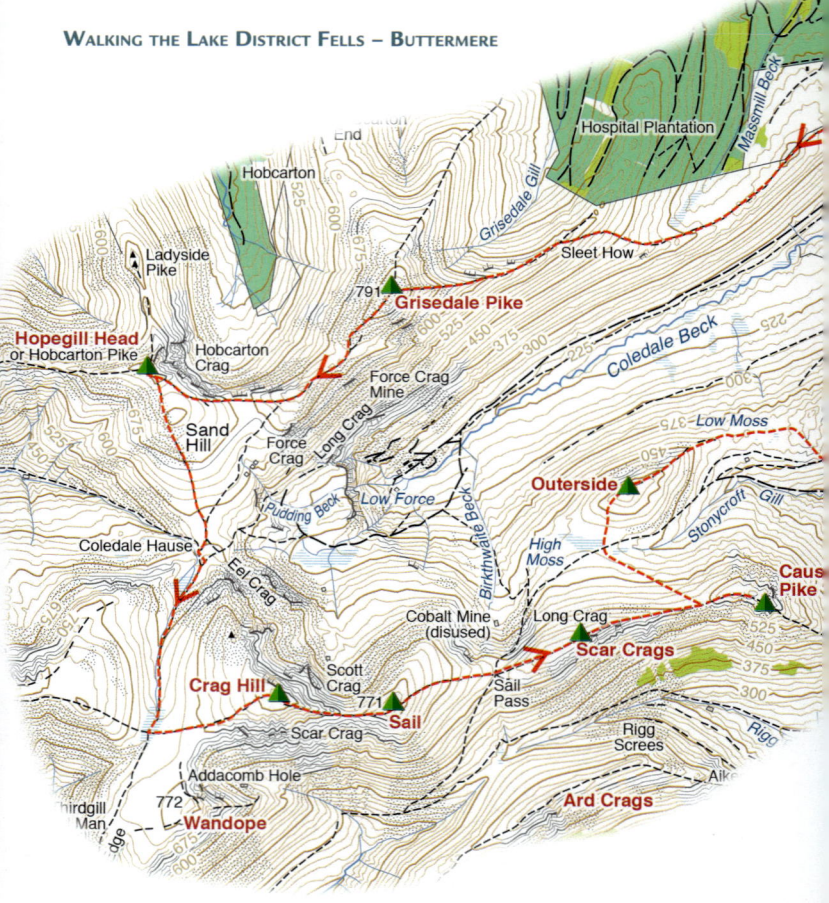

saddle of **Coledale Hause**. Pass the small pool and ignore the first two paths right. Instead keep on to link up with the path climbing out of Coledale, bending right at the foot of the scree bank beneath **Eel Crag**. The valley path at the head of Gasgale Gill leads to a cross-paths saddle where you turn left. Head on to find the airy brink overlooking Addacomb Hole and then bear up the rim path to a prominent cairn marking the edge of the summit plateau of **Crag Hill**. The stone-built Ordnance Survey column provides a grand

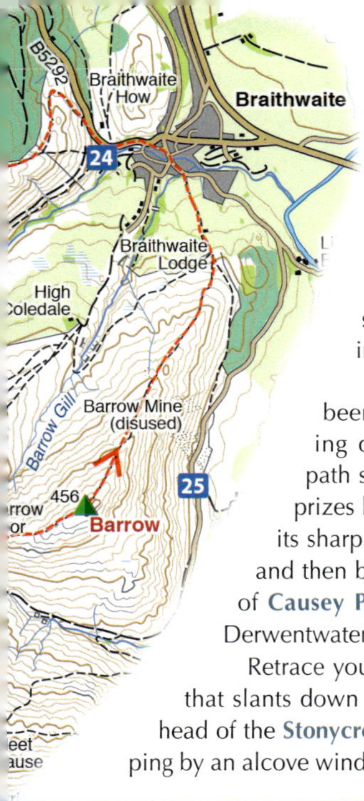

4 THE COLEDALE HORSESHOE

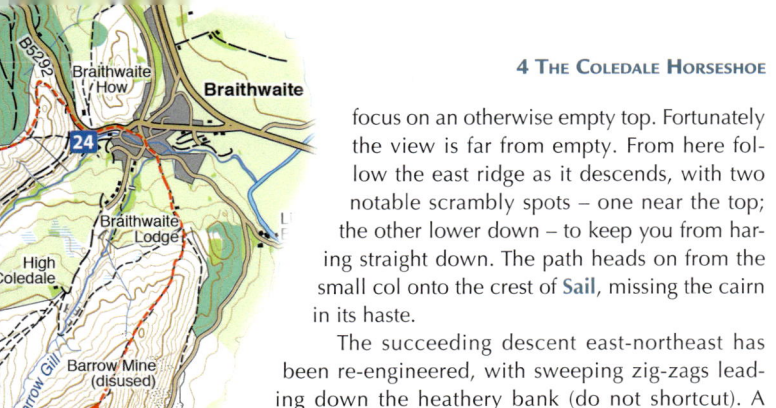

focus on an otherwise empty top. Fortunately the view is far from empty. From here follow the east ridge as it descends, with two notable scrambly spots – one near the top; the other lower down – to keep you from haring straight down. The path heads on from the small col onto the crest of **Sail**, missing the cairn in its haste.

The succeeding descent east-northeast has been re-engineered, with sweeping zig-zags leading down the heathery bank (do not shortcut). A path straddles the next lower depression. Two further prizes lie ahead: firstly **Scar Crags**, a striking ridge with its sharp arêtes falling steeply into the Rigg Beck valley; and then by a set of minor bumps, the mini Pike o'Stickle of **Causey Pike**, a marvellous viewpoint for Catbells and Derwentwater.

Retrace your steps to the obvious grassy dip to find a path that slants down through the heather towards **High Moss** at the head of the **Stonycroft Gill** valley. Traverse the marshy ground, slipping by an alcove wind-break to mount the heather slope on a thin path

Descent from Crag Hill

Final fells of the horseshoe from Crag Hill

direct to the summit cairn of **Outerside**. The ridge dips steeply through the heather northeast and then runs east over **Low Moss** and Stile End and smartly down into **Barrow Door**, continuing east onto **Barrow** where a cairn resting on the bare rock top makes a good spot for a well-earned rest.

Follow on naturally down the north ridge, the flaky rock later becoming a grass path. A small dip in the ridge holds a cairn. From here either keep up and on with the declining ridge, or veer left, sweeping down through the bracken banks, by either route coming to a hand-gate onto a path leading down a field via gates and through the yard and access lane at **Braithwaite Lodge** to the road, where you then turn left into the heart of the village. Walk through Braithwaite to find the foot of Whinlatter Pass and here turn left to walk up a short distance to the parking area.

MORE TO EXPLORE

Circular
- from Buttermere **30**: Red Pike – Starling Dodd – Great Borne
- from Buttermere **30**: Robinson – Hindscarth – Dale Head
- from Maggie's Bridge **15**: Blake Fell – Gavel Fell – Hen Comb

Linear
- from Honister Pass **4** to Buttermere **30**: Dale Head – Hindscarth – Robinson

Northeast from Dodd, Red Pike (photo: Maggie Allan)

USEFUL CONTACTS

Tourist information
The nearest National Park information centre to the area covered by this guide is just a couple of miles to the east, in Keswick. There is, however, lots of information available on the National Park website: www.lakedistrict.gov.uk. If you want to talk to someone face to face there are also other information points in Seatoller and Cockermouth (ring to check opening hours before dropping in).

Keswick tel 0845 901 0845
(calls cost 2p per minute plus your phone company's access charge)
KeswickTIC@lake-district.gov.uk

Seatoller Barn Tourist Information Centre
tel 017687 77714

Cockermouth Tourist Information Centre
(at Cockermouth Library)
tel 01900 822634
cockermouthtic@co-net.com

Accommodation
In addition to the tourist information centres and search engines, the Visit Cumbria website has a good database of local accommodation options: www.visitcumbria.com.

Weather
It is well worth consulting either of these forecasts to gauge the best times to be on the tops.

Lake District Weatherline
tel 0844 846 2444
www.lakedistrictweatherline.co.uk

Mountain Weather Information Service
Full mountain forecasts for 3 days at a time
www.mwis.org.uk (choose English and Welsh Forecast/Lake District)
App: Mountain Forecast Viewer

Transport

Traveline
Information on buses, trains and coaches – such as they are
www.traveline.info

Stagecoach
Bus information
www.stagecoachbus.com
App: Stagecoach Bus

Organisations

The National Trust
The National Trust owns 90% of the farms in the national park, as well as historic sites and properties, camp sites and car parks.
www.nationaltrust.org.uk
App: National Trust – Days Out

Fix the Fells
Fix the Fells repairs and maintains 335 upland paths in the national park. Read about their work, volunteer or donate on this website.
www.fixthefells.co.uk

Mountain Rescue
The Lake District Search and Mountain Rescue Association manages 12 teams of volunteers across the national park. The site has useful safety information. Downloading the free OS Locate app will enable you to tell the team your grid ref, whether you have phone signal or not, should you need to call them.
www.ldsamra.org.uk

Other

Andrew's Walks
Excellent photo-journal blog with mapping, detailing Andrew Locking's walks in the Lake District and beyond
www.andrewswalks.co.uk

A FELLRANGER'S GLOSSARY

Navigational features

Word	Explanation
arête	knife-edge ridge
band	binding strip of land
bank-barn	barn accessible on two levels (often built on a slope or bank)
beck	main stream flowing into and through valleys to lakes and rivers
boiler-plates	non-technical term for exposed broad slabs of rock
cairn/man	small pile of loose stones indicating a path or path junction
clint	block forming part of a natural limestone pavement
combe/cove	hanging valley high in the fells
common	undivided land grazed by several farmers
cop	viewpoint
crag	substantial outcrop of rock
dale	valley
dodd	rounded hilltop
drumlin	large mound that accumulated beneath a melting glacier
dub	dark pool
fell	mountain pasture, frequently attributed to the whole hill
force	waterfall
garth	small enclosure close to farm buildngs
gate	dialect term for a track
ghyll/gill	steeply sloping watercourse
glen	from British term 'glyn' meaning valley
grain	lesser watercourse above a confluence
hag	eroded section of peat moor
hause, saddle, col, dore, scarth	high gap between fells
holm	dry riverside meadow
hope	secluded valley
howe	hill or mound
ill	treacherous
intake	upper limit of valley enclosure
keld	spring
knott	compact or rugged hilltop
laithe	barn in the field or on the fell (rather than next to the farmstead)
ling	heather

A FELLRANGER'S GLOSSARY *continued*

lonnin	quiet lane
man	from Celtic term 'maen' meaning stone marker
mell	bald hill
mere	pool or lake
mire	marshy ground
moraine	residual valley-head pillow-mound debris left after a glacier melts away
nab, naze	hill-spur or nose
ness	promontory
nether	lower
nook	secluded corner
outcrop	crag or obvious collection of rocks
out-gang	shepherd's drove lane to a particular fell pasture
park	enclosed hunting ground
pike	sharp or rocky summit
place	plot of ground
raise	heap of stones
rake	grooved track
ridding	(the action of) clearing
rigg	ridge
scale	summer-pasture shieling (hut)
scarp/scar	steep hillside
scree	weathered rock debris beneath a crag
seat	summer pasture/high place
shaw	small wood
sheep-creep	small field-to-field access-hole/gap for sheep
shelter-cairn	circular wind-break wall
shieling	hut built for use while pasturing
sike	small stream
slack	small, shallow or stony valley
sled-gate	track for pony-drawn sledges
slump	sedimentary rock that has slipped, creating dykes (intrusions), fractures or ridges
stang	pole
stead	site of a farm
sty	steep path

swine	pigs
tarn	small mountain pool, from the Norse 'tjorn' meaning tear
thwaite	clearing
traverse	walking route across the fells
trig point	Ordnance Survey triangulation column
trod	path created by animals
wash-fold	sheepfold where sheep were once gathered for washing in the beck
water	feeder lake to a river
wath	ford
whin	gorse
wick	inlet or bay or subsidiary farm
wray	secluded corner
yeat	gate

Place names

Name	Explanation
Braithwaite	broad clearing (Norse)
Buttermere Dubs	the strong current linking Buttermere and Crummock Water, used as a sheep wash
Crinkley Hill	hill of the circular clearing
Dudman Comb	hollow of the dead man
Eel Crag	evil (dangerous) cliff
Floutern Cop	high lookout above a tarn
Gale (Fell)	bog-myrtle pasture
Gamlin (End)	crooked pool
Gasgale (Gill)	goat's ravine
Grisedale	valley where swine forage
Herdus	contraction of 'herd house', where the keeper of the herd lived
High Snockrigg	high headland
Kinn	cheek (Norse)
Latterbarrow	hill of the lair (once the domain of wild beasts)
Stile End	steep place
Thackthwaite	clearing with a thatched dwelling (Norse) – for reconstructions of such visit Dubwath Nature Reserve or Trotters Farm near the foot of nearby Bassenthwaite

A FELLRANGER'S GLOSSARY *continued*

Thrang (Crag)   narrow passage
Toddell (Bridge)   fox hill
Warnscale   guard barn (Norse?) – a place where stock could be protected from cattle raiders

Fell names
Just the more intriguing ones...

Name	Explanation
Barrow	from berg (Saxon) = hill
Fleetwith Pike	peak by the wath (Norse) = damp ford
Gavel Pike	gabled peak (retaining the original dialect spelling, unlike Great Gable)
Great Borne	large boundary marker – but the fell was originally known as Hardecnut (like Hardknott)
Haystacks	possibly referring to methods of drying hay, or simply a corruption of 'high stack'
Hindscarth	passage of the deer
Knock Murton	boundary hillock, marking the western limit of fell country hereabouts
Mellbreak	possibly 'hill slope like a sandbank' (Norse) or 'dappled bare hill' (Celtic)
Outerside	outer edge (in this case of the Stonycroft valley)
Rannerdale Knotts	from Rannerhals (Norse), 'pass of the raven shieling'
Robinson	named after Richard Robinson who owned it in the 16th century
Scar Crags	possibly a contraction of scarth, 'passage', as a great inter-dale connection point
Starling Dodd	a boundary charter of 1230 refers to the steep ridge path called 'Styalein' (associated with a Viking landholder called Alein)
Whiteless Pike	perhaps truncated from 'the pike of Whiteless Breast'

THE LAKE DISTRICT FELLS

Fell name	Height	Volume
Allen Crags	784m/2572ft	Borrowdale
Angletarn Pikes	567m/1860ft	Mardale and the Far East
Ard Crags	581m/1906ft	Buttermere
Armboth Fell	479m/1572ft	Borrowdale
Arnison Crag	434m/1424ft	Patterdale
Arthur's Pike	533m/1749ft	Mardale and the Far East
Bakestall	673m/2208ft	Keswick
Bannerdale Crags	683m/2241ft	Keswick
Barf	468m/1535ft	Keswick
Barrow	456m/1496ft	Buttermere
Base Brown	646m/2119ft	Borrowdale
Beda Fell	509m/1670ft	Mardale and the Far East
Bell Crags	558m/1831ft	Borrowdale
Binsey	447m/1467ft	Keswick
Birkhouse Moor	718m/2356ft	Patterdale
Birks	622m/2241ft	Patterdale
Black Combe	600m/1969ft	Coniston
Black Fell	323m/1060ft	Coniston
Blake Fell	573m/1880ft	Buttermere
Bleaberry Fell	589m/1932ft	Borrowdale
Blea Rigg	556m/1824ft	Langdale
Blencathra	868m/2848ft	Keswick
Bonscale Pike	529m/1736ft	Mardale and the Far East
Bowfell	903m/2963ft	Langdale
Bowscale Fell	702m/2303ft	Keswick
Brae Fell	586m/1923ft	Keswick
Brandreth	715m/2346ft	Borrowdale
Branstree	713m/2339ft	Mardale and the Far East
Brim Fell	795m/2608ft	Coniston

THE LAKE DISTRICT FELLS *continued*

Fell name	Height	Volume
Brock Crags	561m/1841ft	Mardale and the Far East
Broom Fell	511m/1676ft	Keswick
Buckbarrow (Corney Fell)	549m/1801ft	Coniston
Buckbarrow (Wast Water)	430m/1411ft	Wasdale
Calf Crag	537m/1762ft	Langdale
Carl Side	746m/2448ft	Keswick
Carrock Fell	662m/2172ft	Keswick
Castle Crag	290m/951ft	Borrowdale
Catbells	451m/1480ft	Borrowdale
Catstycam	890m/2920ft	Patterdale
Caudale Moor	764m/2507ft	Mardale and the Far East
Causey Pike	637m/2090ft	Buttermere
Caw	529m/1736ft	Coniston
Caw Fell	697m/2287ft	Wasdale
Clough Head	726m/2386ft	Patterdale
Cold Pike	701m/2300ft	Langdale
Coniston Old Man	803m/2635ft	Coniston
Crag Fell	523m/1716ft	Wasdale
Crag Hill	839m/2753ft	Buttermere
Crinkle Crags	860m/2822ft	Langdale
Dale Head	753m/2470ft	Buttermere
Dodd	502m/1647ft	Keswick
Dollywaggon Pike	858m/2815ft	Patterdale
Dove Crag	792m/2599ft	Patterdale
Dow Crag	778m/2553ft	Coniston
Eagle Crag	520m/1706ft	Borrowdale
Eskdale Moor	337m/1105ft	Wasdale
Esk Pike	885m/2904ft	Langdale
Fairfield	873m/2864ft	Patterdale

Fell name	Height	Volume
Fellbarrow	416m/1365ft	Buttermere
Fleetwith Pike	648m/2126ft	Buttermere
Froswick	720m/2362ft	Mardale and the Far East
Gavel Fell	526m/1726ft	Buttermere
Gibson Knott	421m/1381ft	Langdale
Glaramara	783m/2569ft	Borrowdale
Glenridding Dodd	442m/1450ft	Patterdale
Gowbarrow Fell	481m/1578ft	Patterdale
Grange Fell	416m/1365ft	Borrowdale
Grasmoor	852m/2795ft	Buttermere
Gray Crag	697m/2287ft	Mardale and the Far East
Grayrigg Forest	494m/1621ft	Mardale and the Far East
Graystones	456m/1496ft	Keswick
Great Borne	616m/2021ft	Buttermere
Great Calva	690m/2264ft	Keswick
Great Carrs	788m/2585ft	Coniston
Great Cockup	526m/1726ft	Keswick
Great Crag	452m/1483ft	Borrowdale
Great Dodd	857m/2812ft	Patterdale
Great End	907m/2976ft	Borrowdale, Langdale, Wasdale
Great Gable	899m/2949ft	Borrowdale, Wasdale
Great How	523m/1716ft	Wasdale
Great Mell Fell	537m/1762ft	Patterdale
Great Rigg	767m/2516ft	Patterdale
Great Sca Fell	651m/2136ft	Keswick
Great Worm Crag	427m/1401ft	Coniston
Green Crag	489m/1604ft	Coniston
Green Gable	801m/2628ft	Borrowdale

THE LAKE DISTRICT FELLS *continued*

Fell name	Height	Volume
Grey Crag	638m/2093ft	Mardale and the Far East
Grey Friar	772m/2533ft	Coniston
Grey Knotts	697m/2287ft	Borrowdale
Grike	488m/1601ft	Wasdale
Grisedale Pike	791m/2595ft	Buttermere
Hallin Fell	388m/1273ft	Mardale and the Far East
Hard Knott	552m/1811ft	Coniston
Harrison Stickle	736m/2415ft	Langdale
Hart Crag	822m/2697ft	Patterdale
Harter Fell (Eskdale)	653m/2142ft	Coniston
Harter Fell (Mardale)	778m/2553ft	Mardale and the Far East
Hart Side	758m/2487ft	Patterdale
Hartsop above How	586m/1923ft	Patterdale
Hartsop Dodd	618m/2028ft	Mardale and the Far East
Haycock	798m/2618ft	Wasdale
Haystacks	598m/1962ft	Buttermere
Helm Crag	405m/1329ft	Langdale
Helvellyn	950m/3116ft	Patterdale
Hen Comb	509m/1670ft	Buttermere
Heron Pike	621m/2037ft	Patterdale
Hesk Fell	476m/1562ft	Coniston
High Crag	744m/2441ft	Buttermere
High Hartsop Dodd	519m/1703ft	Patterdale
High Pike (Caldbeck)	658m/2159ft	Keswick
High Pike (Scandale Fell)	656m/2152ft	Patterdale
High Raise (Central Fells)	762m/2500ft	Langdale
High Raise (Haweswater)	802m/2631ft	Mardale and the Far East
High Rigg	355m/1165ft	Borrowdale
High Seat	608m/1995ft	Borrowdale

Fell name	Height	Volume
High Spy	653m/2142ft	Borrowdale
High Stile	807m/2648ft	Buttermere
High Street	828m/2717ft	Mardale and the Far East
High Tove	515m/1690ft	Borrowdale
Hindscarth	727m/2385ft	Buttermere
Holme Fell	317m/1040ft	Coniston
Hopegill Head	770m/2526ft	Buttermere
Ill Bell	757m/2484ft	Mardale and the Far East
Illgill Head	609m/1998ft	Wasdale
Iron Crag	640m/2100ft	Wasdale
Kentmere Pike	730m/2395ft	Mardale and the Far East
Kidsty Pike	780m/2559ft	Mardale and the Far East
Kirk Fell	802m/2631ft	Wasdale
Knock Murton	447m/1467ft	Buttermere
Knott	710m/2329ft	Keswick
Knott Rigg	556m/1824ft	Buttermere
Lank Rigg	541m/1775ft	Wasdale
Latrigg	368m/1207ft	Keswick
Ling Fell	373m/1224ft	Keswick
Lingmell	807m/2649ft	Wasdale
Lingmoor Fell	470m/1542ft	Langdale
Little Hart Crag	637m/2090ft	Patterdale
Little Mell Fell	505m/1657ft	Patterdale
Little Stand	739m/2426ft	Langdale
Loadpot Hill	671m/2201ft	Mardale and the Far East
Loft Crag	682m/2237ft	Langdale
Longlands Fell	483m/1585ft	Keswick
Long Side	734m/2408ft	Keswick
Lonscale Fell	715m/2346ft	Keswick

THE LAKE DISTRICT FELLS *continued*

Fell name	Height	Volume
Lord's Seat	552m/1811ft	Keswick
Loughrigg Fell	335m/1099ft	Langdale
Low Fell	423m/1388ft	Buttermere
Low Pike	507m/1663ft	Patterdale
Maiden Moor	576m/1890ft	Borrowdale
Mardale Ill Bell	761m/2497ft	Mardale and the Far East
Meal Fell	550m/1804ft	Keswick
Mellbreak	512m/1680ft	Buttermere
Middle Dodd	653m/2143ft	Patterdale
Middle Fell	585m/1919ft	Wasdale
Muncaster Fell	231m/758ft	Coniston
Nab Scar	450m/1476ft	Patterdale
Nethermost Pike	891m/2923ft	Patterdale
Outerside	568m/1863ft	Buttermere
Pavey Ark	697m/2287ft	Langdale
Pike o'Blisco	705m/2313ft	Langdale
Pike o'Stickle	708m/2323ft	Langdale
Pillar	892m/2926ft	Wasdale
Place Fell	657m/2155ft	Mardale and the Far East
Raise	884m/2900ft	Patterdale
Rampsgill Head	792m/2598ft	Mardale and the Far East
Rannerdale Knotts	355m/1165ft	Buttermere
Raven Crag	463m/1519ft	Borrowdale
Red Pike (Buttermere)	755m/2477ft	Buttermere
Red Pike (Wasdale)	828m/2717ft	Wasdale
Red Screes	777m/2549ft	Patterdale
Rest Dodd	697m/2287ft	Mardale and the Far East
Robinson	737m/2418ft	Buttermere
Rossett Pike	651m/2136ft	Langdale

Fell name	Height	Volume
Rosthwaite Fell	551m/1808ft	Borrowdale
Sail	771m/2529ft	Buttermere
Sale Fell	359m/1178ft	Keswick
Sallows	516m/1693ft	Mardale and the Far East
Scafell	964m/3163ft	Wasdale
Scafell Pike	977m/3206ft	Borrowdale, Langdale, Wasdale
Scar Crags	672m/2205ft	Buttermere
Scoat Fell	843m/2766ft	Wasdale
Seatallan	693m/2274ft	Wasdale
Seathwaite Fell	631m/2070ft	Borrowdale
Seat Sandal	736m/2415ft	Patterdale
Selside Pike	655m/2149ft	Mardale and the Far East
Sergeant Man	736m/2414ft	Langdale
Sergeant's Crag	574m/1883ft	Borrowdale
Sheffield Pike	675m/2215ft	Patterdale
Shipman Knotts	587m/1926ft	Mardale and the Far East
Silver How	395m/1296ft	Langdale
Skiddaw	931m/3054ft	Keswick
Skiddaw Little Man	865m/2838ft	Keswick
Slight Side	762m/2500ft	Wasdale
Souther Fell	522m/1713ft	Keswick
Stainton Pike	498m/1634ft	Coniston
Starling Dodd	635m/2083ft	Buttermere
Steel Fell	553m/1814ft	Langdale
Steel Knotts	433m/1421ft	Mardale and the Far East
Steeple	819m/2687ft	Wasdale
Stickle Pike	376m/1234ft	Coniston
Stone Arthur	503m/1650ft	Patterdale

THE LAKE DISTRICT FELLS *continued*

Fell name	Height	Volume
St Sunday Crag	841m/2759ft	Patterdale
Stybarrow Dodd	846m/2776ft	Patterdale
Swirl How	804m/2638ft	Coniston
Tarn Crag (Easedale)	485m/1591ft	Langdale
Tarn Crag (Longsleddale)	664m/2179ft	Mardale and the Far East
Thornthwaite Crag	784m/2572ft	Mardale and the Far East
Thunacar Knott	723m/2372ft	Langdale
Troutbeck Tongue	363m/1191ft	Mardale and the Far East
Ullock Pike	690m/2264ft	Keswick
Ullscarf	726m/2382ft	Borrowdale
Walla Crag	379m/1243ft	Borrowdale
Wallowbarrow Crag	292m/958ft	Coniston
Walna Scar	621m/2037ft	Coniston
Wandope	772m/2533ft	Buttermere
Wansfell	489m/1604ft	Mardale and the Far East
Watson's Dodd	789m/2589ft	Patterdale
Wether Hill	673m/2208ft	Mardale and the Far East
Wetherlam	762m/2500ft	Coniston
Whinfell Beacon	472m/1549ft	Mardale and the Far East
Whinlatter	517m/1696ft	Keswick
Whin Rigg	536m/1759ft	Wasdale
Whiteless Pike	660m/2165ft	Buttermere
Whiteside	707m/2320ft	Buttermere
White Side	863m/2831ft	Patterdale
Whitfell	573m/1880ft	Coniston
Winterscleugh	464m/1522ft	Mardale and the Far East
Yewbarrow	628m/2060ft	Wasdale
Yoadcastle	494m/1621ft	Coniston
Yoke	706m/2316ft	Mardale and the Far East

LISTING OF CICERONE GUIDES

SCOTLAND

Backpacker's Britain: Northern Scotland
Ben Nevis and Glen Coe
Cycle Touring in Northern Scotland
Cycling in the Hebrides
Great Mountain Days in Scotland
Mountain Biking in Southern and Central Scotland
Mountain Biking in West and North West Scotland
Not the West Highland Way
Scotland
Scotland's Best Small Mountains
Scotland's Mountain Ridges
Skye's Cuillin Ridge Traverse
The Ayrshire and Arran Coastal Paths
The Border Country
The Borders Abbeys Way
The Cape Wrath Trail
The Great Glen Way
The Great Glen Way Map Booklet
The Hebridean Way
The Hebrides
The Isle of Mull
The Isle of Skye
The Skye Trail
The Southern Upland Way
The Speyside Way
The Speyside Way Map Booklet
The West Highland Way
The West Highland Way Map Booklet
Walking Highland Perthshire
Walking in Scotland's Far North
Walking in the Angus Glens
Walking in the Cairngorms
Walking in the Ochils, Campsie Fells and Lomond Hills
Walking in the Pentland Hills
Walking in the Scottish Borders
Walking in the Southern Uplands
Walking in Torridon
Walking Loch Lomond and the Trossachs
Walking on Arran
Walking on Harris and Lewis
Walking on Jura, Islay and Colonsay
Walking on Rum and the Small Isles
Walking on the Orkney and Shetland Isles
Walking on Uist and Barra
Walking the Cape Wrath Trail
Walking the Corbetts Vol 1 South of the Great Glen
Walking the Corbetts Vol 2 North of the Great Glen
Walking the Galloway Hills
Walking the Munros Vol 1 – Southern, Central and Western Highlands
Walking the Munros Vol 2 – Northern Highlands and the Cairngorms
Winter Climbs Ben Nevis and Glen Coe
Winter Climbs in the Cairngorms

NORTHERN ENGLAND TRAILS

Hadrian's Wall Path
Hadrian's Wall Path Map Booklet
The Coast to Coast Walk
The Coast to Coast Map Booklet
The Dales Way
The Dales Way Map Booklet
The Pennine Way
The Pennine Way Map Booklet

LAKE DISTRICT

Cycling in the Lake District
Great Mountain Days in the Lake District
Lake District Winter Climbs
Lake District: High Level and Fell Walks
Lake District: Low Level and Lake Walks
Mountain Biking in the Lake District
Outdoor Adventures with Children – Lake District
Scrambles in the Lake District – North
Scrambles in the Lake District – South
Scrambles in the Lake District – South and East
Short Walks in Lakeland Book 2: North Lakeland
The Cumbria Way
Trail and Fell Running in the Lake District
Walking the Lake District Fells – Buttermere
Walking the Lake District Fells – Keswick
Walking the Lake District Fells – Langdale
Walking the Lake District Fells – Mardale and the Far East
Walking the Lake District Fells – Patterdale
Walking the Lake District Fells – Wasdale

NORTH WEST ENGLAND AND THE ISLE OF MAN

Cycling the Pennine Bridleway
Cycling the Way of the Roses
Hadrian's Cycleway
Isle of Man Coastal Path
The Lancashire Cycleway
The Lune Valley and Howgills
The Ribble Way
Walking in Cumbria's Eden Valley
Walking in Lancashire
Walking in the Forest of Bowland and Pendle
Walking on the Isle of Man
Walking on the West Pennine Moors
Walks in Silverdale and Arnside

NORTH EAST ENGLAND, YORKSHIRE DALES AND PENNINES

Cycling in the Yorkshire Dales
Great Mountain Days in the Pennines
Mountain Biking in the Yorkshire Dales
St Oswald's Way and St Cuthbert's Way
The Cleveland Way and the Yorkshire Wolds Way
The Cleveland Way Map Booklet
The North York Moors
The Reivers Way
The Teesdale Way
Trail and Fell Running in the Yorkshire Dales
Walking in County Durham
Walking in Northumberland
Walking in the North Pennines
Walking in the Yorkshire Dales: North and East
Walking in the Yorkshire Dales: South and West

WALES AND WELSH BORDERS

Cycle Touring in Wales
Cycling Lon Las Cymru
Glyndwr's Way
Great Mountain Days in Snowdonia
Hillwalking in Shropshire
Hillwalking in Wales – Vols 1&2
Mountain Walking in Snowdonia
Offa's Dyke Path
Offa's Dyke Map Booklet
Ridges of Snowdonia
Scrambles in Snowdonia
Snowdonia: 30 Low-level and easy walks – North
Snowdonia: 30 Low-level and easy walks – South
The Cambrian Way
The Ceredigion and Snowdonia Coast Paths
The Pembrokeshire Coast Path
The Pembrokeshire Coast Path Map Booklet
The Severn Way
The Snowdonia Way
The Wales Coast Path
The Wye Valley Walk
Walking in Carmarthenshire
Walking in Pembrokeshire
Walking in the Forest of Dean
Walking in the Wye Valley
Walking on the Brecon Beacons
Walking on the Gower
Walking the Shropshire Way

LISTING OF CICERONE GUIDES *continued*

DERBYSHIRE, PEAK DISTRICT AND MIDLANDS
Cycling in the Peak District
Dark Peak Walks
Scrambles in the Dark Peak
Walking in Derbyshire
Walking in the Peak District
 – White Peak East
White Peak Walks:
 The Southern Dales

SOUTHERN ENGLAND
20 Classic Sportive Rides in South East England
20 Classic Sportive Rides in South West England
Cycling in the Cotswolds
Mountain Biking on the North Downs
Mountain Biking on the South Downs
Suffolk Coast and Heath Walks
The Cotswold Way
The Cotswold Way Map Booklet
The Great Stones Way
The Kennet and Avon Canal
The Lea Valley Walk
The North Downs Way
The North Downs Way Map Booklet
The Peddars Way and Norfolk Coast Path
The Pilgrims' Way
The Ridgeway National Trail
The Ridgeway Map Booklet
The South Downs Way
The South Downs Way Map Booklet
The South West Coast Path
The South West Coast Path Map Booklet – Vol 1: Minehead to St Ives
The South West Coast Path Map Booklet – Vol 2: St Ives to Plymouth
The South West Coast Path Map Booklet – Vol 3: Plymouth to Poole
The Thames Path
The Thames Path Map Booklet
The Two Moors Way
The Two Moors Way Map Booklet
Walking Hampshire's Test Way
Walking in Cornwall
Walking in Essex
Walking in Kent
Walking in London
Walking in Norfolk
Walking in the Chilterns
Walking in the Cotswolds
Walking in the Isles of Scilly
Walking in the New Forest
Walking in the North Wessex Downs
Walking in the Thames Valley
Walking on Dartmoor
Walking on Guernsey
Walking on Jersey
Walking on the Isle of Wight
Walking the Jurassic Coast
Walks in the South Downs National Park

BRITISH ISLES CHALLENGES, COLLECTIONS AND ACTIVITIES
The Big Rounds
The Book of the Bivvy
The Book of the Bothy
The C2C Cycle Route
The End to End Cycle Route
The Mountains of England and Wales: Vol 1 Wales
The Mountains of England and Wales: Vol 2 England
The National Trails
Three Peaks, Ten Tors
Walking The End to End Trail

ALPS CROSS-BORDER ROUTES
100 Hut Walks in the Alps
Alpine Ski Mountaineering Vol 1 – Western Alps
Alpine Ski Mountaineering Vol 2 – Central and Eastern Alps
Chamonix to Zermatt
The Karnischer Hohenweg
The Tour of the Bernina
Tour of Monte Rosa
Tour of the Matterhorn
Trail Running – Chamonix and the Mont Blanc region
Trekking in the Alps
Trekking in the Silvretta and Ratikon Alps
Trekking Munich to Venice
Trekking the Tour of Mont Blanc
Walking in the Alps

PYRENEES AND FRANCE/SPAIN CROSS-BORDER ROUTES
Shorter Treks in the Pyrenees
The GR10 Trail
The GR11 Trail
The Pyrenean Haute Route
The Pyrenees
Walks and Climbs in the Pyrenees

AUSTRIA
Innsbruck Mountain Adventures
The Adlerweg
Trekking in Austria's Hohe Tauern
Trekking in the Stubai Alps
Trekking in the Zillertal Alps
Walking in Austria

SWITZERLAND
Switzerland's Jura Crest Trail
The Swiss Alpine Pass Route – Via Alpina Route 1
The Swiss Alps
Tour of the Jungfrau Region
Walking in the Bernese Oberland
Walking in the Engadine – Switzerland
Walking in the Valais

FRANCE
Chamonix Mountain Adventures
Cycle Touring in France
Cycling London to Paris
Cycling the Canal de la Garonne
Cycling the Canal du Midi
Mont Blanc Walks
Mountain Adventures in the Maurienne
The GR20 Corsica
The GR5 Trail
The GR5 Trail – Vosges and Jura
The Grand Traverse of the Massif Central
The Loire Cycle Route
The Moselle Cycle Route
The River Rhone Cycle Route
The Robert Louis Stevenson Trail
The Way of St James – Le Puy to the Pyrenees
Tour of the Oisans: The GR54
Tour of the Queyras
Vanoise Ski Touring
Via Ferratas of the French Alps
Walking in Corsica
Walking in Provence – East
Walking in Provence – West
Walking in the Auvergne
Walking in the Briançonnais
Walking in the Dordogne
Walking in the Haute Savoie: North
Walking in the Haute Savoie: South

GERMANY
Hiking and Cycling in the Black Forest
The Danube Cycleway Vol 1
The Rhine Cycle Route
The Westweg
Walking in the Bavarian Alps

ICELAND AND GREENLAND
Trekking in Greenland – The Arctic Circle Trail
Walking and Trekking in Iceland

IRELAND
The Wild Atlantic Way and Western Ireland

ITALY
Italy's Sibillini National Park
Shorter Walks in the Dolomites
Ski Touring and Snowshoeing in the Dolomites
The Way of St Francis
Trekking in the Apennines
Trekking in the Dolomites
Via Ferratas of the Italian Dolomites Vols 1 & 2

Walking and Trekking in the Gran Paradiso
Walking in Abruzzo
Walking in Italy's Cinque Terre
Walking in Italy's Stelvio National Park
Walking in Sardinia
Walking in Sicily
Walking in the Dolomites
Walking in Tuscany
Walking in Umbria
Walking Lake Como and Maggiore
Walking Lake Garda and Iseo
Walking on the Amalfi Coast
Walks and Treks in the Maritime Alps

BELGIUM AND LUXEMBOURG
The GR5 Trail – Benelux and Lorraine
Walking in the Ardennes

SCANDINAVIA: NORWAY, SWEDEN, FINLAND
Trekking in Southern Norway
Trekking the Kungsleden
Walking in Norway

POLAND, SLOVAKIA, ROMANIA, HUNGARY AND BULGARIA
The Danube Cycleway Vol 2
The High Tatras
The Mountains of Romania
Walking in Bulgaria's National Parks
Walking in Hungary

SLOVENIA, CROATIA, SERBIA, MONTENEGRO, ALBANIA AND KOSOVO
Mountain Biking in Slovenia
The Islands of Croatia
The Julian Alps of Slovenia
The Mountains of Montenegro
The Peaks of the Balkans Trail
The Slovene Mountain Trail
Walking in Slovenia: The Karavanke
Walks and Treks in Croatia

SPAIN
Camino de Santiago: Camino Frances
Coastal Walks in Andalucia
Cycle Touring in Spain
Cycling the Camino de Santiago
Mountain Walking in Mallorca
Mountain Walking in Southern Catalunya
Spain's Sendero Historico: The GR1
The Andalucian Coast to Coast Walk
The Camino del Norte and Camino Primitivo
The Camino Ingles and Ruta do Mar
The Mountains of Nerja
The Mountains of Ronda and Grazalema
The Sierras of Extremadura

Trekking in Mallorca
Trekking in the Canary Islands
Walking and Trekking in the Sierra Nevada
Walking in Andalucia
Walking in Menorca
Walking in the Cordillera Cantabrica
Walking on Gran Canaria
Walking on La Gomera and El Hierro
Walking on La Palma
Walking on Lanzarote and Fuerteventura
Walking on Tenerife
Walking on the Costa Blanca
Walking the Camino dos Faros

PORTUGAL
Portugal's Rota Vicentina
The Camino Portugues
Walking in Portugal
Walking in the Algarve
Walking in Madeira
Walking on the Azores

GREECE
The High Mountains of Crete
Trekking in Greece
Walking and Trekking in Zagori
Walking and Trekking on Corfu
Walking on the Greek Islands – the Cyclades

CYPRUS
Walking in Cyprus

MALTA
Walking on Malta

INTERNATIONAL CHALLENGES, COLLECTIONS AND ACTIVITIES
Canyoning in the Alps
Europe's High Points
The Via Francigena Canterbury to Rome – Part 2

MOROCCO
The High Atlas
Walks and Scrambles in the Moroccan Anti-Atlas

TANZANIA
Kilimanjaro

SOUTH AFRICA
Walking in the Drakensberg

TAJIKISTAN
Trekking in Tajikistan

JAPAN
Hiking and Trekking in the Japan Alps and Mount Fuji
Japan's Kumano Kodo Pilgrimage

JORDAN
Treks and Climbs in Wadi Rum, Jordan

NEPAL
Annapurna
Everest: A Trekker's Guide
Trekking in the Himalaya

BHUTAN
Trekking in Bhutan

INDIA
Trekking in Ladakh

CHINA
The Mount Kailash Trek

NORTH AMERICA: USA AND CANADA
The John Muir Trail
The Pacific Crest Trail

SOUTH AMERICA: ARGENTINA, CHILE AND PERU
Aconcagua and the Southern Andes
Hiking and Biking Peru's Inca Trails
Torres del Paine

NEW ZEALAND & AUSTRALIA
Hiking the Overland Track

TECHNIQUES
Fastpacking
Geocaching in the UK
Map and Compass
Outdoor Photography
Polar Exploration
The Mountain Hut Book

MINI GUIDES
Alpine Flowers
Navigation
Pocket First Aid and Wilderness Medicine
Snow

MOUNTAIN LITERATURE
8000 metres
A Walk in the Clouds
Abode of the Gods
Fifty Years of Adventure
The Pennine Way – the Path, the People, the Journey
Unjustifiable Risk?

For full information on all our guides, books and eBooks, visit our website:
www.cicerone.co.uk

Explore the world with Cicerone

walking • trekking • mountaineering • climbing • mountain biking • cycling • via ferratas • scrambling • trail running • skills and techniques

For over 50 years, Cicerone have built up an outstanding collection of nearly 400 guides, inspiring all sorts of amazing experiences.

www.cicerone.co.uk – where adventures begin

- Our **website** is a treasure-trove for every outdoor adventurer. You can buy books or read inspiring articles and trip reports, get technical advice, check for updates, and view videos, photographs and mapping for routes and treks.

- **Register this book** or any other Cicerone guide in your member's library on our website and you can choose to automatically access updates and GPX files for your books, if available.

- Our **fortnightly newsletters** will update you on new publications and articles and keep you informed of other news and events. You can also follow us on Facebook, Twitter and Instagram.

We hope you have enjoyed using this guidebook. If you have any comments you would like to share, please contact us using the form on our website or via email, so that we can provide the best experience for future customers.

CICERONE

Juniper House, Murley Moss Business Village, Oxenholme Road, Kendal LA9 7RL

✉ info@cicerone.co.uk   cicerone.co.uk